◁ W9-BKP-732

ackling Complex Texts

VOLUME 2

HISTORICAL FICTION IN BOOK CLUBS

LUCY CALKINS ◆ **MARY EHRENWORTH**

firsthand
HEINEMANN

DEDICATED TO TEACHERS

Dedicated to all the school principals who have graciously opened their doors to us, and especially to Katy Rosen, Elsa Nuñez, Peter MacFarlene, Maria Stiles, Melanie Woods, Adele Schroeder, Lauren Fontana, Ellen Foote, and Liz Phillips.

HEINEMANN

DEDICATED TO TEACHERS

firsthand
An imprint of Heinemann
361 Hanover Street, Portsmouth, NH 03801
www.heinemann.com

Offices and agents throughout the world

"Dedicated to Teachers" is a trademark of Greenwood Publishing Group, Inc.

© 2010 by Lucy Calkins and Kathleen Tolan

All rights reserved. No part of this book may be reproduced in any form or by any electronic or mechanical means, including information storage and retrieval systems, without permission in writing form the publisher, except by a reviewer, who may quote brief passages in a review, and with the exception of reproducible pages, which are identified by the *Units of Study for Teaching Reading* copyright line, and may be photocopied for classroom use only.

The asterisked tradebook titles in this text have been officially leveled by Irene Fountas, Gay Su Pinnell, and their trained levelers. Other systems that use level designations are not equivalent to theirs.

Post-its ® is a registered trademark of the 3M company.

The authors and publisher wish to thank those who have generously given permission to reprint borrowed material:
Excerpts from NUMBER THE STARS by Lois Lowry. Copyright © 1989 by Lois Lowry. Reprinted by permission of Houghton Mifflin Harcourt Publishing Company. All rights reserved.

"A Tent of Pain" from OUT OF THE DUST by Karen Hesse. Used by permission of Scholastic, Inc.

"Things" from *Honey, I Love and Other Love Poems* by Eloise Greenfield. Text copyright © 1978 by Eloise Greenfield.

Excerpts from *Rose Blanche* by Roberto Innocenti. Published by Creative Paperbacks, an imprint of the Creative Company, Mankato, MN.

Anne Frank photograph from Getty Images

Miep Gies photograph courtesy of AP/Wide World Photos.

Irish Peasant Girl photograph © 2007 WHA United Archives

Two Young Brothers photograph from the United States Holocaust Memorial Museum

Two Buchenwald Survivors © the Federation Nationale des Deportes et Internes Resistants et Patriots.

Photographers: Peter Cunningham and Melanie Brown
Cover and Interior Design: Jenny Jensen Greenleaf
Composition: Publishers' Design and Production Services, Inc.

Library of Congress Cataloging-in-Publication Data
CIP data on file with the Library of Congress

ISBN 10: 0-325-03069-3
ISBN 13: 978-0-325-03069-2

Printed in the United States of America on acid-free paper
14   13   12   11   10   ML   1   2   3   4   5

Tackling Complex Texts
Historical Fiction in Book Clubs

VOLUME
2

INTERPRETATION AND CRITICAL READING

Units of Study for Teaching Reading, Grades 3–5

Contents

TACKLING COMPLEX TEXTS — HISTORICAL FICTION IN BOOK CLUBS

VOLUME 1: Synthesizing Perspectives

PART ONE TACKLING COMPLEX TEXTS IN THE COMPANY OF FRIENDS

TACKLING COMPLEX TEXTS — HISTORICAL FICTION IN BOOK CLUBS
VOLUME 2: Interpretation and Critical Reading

PART TWO   INTERPRETING COMPLEX TEXTS

Contents

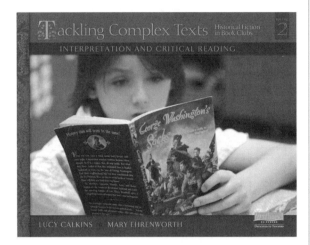

Interpreting Complex Texts

PART TWO

Authoring Our Own Responses to Texts

t's no easy task for young readers to read in ways that allow them to construct coherent and full understandings of complex fictional texts—and for most young readers, historical fiction books tend to be as complex as any other fiction that they encounter. During the previous bend in the road of this unit, you taught readers ways to get their minds around the story line and the settings in their books. By now, most of your readers have had several satisfying experiences reading full-length historical fiction novels. This new bend in the road of the unit aims to support deep and interpretive readings and to help students learn that historical fiction allows a person to not only learn to read but also to learn to live.

If the unit is truly going to help readers develop new muscles, we need not only to *say* new things in our mini-lessons, we also need to rally young people to *do* different sorts of work. By this time in the year, you'll want to encourage children to work harder at developing their ideas through talking and writing at length, using both deep conversation and writing as ways to grow ideas as they read. By now, many of your children have become avid readers, carrying books with them everywhere, finding lots of moments

GETTING READY

- This bend in the road continues the clubs that were begun in the first portion of the unit, but it will be increasingly likely that clubs will meet on alternate days rather than every day. Children will still sit near club mates while in the meeting and while reading, but they will sometimes work with a partner (from within the club) rather than with the entire club. Today the club works together, but on a special activity—not a regular club meeting.

- During the connection you will read an excerpt from the read-aloud book that you've been weaving throughout your unit. If you've selected *Number the Stars*, as we've done, you could read aloud the part from Chapter 3 that begins with, "Soon we will have to add another blanket. . . ." This puts you back in the novel just where you left off in the prior session. If possible, copy the excerpt you'll use onto chart paper so that kids can see as well as hear it. Or distribute copies to some children, encouraging others to look on.

- Assuming you have some readers who struggle and who receive extra help in reading at another time of the day, you could use a bit of that time to read the passage to them that you'll later be reading in this session. As you read the passage during that after-school time, you could react to it in ways that help readers take in the plot and prepare them for later taking in more than plot. This way, during the minilesson, those strugglers will be more able to do the intellectual work of sifting through the text.

- If you have selected a different read-aloud book, pick a passage you've already read aloud that particularly reveals a character.

for reading throughout their lives. Many read well beyond your requisite half an hour a night. It is time to be sure they are given the support they need to develop interpretations as they read and to carry those interpretations into their lives.

The upcoming bend in the road of this unit, then, will provide you with an opportunity to help youngsters learn to read interpretively. This particular minilesson helps readers become invested and interested in their thoughts and

> *In the name of teaching interpretation, too many readers have been silenced by the message that there is one right interpretation to a text. . . .*

reactions as they read so they can eventually develop these into mature interpretations.

A word of caution. It is important to guard against the instinct to teach interpretive reading as it was perhaps taught to us. The results are clear: The high school English classes of yesteryear did not produce a generation of avid, thoughtful readers. In fact, the average college graduate in America reads one book a year. In the name of teaching interpretation, too many young readers have been silenced and disenfranchised by the message that there is one right interpretation to a text and that they do not have access to that one right interpretation. Did your high school English teacher ask you questions such as, "What does the light at the end of the dock *mean*?" I distinctly remember my

teacher asking that question, then scanning the room for answers. I remember, too, thinking, "What do *you* mean, 'What does the light at the end of the dock *mean*?' It means a light, a lantern, at the end of the dock, the pier." And I remember also thinking, "That couldn't be the answer he wants," and, after straining to think symbolically, raising my hand to say, "Does it mean heaven?"

My teacher said nothing in response, but when his eyes searched the rest of the room in hopes of a better suggestion, and he asked, "Anybody? Anybody?" I decided that I don't have a symbolic mind. Apparently my classmates were learning a similar lesson because I distinctly remember that no one took the bait, so my teacher delivered his Right Answer, a complicated discourse on themes and symbols. I recall listening to what he said, looking down at the text before me, and thinking, "How did he get *that* from *this*?"

Only years later did I realize that my teacher's interpretation of the text was not inherent in the text, nor did it reflect a deeply felt personal response to the text. It was the same interpretation that was inside the CliffsNotes on the novel. In my town, the CliffsNotes still sell out the very first day that a teacher embarks on the study of a new text.

My high school English teacher taught me lessons that lasted for a very long time. He taught me that he had some acuity that I didn't have. He taught me that I didn't have a "symbolic mind." This was sad news for me, because I'd always assumed I would major in English at college and devote my career to reading and writing. For a chunk of my life, my light-at-the-end-of-the-dock disability put an end to those ambitions. During my first years at college, whenever I was asked to write about a book, I dug through what the critics said, translating their high-flown interpretations into my own words so I could mask my deficits. And when professors asked, "What does this passage mean?" I scrunched low in my seat, kept my eyes trained on my desk, and prayed that I wouldn't be called on. None of that changed until my junior year of college when I began studying with teachers who taught *the process* of reading, not the

products of their sanctioned (and completed) interpretations.

There needs to be a revolution in the teaching of reading (and especially of interpretation) that resembles the revolution that has transformed the field of writing. At one time, teachers believed that some people had the DNA to be Talented Writers: When these writers picked up their plumed pens, they scribed exquisite *literature*. Then there were the nonwriters whose drafts were full of contradictions and incomplete thoughts and stops and starts. Since then, research has shown that the best of literature begins as scraps of thoughts, jotted ideas, and rough incoherent drafts. Writers who are "talented" are writers with the perseverance and the strategies to rework first drafts over and over to eventually produce final pieces. This, of course, has had profound implications on the teaching of writing because now the message is that children (and you and I, their teachers) need not despair when we look at what they (or we) put first onto the page. Instead, we can see kernels of possibility and roll up our sleeves. Young *readers* need similar instruction.

I wish my third-, fourth-, and fifth-grade teachers had let me in on the truth that even the most experienced readers don't look up from a text they are reading and immediately generate astute interpretations of dense, heady texts; instead, they respond with muttered questions and incoherent ideas. What a difference it would have made if my high school teacher had listened to my suggestion that the light at the end of the dock represented heaven and helped me to see how I could put that idea to the test, checking to see whether my hypothesis linked to the larger meanings of the text. That is, what a difference it would have made had more of my teachers led me to understand that experienced readers are people with tools and strategies and habits that are within reach for everyone. Experienced readers know that good reading, like good writing, is the result of time and thought and work. It is a process—one that we can all learn.

Today's session conveys that the process begins with each of us, as a reader, trusting that our own idiosyncratic response to a text is the starting place. William Sloane, author of *The Craft of Writing*, points out that when any of us read a novel, we are not saying to that book, to that author, "Tell me, Dear Author, about yourself and what you think about the world, art, life, the eternal verities." No. Instead, we read, and the first thing we say is: "Tell me about me. I want to be more alive. Give me me."

This session issues an invitation to readers to realize that thinking deeply about texts is something that all of us can do. You will show readers that finding meaning in a text is not about locating examples of some theme you have already decided upon that they need to prove. Instead, as Louise Rosenblatt has suggested, we need to teach readers that the meaning of a text lies between each text and what *each reader* brings to it. Each reader's response to a text is a response that is worth respecting, pondering, and developing. In this session, there is no place for worrying about the qualities of a "good" response. That will come in time, but for now you will focus on the deep connections between a reader's response to a text and that reader's history and identity. This will be your first, and perhaps most important, teaching.

MINILESSON EIGHT

Authoring Our Own Responses to Texts

CONNECTION

Find ways to illustrate that characters grow by understanding more and becoming more aware than they were.

"Do you remember the passage from *Number the Stars* that we talked about yesterday? After Annemarie reminded her mother of the time when Kirsti used to sleep between her parents, Annemarie glanced over at her Mom's face, worrying that the memory of those days would bring a pained look onto it. 'Those days' were the days when the big sister, Lise, had still been alive.'

"I want to point out that when Annemarie was Kirsti's age, she probably didn't even notice the pained looks that sometimes crossed her mother's face; part of being older is that you see more of what's going on. Is that true in your family? Do you think that when you were younger, there were looks or worries or laughter exchanged between the grown-ups that went right by you—looks that now you see?

"So, could you say that for you, one of the ways in which you've grown is that now you see more, even seeing the dark side of things, the pained looks, the fears?

"I'm asking this because it seems to me that one of the ways that *characters* grow, in stories, is that over time some characters come to see more, and I think this is true for people and readers as well. In my family, we had a giraffe laminated onto the back of one of our kitchen doors, and my Mom would register the increasing height of each of us kids as we grew, and grew, and grew. She could record that I was four feet, eight inches, then that I was five feet, and so forth. That kind of growth is easy to see and to chart. But my parents couldn't easily measure that as I became older, I began to see more of what was going on around me. But I did.

COACHING TIPS

You may want to pause and look back across scores of minilessons, collecting a list of the sorts of things that a teacher can do to start a minilesson. You'll have seen many minilessons that begin with an anecdote from the teacher's life or with a story about a particular reader. This minilesson begins with a glimpse of the read-aloud book and then an effort to use that passage to illuminate an idea. It's always useful to remember that we, as teachers, are able to use authors as coteachers, as guest lecturers in the course we are teaching. What a resource!

There are lots of ways to scaffold children's abilities to read well. Authors of books in the M-Q band of text difficulty, for example, often find ways for someone in the text to come right out and talk about the protagonist's complicated emotional feelings. Then when readers read on and the character acts in ways that match the earlier description, the reader is able to bring the earlier description of the character's feelings to the passage conveying the character's actions, and bingo! The reader has an idea about the character and evidence aligned to that idea. The reader will feel as if she grew this idea herself, when in fact she probably leaned a lot on help she was given. In this unit, you'll see that when the minilesson is not yet asking readers to interpret, I sometimes let readers in on an interpretation of the text. Then, when readers are asked to grow "their own big ideas" about this book, their ideas are remarkably sophisticated. This is the case in part because they accumulate the ideas that have leaked out along the way.

Here, my point is that as characters grow older, they see more. I slip in the added idea that paying attention to small fleeting looks means bringing big meaning to those looks. Many children will not grasp that I'm suggesting that in order to pay attention to details, one brings meaning to those details—but some might. This is not formally taught; it is not explicitly named, but it is implicit. In a later conference, the point could be named explicitly.

"You know, some of you have grown as readers even just over the past few days. You are seeing more, and that is important. And I think many of your characters are growing in just this way. Think for a moment about whether you have a character in one of your books who has grown in that he or she is able to see, to recognize, more of what's going on." I gave children a moment to think, then said, "Turn and talk.

"I'm telling you this because yesterday we looked closely at one passage," I said, opening my copy of *Number the Stars* to the passage I'd written on chart paper. *[Fig. VIII-1]*

"And we realized that one of the best things about reading with others is that when we have lots of eyes looking closely together, we see more, discover more, think more."

Use the story of a child to suggest that seeing more can be hard because we, as readers, aren't always sure what we are expected to see.

"Kobe, though, came up to me at one point yesterday and asked a really important question. He said, 'I know we are supposed to *see more* in our stories, but I am confused. What, exactly, are we looking for?'

"I didn't have the right words then to explain what I meant by 'seeing more.' I told Kobe we'd talk about that important question today in our minilesson."

Name your teaching point. Specifically, teach children that each reader decides what he or she will notice in texts. This is part of what it means to author one's own reading, one's interpretation.

"So today, I want to teach you that when we read novels and specifically when we study texts really closely, we are looking at . . . (I held up a giant question mark on chart paper). We are looking at . . . *something*.

"And here is the thing. No one can tell you, as a reader, what to look at, what to notice, what to think. One reader and another will tend to notice similar things about *what is happening* in the story—about the plot. But each reader brings his or her own meaning to the story, and to do that, we let different parts reverberate in our lives. Each one of us is the author of his or her own reading."

This is surely the case for Annemarie and Kirsti in Number the Stars, *for Rose in* Rose Blanche, *for Cassie in* Roll of Thunder, Hear My Cry, *and for Anna in* Sarah, Plain and Tall. *In a way, many of the great historical fiction books and realistic children's fiction novels are about children coming to realize a truth about the world that they hadn't known at the beginning of the book.*

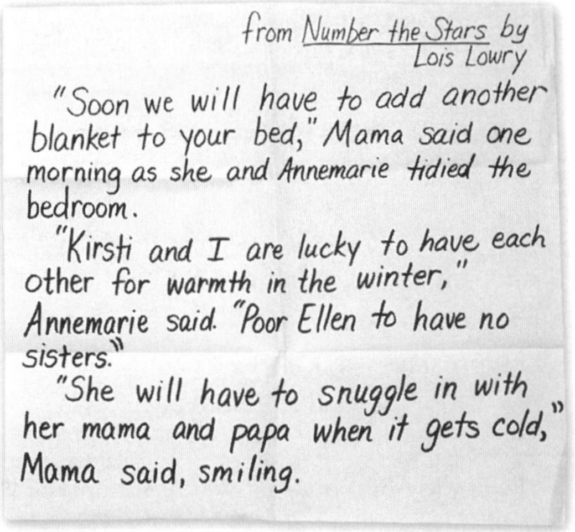

from *Number the Stars* by Lois Lowry

"Soon we will have to add another blanket to your bed," Mama said one morning as she and Annemarie tidied the bedroom.
"Kirsti and I are lucky to have each other for warmth in the winter," Annemarie said. "Poor Ellen to have no sisters."
"She will have to snuggle in with her mama and papa when it gets cold," Mama said, smiling.

Figure VIII-1

By now, you will begin to see that I've emphasized that as readers grow, we see more because today's session is all about the question, "How do I know what to look at?" Notice that I put that question into the mouth of one lad who, like the boy in The Emperor's New Clothes, *voices the question that others didn't dare ask.*

If you can actually hold up a giant question mark, this will help the minilesson. Using physical objects adds a lot to your minilesson.

You might decide to add a line to your teaching point such as, "We call what we're doing interpretation, *which involves looking inside the story, and beginning to see more than simply what is happening," I do not do this because I generally find it helps to teach readers to do something, and only later, to provide the technical name for what they are doing. By then, the term (in this case,* interpretation, *but later in this unit,* symbolism *and* allusion) *means something. But if you think that one way to rally kids around the big work of this upcoming bend in the road is to use the phrase, then by all means do so.*

Teaching

Acknowledge that earlier you provided readers things to think about when reading—training wheels—and tell readers that actually in life, readers themselves decide what to notice.

"I know, I know. Earlier this year I taught you that when you are reading a story, it often pays to think about what a character *wants* and to think also about *what gets in the way* for that character, what causes the character to *struggle*. And I told you that it often pays to think about how characters *change* and what they *learn*. All of that is still true. Stories are written in such a way that it often pays off to think about characters' wants and struggles, changes and lessons. That work is probably second nature to you now.

"But when I asked you to read books in such a way that you were thinking about those things, I was propping you up, I was giving you training wheels so that you'd get the feel for what strong readers do. I was giving you things to think about that many readers often find interesting. 'Try thinking about these things,' I said. I'll probably continue to give you training wheels, from time to time, so that I help you get the feel for the sorts of thinking that experienced readers often practice."

Explain that different readers attend to different aspects of a text. Make your point by showing that in the same way, if each observed a particular school setting, each would note different aspects of it.

"But in real life, people get books out of the library and start reading those books without anyone telling us, 'Think about this,' or 'Look closely at that.' For all the years of your life, *you* will decide what interests you.

Teachers, it is important for you to realize a couple of things. First, it is going to be true that sometimes we teach kids a rather methodical, procedural way of doing things, and we do this knowing that in the end, they'll develop automaticity with that procedure, and they'll no longer think about the distinct steps one takes, nor will they proceed in such a methodical fashion. So it should not surprise you if, at one point, we teach readers to grow ideas by attending to the character's traits, wants, troubles, and so forth, and then at another time we say that each reader will attend to the idiosyncratic stuff that speaks to that reader. That is, one way of understanding the apparent contradiction is to realize that there is a progression from more procedural, concrete processes toward internalizing those processes.

But the other thing to bear in mind is that often in life, two seemingly contradictory things can both be true. In this instance it is definitely true that as readers, we each author our own responses to and interpretations of texts, and at the same time, there are certain elements that prove especially fruitful when we think and talk about them. In fact, the elements that provide the most room for interpretation are the most universal elements: the characters' yearnings, relationships, families, disappointments, times when they chafe against others' needs or expectations, moments of enlightenment or change.

This will no doubt feel as if it should be the active involvement component of your minilesson, and you could rewrite this minilesson so that this is the case, perhaps dividing it into two sessions. For now, pat yourself on the back for the fact that you noticed this, because it suggests you have internalized the template of minilessons, but note that none of us necessarily follow that template all the time. As you will see, the active involvement slot of the minilesson will provide an opportunity for children to transfer what you help them to do to the text they're reading in clubs.

"For example—right now, let's pretend you have been asked to do some research while first graders have lunch. Picture that you are walking into the lunchroom, a clipboard in hand. Are you with me? Your job is to interpret the lunchroom—to be a serious researcher of something that you find interesting and important, something that you can see right now while you walk around the lunchroom as those first graders are having lunch. Right now, imagine you are looking around that lunchroom. Decide what you will record. Pretend you see that lunchroom and imagine what, exactly, you might be writing on your page. Jot some notes." [Fig. VIII-2]

Kids could be shouting because when I am at lunch a lot of kids are shouting. Teachers would be walking around because when I have lunch at least 3 teachers are walking around. I don't think they should be because sometimes they get kids in trouble even though they shouldn't be. I got a bun thrown at me and I threw it somewhere else, and I got in trouble.

Figure VIII-2

As children started doing the work, I voiced over in a way that scaffolded them. "Some of you will be noticing differences in that cafeteria between boys and girls. Some of you will notice kids who are left out versus the kids who have social power, or you'll think about nutrition, or about trash and waste. Some will think about ways that adults treat kids. Jot whatever you are seeing and thinking about as you pretend to look over the cafeteria during the first graders' lunchtime."

Notice that I went through a nice list of possibilities while children were sitting there, trying to write what they noticed. I'm providing them with a leg up so they have success with this little activity. It'll help me make the larger point more easily if they are successful.

If your children write slowly, you'll probably ask them to think of what they see, of the ideas this gives them, and then turn and talk. The instructions to stop and jot work best if children write fluently and quickly.

Extend your argument by pointing out that the things each person noticed reflect that person's autobiography and values.

"Now, let me take this a step further. Your *interpretation* of what is going on in the cafeteria—what you noticed—is not accidental. It has something to do with who you are, with your own childhood, with your own family, or with what you care about. You bring your life into this kind of 'seeing more.' I know you may not believe me, but for now, try buying into this idea. Think, 'What, in my own life, explains why I saw what I did in that lunchroom? Have I encountered bullies? Do my parents make a fuss about recycling?'"

I let the children think for long enough that many had an answer. "Thumbs up when you have an answer," I said. Malik wrote his thoughts in his notebook. *[Fig. VIII-3]*

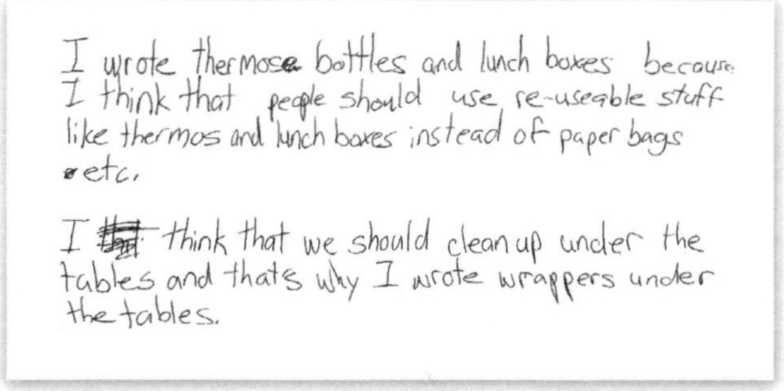

When many thumbs went up, I said, "Turn and talk. Be sure to ask each other, 'What in your life drew you to interpret the cafeteria scene like that? What in your life made you notice whatever you noticed?'" I gestured to those two questions, scrawled on chart paper.

I heard Brianna say, "I notice kids sitting alone and kids who don't seem to have friends."

With my prompting, Grace responded, "Why do you notice that?"

"No reason, really," Brianna said, shrugging. Then, when she saw me gesture in a 'Come on' way to elicit more, she added, her voice unsure, "Because I'm always taking care of my little sister and her friends and so I notice kids getting left out, 'cause they do that *all* the *time*?"

I signalled for Brianna to now ask Grace the same "What did you notice?" question, and Grace said, "I notice how girls and boys are sitting, with all the girls at one table and the boys are all talking together at the next one."

I pointed to the second question, and on cue, Brianna asked, "How does that go with your life?"

"I have no idea. I dunno. We don't sit like that in my family or if we did, I'd be all alone on one side. With my mom."

"Maybe it is 'cause you are friends with boys and you sit with them, so it would be really strange for you if there was a girls' table and a boys' table?" Brianna said, offering an explanation.

If you know much about reader response theories of reading, you'll grasp where I am going with this. When we read, the things we notice in a text come as much from our own experiences and beliefs as from the text itself. A researcher, Denny Taylor, once said, "We do not see with our eyes or hear with our ears but with our beliefs." There is a great deal of truth to that. This means that it is especially interesting to reflect on one's own reading and to share one's reading with others. When several people read the same text and our responses to that text vary in big ways, those variations say a lot about what different readers bring to the texts. Scholes writes that "we bring the book of ourselves to the text in front of us." Here, I am opening up the children's books of their lives.

> I wrote thermose bottles and lunch boxes because I think that people should use re-useable stuff like thermos and lunch boxes instead of paper bags ✗ etc.
>
> I think that we should clean up under the tables and thats why I wrote wrappers under the tables.

Figure VIII-3
Malik suggests his belief values influenced what he attended to while observing the first graders at lunchtime.

Remember that your point here is not about the cafeteria. Your point is that what people tend to see and to note comes in part from our own life stories. In general, you can always remember that most so-called reading skills are in fact life skills or thinking skills. So this means you can teach most things by referencing examples that are not actual reading stories. Especially when you are diving into the heady intellectual terrain of interpretation, it makes sense to compare the work to real-life experience—to ground this new thinking in examples that are familiar.

Build a bridge to reading, telling children that what a reader sees in a text is also a reflection of the reader (as well as the text).

"You are probably wondering what any of this lunchroom conversation has to do with reading. This is my point. When we read a book, we each notice and think different things, and what we notice says something about who we are, what we care about."

ACTIVE INVOLVEMENT

Reiterate that when we read, what we see in a text is largely up to us. Read aloud the upcoming section of the read-aloud book, setting children up to record what they notice and think.

"I'm going to read the upcoming section of *Number the Stars,* and this time, let's all try to 'see more' in the story. As you do this, allow yourself to see more of the things that you care about! If you care about relationships, go ahead, see more of that. If you're starting to see signs of danger everywhere, because of your World War II reading, you may see more of that. *It is up to you!* My expectation is simply that you will be thinking hard. The content that you think about, will be . . . ," and I finished the sentence by pointing to the question mark that I'd held high during my teaching point.

"So, readers, notice *whatever* you notice. Think *whatever* you think. I'm not going to say, 'Think about this' or 'Think about that.' I *am* saying, 'Think in ways that reflect who you are and what you care about.' Later, I'm going to ask you to notice ways in which your thinking about a book is as individual and idiosyncratic as your fingerprint."

Teachers, you may have noticed that I haven't said a lot yet about how readers accumulate their observations and make more of what they notice. The unit will get to that work soon. Part of teaching is deciding what not to teach on a given day, and it feels as if helping children reflect on what they bring to a text that allows them to see more is enough. Don't worry, we'll get to a lot of interpretive practices in the rest of this unit.

I will often tell a child that his writing about reading shows his thinking in a manner that is as idiosyncratic as a fingerprint. I am hoping to encourage that child to be invested in this record. And I know that when I pull alongside children in conferences and say, "Will you walk me through your thinking?" and then look at their written responses to reading, I'm conveying that of course the Post-its and notebook entries are the fingerprints that reveal the minds and hearts of the readers.

Opening *Number the Stars*, I said, "*Previously in* this chapter, we learned about the electricity being rationed, and we learned that the two mothers knit mittens as they brace themselves for the oncoming winter. We learned, too, that the girls took the long way home every day to avoid the soldiers on the corner. As I read on, you'll especially notice some things. Record these and think, 'What do I make of this?'"

Mama, still laughing, knelt and kissed Kirsti on the cheek. "Time to leave for school, girls," she said. She began to button Kirsti's jacket. "Oh, dear," she said, suddenly. "Look. This button has broken right in half. Annemarie, take Kirsti with you, after school, to the little shop where Mrs. Hirsch sells thread and buttons. See if you can buy just one, to match the others on her jacket. I'll give you some kroner—it shouldn't cost very much."

But after school, when the girls stopped at the shop, which had been there as long as Annemarie could remember, they found it closed. There was a new padlock on the door, and a sign. But the sign was in German, They couldn't read the words.

"I wonder if Mrs. Hirsch is sick," Annemarie said as they walked away.

"I saw her Saturday," Ellen said. "She was with her husband and her son. They all looked just fine. Or at least the parents looked just fine—the son always looks like a horror." She giggled.

Annemarie made a face. The Hirsch family lived in the neighborhood, so they had seen the boy, Samuel, quite often. He was a tall teenager with thick glasses, stooped shoulders, and unruly hair. He rode a bicycle to school, leaning forward and squinting, wrinkling his nose to nudge his glasses into place. His bicycle had wooden wheels, now that rubber tires weren't available, and it creaked and clattered on the street.

"I think the Hirsches all went on a vacation to the seashore," Kirsti announced.

"And I suppose they took a big basket of pink-frosted cupcakes with them," Annemarie said sarcastically to her sister.

If you can distribute copies of these passages, you might decide to do so. You might want children to simply listen as you read, and to only afterward receive a printout of the passage. Alternatively, you can simply ask children to jot what they recall and think as they listen.

Teachers, in an ideal world, you might choose to read this passage twice, but chances are you won't have time while staying within the ten minute boundary for a minilesson. Still, rereading helps. Many readers read hard or exciting texts the first time just for plot.

I've asked children to record what they notice. I could have instead given each child a copy of this passage and simply asked the child to underline parts of it that seem especially interesting to that child. Even those choices, alone, will show differences, one person to another. Then later I could ask the students to glance to their right and left, noticing if others underlined the same lines.

Some of your readers may struggle a bit just to make sense of what is happening here, figuring out who these Hirsches are, tracking the time shift as Annemarie thinks back to the Hirsch boy's habits of bicycling to school.

"Yes, I suppose they did," Kirsti replied.

Annemarie and Ellen exchanged looks that meant: Kirsti is so *dumb*. No one in Copenhagen had taken a vacation at the seashore since the war began. There *were* no pink-frosted cupcakes: there hadn't been for months.

"Stop and jot." I said. "What did you notice? What do you make of it? What part of it do you care about? Let your response to this be as individual as your fingerprint." Jasmine quickly wrote in her notebook. *[Fig. VIII-4]*

Remind children that the challenge is not only to notice stuff in texts but to reflect on what one notices and on what this reveals about us.

After children jotted for a few minutes, I said, "Right now, be sure you have asked that question that readers ask a lot: 'What in my life helps me notice whatever it is that stands out for me in this text?'" I gestured toward the chart-paper record of the earlier question: "What did you notice, and what do you make of it?" and of this new question: "What in my life helps me notice whatever it is that stands out for me?"

After giving children a moment to reflect on this, I said to them, "Share what you are noticing about the things you tend to pay attention to and the sorts of things you tend to bypass. And talk, too, about what in your childhood or your personality explains why some things do or don't stand out for you." *[Fig. VIII-5]*

I leaned in to listen to Lily, who said, "I noticed that Annemarie and Kirsti seem to know the Hirsches pretty well. They say the shop has been there forever and talk about the son riding his bike around the neighborhood. Where I live, people wouldn't notice the son of the store owner. I don't really know any of the families who own the shops in my neighborhood. Maybe because New York is so big."

Jasmine jumped in. "Yeah, and you noticed that part about the Hirsches' son because, it was like, 'Whoa! That's different.' Some kids would read that part and not blink an eye 'cause in their town, everyone knows everyone's family." Then she added, "The part I noticed was how the Hirsches' son rides his bicycle with wooden wheels because they can't get rubber ones and how the mothers met for their coffee but it was really just hot water. When I don't get stuff like a new iPod, I get mad and say, 'It's not fair how . . . ,' and my mom always says I should be grateful for what I have. I was thinking that these characters seem like they hardly complain."

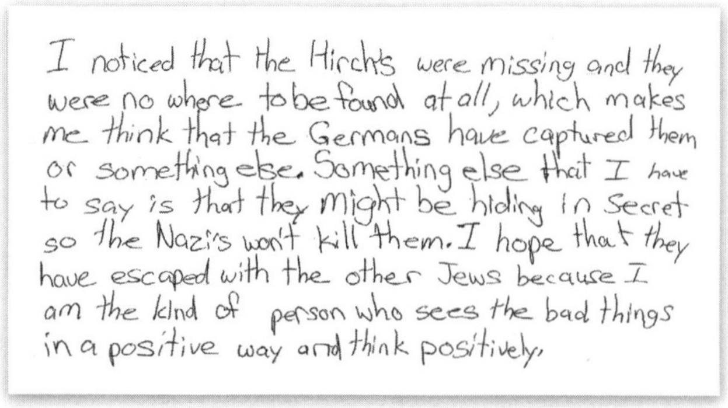

I noticed that the Hirch's were missing and they were no where to be found at all, which makes me think that the Germans have captured them or something else. Something else that I have to say is that they might be hiding in secret so the Nazi's won't kill them. I hope that they have escaped with the other Jews because I am the kind of person who sees the bad things in a positive way and think positively.

Figure VIII-4
One child's stop-and-jots

I could also have said, "You know how, in the writing workshop, we sometimes do author studies? For a moment look over what you've noticed and written—also look over the Post-its in your book, the ones that show a trail of thought over the last few days—and think, 'What sorts of things do I tend to notice and think about as I read?'"

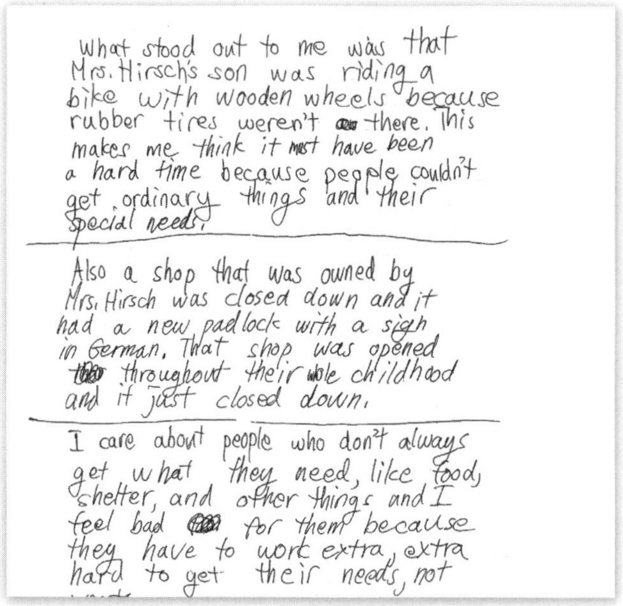

What stood out to me was that Mrs. Hirsch's son was riding a bike with wooden wheels because rubber tires weren't there. This makes me think it must have been a hard time because people couldn't get ordinary things and their special needs.

Also a shop that was owned by Mrs. Hirsch was closed down and it had a new padlock with a sign in German. That shop was opened throughout their whole childhood and it just closed down.

I care about people who don't always get what they need, like food, shelter, and other things and I feel bad for them because they have to work extra, extra hard to get their needs, not

Figure VIII-5
One child's noticings from the read-aloud passage.

Point out that when we read, we bring all the parts of ourselves to the book. Show that what you saw in the excerpt reflects one part of who you are and demonstrate how these connections led you to think more about the text.

"Readers, as I listen to the parts of the passage that each of you cared about, and your reasons for caring, I'm getting glimpses of you as interpretive readers. I am realizing that when you sit with your books, I call you readers, which you are. But you're not *only that,* and neither am I. When I sit with a book, I am also a friend, a daughter, a teacher, a sister, a lover of mountains and dogs, and a person who is intimidated by formal parties. Sometimes, I bring more of one part of me than another to a text. For example, in the part of this book that we just read, I found myself bringing the part of me that is an older sister.

"Let me show you for a minute how this helps me grow ideas. Because I bring myself as a big sister to my reading, I am extra alert to parts of the story that show Annemarie as a sister. Then, I actually *think* about what I notice and how I am the same or different. I think that like Annemarie, I try to protect my sister from things that are difficult, and like her, sometimes I can't protect my little sister. Pretty soon I'm thinking about all the people in this book who try to protect other people and can't always (like the King and the parents)."

Name what you and the children have just done in ways that are transferable to another reader, another text, and another day. Show that in reading, as in writing, people layer moments with meanings.

Shifting into debriefing, I said, "Do you see how each of us started out noticing what we paid attention to as we read, and then we realized we notice stuff because it connects with part of what we bring to the text. Then we realized after we realize this, we can try to see *even more* about whatever stands out for us, and we do that partly by thinking about how our lives are and are not the same as the book. What we are doing is what people call interpretation. We start by see more in a story, and then we end up seeing more also in our lives. This is something I want for you for your whole life."

When I read Number the Stars, *I read it as a big sister, and I relate to how Annemarie tries to protect Kirsti. I have done the same with my own sister—tried to protect her from things that are hard to understand. That leads me to think about protection in my life and in this story—how there comes a time when a person can no longer be protected from life and its hardships. I think about Annemarie's parents having to let Annemarie be in dangerous situations, about not being able to protect her. And I think about the earlier passage in which Annemarie's father describes their king, talking about how he tried to protect his people the best way he knew how. Mary, on the other hand, read the passage and thought about all the little signs that things are going amuck in this place. She locked on the sign being in German, the wheels being wooden, the sweets that are only memories. She read it from a perspective of a person who in her past missed some signs when things were falling apart, and she felt the kids were missing all those signs now. They told the signs, but didn't put them all together, which she found wildly frustrating. Our perspectives couldn't have been more different.*

You may worry that this session has not instilled in readers a real knowledge of what constitutes an interpretation of a text, and that is true. You are wise to think about this. Perhaps because of my own long history of being taught about the right way to interpret texts, I've made the decision to start this bend in the road by issuing kids the most generous invitation possible to respond deeply to texts, to approximate interpreting. You'll see that in the sessions that follow, kids are equipped to lift the level of this work.

Rather than teaching kids that the theme of this book is x, and our job is to prove this, I want to teach students that their ideas are worth pursuing and developing. Many researchers believe that the way English was taught when you and I were secondary school students has driven a good many young people away from reading.

LINK

Send children off to read and respond in their idiosyncratic and revealing ways to what they read. Set them up to spend today's workshop reading and also writing about reading.

"Readers, let's head off to continue reading. As you read today, leave some bread-crumbs that can show you, later, the trail of thought you take as you read, the things that stand out for you. You'll be especially noticing. . . . (I completed the sentence by holding up the giant question mark I'd used earlier in the minilesson and shrugging.) As the author of your reading, *you* need to decide what it is you will notice and think about.

"For today, we will not have our regular club meetings (although you will do some work with your club-mates during our share—just not talking) because I want to give you as much time as possible to read and to pay attention to your own unique fin-gerprint as a reader."

You will want to be careful that writing and talking about read-ing do not swamp the actual reading that your kids do in this unit. It could be that you teach a class of extremely proficient readers and that you decide that it is okay for the volume of texts that they read to be a bit lighter this month, with more empha-sis on writing about texts. And it could be that you teach a writ-ing workshop unit parallel to this portion of the reading unit, and that during writing workshop time your children are learning to write well about reading. But in most classrooms, with most kids, you will need to gauge how much writing (versus talking) you can ask your students to do by keeping an eye on their volume of read-ing and making sure this does not lag. For most classrooms, it would be a very bad decision to stuff the reading workshop so full of talking and writing that kids do very little reading. Instead, you'll want to teach interpretive strategies in such a way that readers can use them "on the run," as they read.

Responding from my LIFE HISTORY

* What do I notice and what can I make of it?

* What in my life is leading me to whatever it is that stands out for me in this text?

* How is this text sending me to my life history?

CONFERRING AND SMALL-GROUP WORK

Readers Look Across Responses to Find Ourselves

At the start of the minilesson, I pointed out to students that characters grow by seeing things that they may at one time have overlooked. Teachers, too, grow by learning to see more. Minilessons that put a new spin on the ongoing work readers do (that is, on the work of reading, writing, thinking, and talking) can sometimes help us look at students' ongoing work with new eyes, seeing more that interests *us* in their work. Today's teaching point certainly gave me new eyes because this time, as I looked at the notations readers were making to signal that one passage or another meant something to them, I was especially touched to see ways in which students' own personalities did, indeed, seem to be shaping what they saw in texts. This was a beautiful thing to see because I found myself treating responses to reading as I'm apt to treat children's writing entries. Each seemed intimate, revealing, and delicate.

Sarah and José were both reading silently when I approached first one and then the other, and with both children, I asked them if it would be okay for me to look over the entries they'd been jotting about their club

book, *Bud, Not Buddy*. They were happy to continue reading, so I had a minute to look between their responses. I quickly found a place where the two readers had responded quite differently to the same passage, and I sensed this would help them grasp the point I'd tried to make in the minilesson. The passage they'd written about was one in which the main character, Bud, begins to weep in the middle of a dinner at a restaurant (his first). Sarah had taken his tears in stride and worried only that he was embarrassed over them. "Bud is embarrassed for crying. Bud, you don't always have to be so brave. You don't."

José, on the other hand, had been perplexed over the tears in the first place, writing "Why is Bud crying? He was having the time of his life and now he's crying. He never cried before, even with all the bad stuff that happened to him."

We Can Show Readers How to Notice Patterns in Their Responses to Texts

Asking Sarah and José if I could interrupt for a moment, I said, "I just

---

> **MID-WORKSHOP TEACHING POINT**
>
> #### Characters—and Readers—Learn to See Below the Surface
>
> "Readers, can I have your attention?" I asked and waited for their eyes. "At the start of today, we talked about how Annemarie, after reminding her mother of the time when Kirsti used to sleep between her parents, glanced over at her mom's face, worrying that the memory of those days would bring a pained look to it. And we talked about how part of growing up seems to be that people notice pained looks and other tiny signals of what's going on. Some of you agreed that now that you are older, you see things in your families and among friends that you didn't even notice when you were littler. Your characters are growing more aware, and you are as well.
>
> "So I want to remind you that part of becoming better readers means becoming more aware readers. No one can be aware of everything, but if you are especially drawn to a particular relationship in your book, then watch that relationship and try to see little things that others might not see.
>
> "Right now, look back at what you have noticed so far in the text, and think about whether you are noticing the most obvious things in the world, things that anyone would see, or whether your observations show that like Annemarie, you're growing up, and you're seeing more.
>
> "If your observations seem like they're ones you could have made when you were younger, before you got the eyes to really see, try making some new ones. One way to do this is to just open your reader's notebook and write, 'I will remember . . . ' and then something that you're carrying with you from the book. As you work, I'm going to read aloud some of the observations that my son collected when he was in middle school. These are about a book called *The Chosen*, which is set in the time of World War II. The story opens with a baseball game played between two teams from Jewish schools that were usually kept really separate. Danny Saunders, who
>
> *continued on next page*

found something really interesting." I placed a hand on each notebook to underscore the two jottings I found so fascinating. "This is magical," I whispered. "Just like we talked about in the minilesson; right here you two responded to the exact same passage in your book—and your ideas are so different! Here's the thing. I bet if we look at what you each saw in the passage, I bet we will see something not just about the passage but also about each of you. I bet if we reread your entries, we'll learn not only about Bud, but also about you, Sarah, and you, José."

José read Sarah's entry: [Fig. VIII-6]

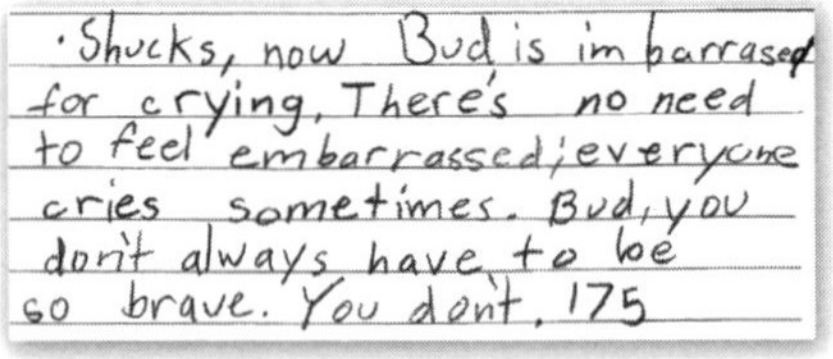

Figure VIII-6

Meanwhile, Sarah read José's, response to the exact same passage: [Fig. VIII-7]

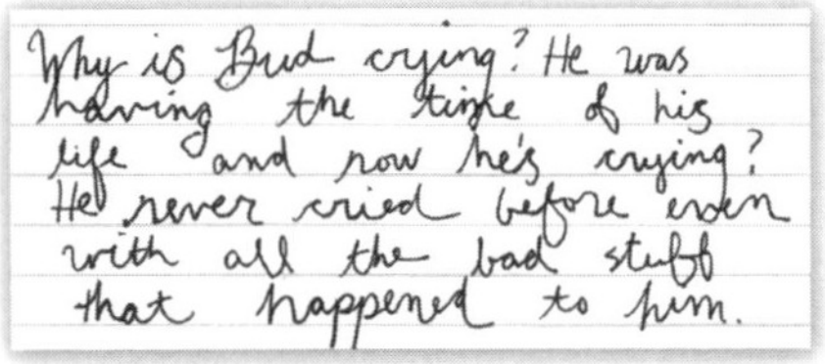

Figure VIII-7

Sarah said to José, who had been baffled about why Bud was upset, "It's like *you* are embarrassed he is crying. That's probably because you are the same as him and you don't, like, cry for happiness or anything."

MID-WORKSHOP TEACHING POINT

continued from previous page

has been chosen by birth to eventually grow to be the leader of his ultraconservative sect, hits a baseball into the face of a player from the other team, Reuven, breaking his glasses and sending a glass shard deep into Reuven's eye. Listen to my son's observations and listen to the nuance, the detail, because as you get older, and more aware, it's the little looks, the unspoken ahhas that you, also, will begin to notice."

I then read aloud an entry my son had written, capturing details he held onto from the start of *The Chosen*. [Fig. VIII-9]

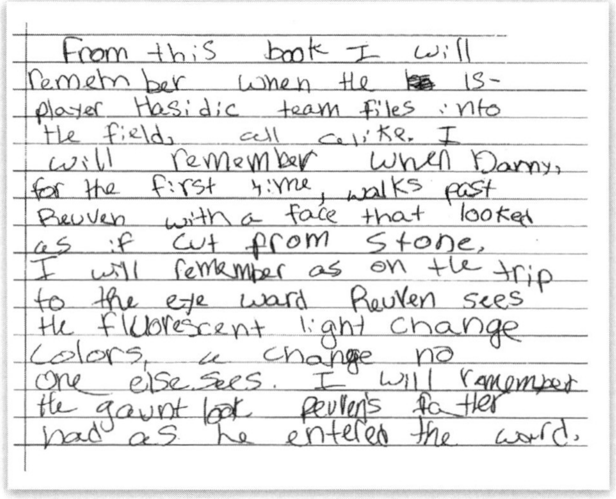

Figure VIII-9

continued on next page

I nodded. "Interesting, Sarah. So you think that for you it makes total sense why Bud would be crying at his first dinner out ever?"

Sarah nodded. "'Cause I'm the same way. I don't just cry when I am sad. Even though he partly *is* sad, I think."

I added on to her interpretation. "And Sarah, I think José and I notice that in your Post-it, you talk right to the person. It's like you can't resist trying to cheer someone up who is miserable, even if it is a person in a book! So it is not just what you think about that reveals you but also how you think. It's like you've sort of put your arm around Bud, saying, 'It's okay to cry.'" Then, to extrapolate my point, I said "Do you see Sarah, how your response to this section shows stuff about you as well as about Bud?"

We Can Scaffold Students to Try What We've Demonstrated, Searching for Patterns across Their Responses to Texts

Then, to rope José into the work of looking over Sarah's responses, I said, "José, I need to check with some other readers to see what they're up to, but do you think that before I come back, you two could look over Sarah's other responses to her book and see if this is sort of a fluke, or if you can almost see a pattern in the ways she responds to books? Then look at what you notice about your responses, José, and what they reveal."

I headed off to work with some other readers, leaving José and Sarah to leaf through other entries Sarah had made. I'd taken a quick glance at them and knew that her notebook was full of phrases like, "Come on Bud! This is a wonderful opportunity to have food, company, a shack" or "Uh oh! Bud is busted!" which seemed to me to very much show how invested she was in rooting for the character. *[Fig. VIII-8]*

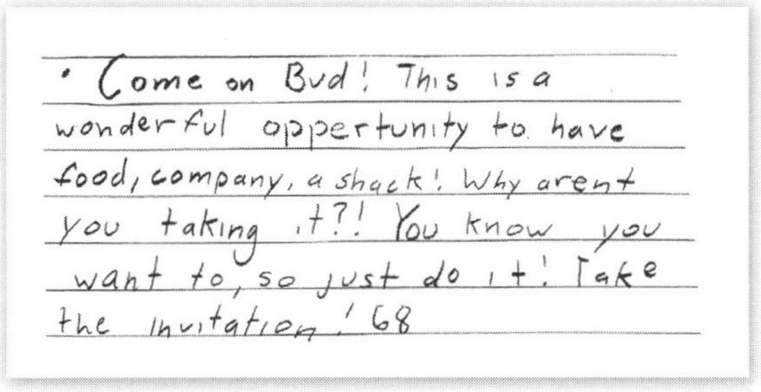
• Come on Bud! This is a wonderful oppertunity to have food, company, a shack! Why arent you taking it?! You know you want to, so just do it! Take the invitation! 68

Figure VIII-8

When I circled back, Sarah and José were waiting. Sarah pointed out other responses that all showed that she can't resist trying to cheer up her characters and then, blushing, said, "Actually, it's sort of true. My friends come to me for help a lot." José capped that off with the point that for her, the characters are like friends.

They then tried to explain how José's Post-its also reflected a pattern, suggesting that he had more facts. I found myself resisting this a little bit because it felt like gender stereotyping (Sarah cares for the characters; José collects facts), but my main goal was to help the readers see that their responses to a text revealed not only the text, but them as well. I also wanted them to feel supported for their responses. "So you are thinking, José, that your thoughts reveal you because they show that you are always gathering information as you read and fitting things together like a puzzle? And here, Bud's crying didn't really fit with the other information you had about him, so you tried to figure it out. It's great how you're thinking of everything you've learned *over the course of the whole book*, not just about this one little part in isolation. 'Cause he's gone through terrible things before and never got really upset, never cried."

José picked up the thread of my thinking. "Yeah, he *never* cried. And now he seems to be actually having a fun time for the first time in the whole book. So it doesn't fit with the rest of the information that he is crying now."

I nodded, "Yeah, and that idea reflects who you are because you are always trying to gain information and to figure out how things work. Not just in reading, but in other subjects, like science and math, too." José was nodding now, too. I said to the two children, "I congratulate you both on the way your responses to reading reflect who you are. Can I teach you one more tip?" They nodded.

MID-WORKSHOP TEACHING POINT

continued from previous page

For a moment, the children borrowed the incantation, "I will remember . . ." and jotted. Then I said, "When you've finished marking what you notice or capturing it in your reader's notebook, shift back to reading. Remember that you can deliberately try to read seeing not just who's coming and who's going, but the looks that pass between them, the raised eyebrows that no one else sees, the person whose fingernails are bitten to the quick. You'll especially want to see what's often unseen and also what's invisible, what lies under the surface of whatever it is that matters especially to you in your book."

We Can Teach Readers that Once We Realize Others Respond Differently than We Do, We Can Try to Take On Their Lenses

"What I want to teach you today is that because your ideas reflect your own experiences and values, it is really powerful in a partnership or a club to try to see the way the other person has been seeing things. So, now that you have noticed your reactions to this one passage are different, can the two of you try on each other's way of seeing in the book? Sarah, as you read on today, continue to read your way, but sometimes push yourself to read José's way and to collect information and put the pieces of Bud together like a puzzle."

José, visibly puffing himself up, said, "Yeah, Bud is brave in the whole book, like I said. All these terrible things happen to him, and he has to take care of himself and act like a grown-up."

I intervened. "There you go again, José, putting all the pieces of the book and of Bud together like the pieces are parts of a puzzle. That's good work, but José, your goal now is to not just do that sort of thinking but to also try to let Sarah *change your mind*, because her ideas are different than yours."

Turning to Sarah, I nudged her, saying, "Get José started thinking like you, Sarah. Which of your thoughts do you want him to carry as he reads on?"

Sarah said, "Well, 'cause, Bud doesn't have to be brave anymore. It's not that he *isn't*, but he doesn't have to be. He cries because he's acting like a kid because he has someone to take care of him for the first time in the book."

I interrupted. "I'm going to leave you two to get back to your reading, and this time remember to try to think like yourself *and* like each other. In the future, maybe you can help the rest of the class learn that we share our ideas with partners, clubs, or the whole class partly because this gives us chances to change as thinkers and readers. It's not just *nice* that people have unique responses. It's necessary. This is how we outgrow our own ideas."

TEACHING SHARE

Readers Realize Our Responses Come from Our Lives and the Texts

Ask children to find an important passage from their independent books and read it aloud to their club mates, and then ask them to stop and jot their thinking at the end of it.

"Readers, make sure you are sitting with your club and ready to give me your attention," I said and waited. "In the minilesson earlier today, we found a passage that seemed significant, and I read it aloud, and then all of us wrote and talked about what that particular passage made us think. You aren't going to be surprised when I tell you that the work we did together is work you can do too, without me. In fact, it is really the most natural thing in the world to look up from a great book or to walk out of a great movie and to say, 'What'd you think of the part when . . . ,' and then everyone shares what they thought about that one part.

"Let's try it. You and your club mates take ten seconds, no more, to find a passage from a section you have read recently that seems important. Do this super quickly." I waited for a minute while most of the children located such a page.

"Now I'm going to ask one person from each club to read the section you marked aloud to your club mates. You'll be doing my job. Read it as if this was read-aloud time. Think about the meaning, the feeling, of the words as you read them. And—here is the important part—after reading just a few sentences or a paragraph, when you feel your own mind is brimming with ideas, say, 'Stop and jot,' and then you and the others in your club *quickly* jot whatever thoughts each one of you has about that part of the story. Each one of you will be bringing yourselves to that one shared passage, and you'll each see different things in it.

"After you and your club mates write for a minute, resume reading aloud just like I do, and then say another 'Stop and jot.' See what I'm getting at?"

After children did this for a bit, I stopped them.

Sam had read a passage from *Roll of Thunder, Hear My Cry* to the other members of the Freedom Fighters. It was the passage where Cassie and her brothers have caused the school bus to break down, and now, in the middle of the night, they are afraid the Klan are coming for them:

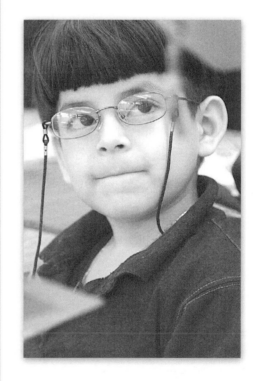

The lead car swung into the muddy driveway and a shadowy figure outlined by the headlights of the car behind him stepped out. The man walked slowly up the drive.

I stopped breathing.

The driver of the next car got out, waiting. The first man stopped and stared at the house for several long moments as if uncertain whether it was the correct destination. Then he shook his head, and without a word returned to his car. With a wave of his hand he sent the other driver back inside, and in less than a minute the lead car had backed into the road, its headlights facing the other cars. Each of the cars used the driveway to turn around, then the caravan sped away as swiftly as it had come, its seven pairs of rear lights glowing like distant red embers until they were swallowed from view by Granger forest.

At this point, he called, "Stop and jot." Aly wrote in her notebook. *[Fig. VIII-10]*

Ask children to share their responses and responses they've written lately and study them, looking for patterns and reflecting on what those patterns might mean.

"Now, put the writing everyone in your group has done just now at the center of the table, and look between each other's writing as if you are scientists, studying patterns. Look at differences between what one person saw in the passage and what another saw. Think, 'How does looking at this help me to see *my* reading as idiosyncratic and revealing, like a fingerprint?' You *might* think, 'What in my life makes me see what I see?' Right now just look and don't say anything, but if you find something interesting, you can point it out (without talking) to your club mate. Jot if you want." *[Fig. VIII-11]*

After a bit I said, "Thumbs up when you have some ideas."

Ask readers to take what they are learning about how they read and let it change the work they choose to do in their clubs.

I said, "I'm not going to ask you to talk about this quite yet. But as you read on, tomorrow, remember that your interpretations will not only show stuff about *the book,* but they'll also show stuff about *you.*

"Before we stop, I want to suggest that you might begin to be more thoughtful about the homework you and your club assign yourselves. I heard members of American

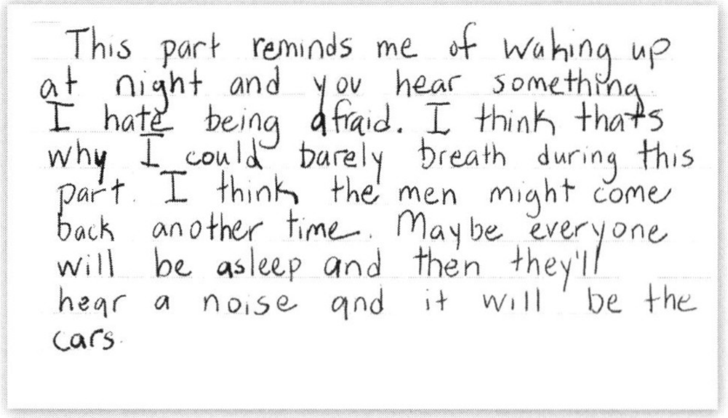
This part reminds me of waking up at night and you hear something I hate being afraid. I think that's why I could barely breath during this part. I think the men might come back another time. Maybe everyone will be asleep and then they'll hear a noise and it will be the cars.

Figure VIII-10
Aly's stop-and-jot response to the passage from *Roll of Thunder, Hear My Cry.*

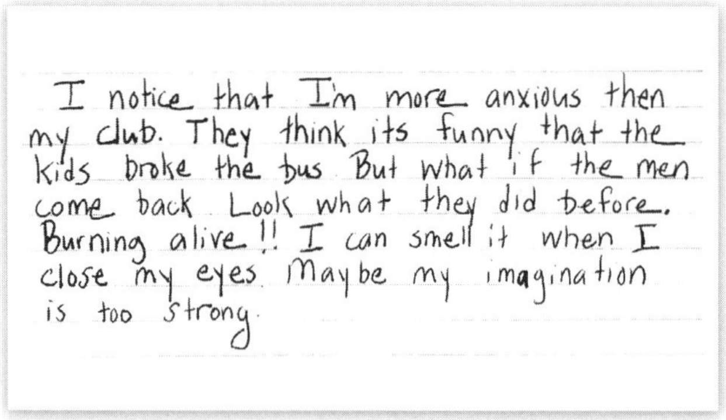
I notice that I'm more anxious then my club. They think its funny that the kids broke the bus But what if the men come back. Look what they did before. Burning alive!! I can smell it when I close my eyes. Maybe my imagination is too strong.

Figure VIII-11
Aly reflected on why her response to the passage was so different from her club mate's responses.

Dreamers say to each other, 'Let's read the next two chapters of *Letters from Rifka*, and write six Post-its.' I was glad the group talked through a homework assignment, but I was surprised that all you talked about was how much you'd read and write, and that was it!

"The amazing thing is that just before they had this talk, this group had an incredible conversation about the fact that *Letters from Rifka* is written as letters written by the main character as she immigrated to the U.S., and—here is the amazing part—the club had just realized that the character wrote the letters in a book of Pushkin's poetry and used a different passage from a Pushkin poem to open each of her letters! It was really easy to overlook that, but they'd just spotted the pattern. The club could have said, "For homework, let's go back and study the book to figure out why she selected the particular Pushkin quote for each of her letters." Instead, they just assigned themselves pages to read. All of you, in your clubs, have gotten great at inventing things to do so use that inventive spirit of yours to come up with homework that pulls the club together and sets you up for grand conversations."

This tip about the homework makes the teaching share especially long, and you may want to find a different moment to help your children think about the homework they're doing in preparation for club conversations. But you definitely will want to make sure that children learn the power of generating a shared focus for the reading and writing about reading that they do at home. If every reader simply reads the requisite chapters and Post-its or writes about whatever occurs to that reader, then when kids convene in clubs, it's bound to be difficult for them to come together around a shared focus. Each child will be prepared for an entirely different conversation. But if, on the other hand, the members of a club have all thought about one thing—as in the example here, where they decided to figure out how Karen Hesse chose particular Pushkin quotes for each of the chapters of this book—then they enter the conversation already angled toward collaborative talk. Ideally, the homework is not only shared, but it also grows out of one day's club conversation, helping children to become even better at advancing an idea across time.

Developing an Assessment Tool for Writing About Reading

In planning your formative assessments, you may eventually want to develop a tool for tracking your students' abilities to write about their reading.

A Framework for a New Tool for Assessing Literary Essays

Although my colleagues and I have not developed the tool I'm imagining, we do have ideas to bring to the table. First, it may help you to know that most of the schools in which the Teachers College Reading and Writing Project works have devised a system for assessing students' *narrative* writing, and we know a similar system could be developed to assess students' literary essays.

Ask Students to Complete a Piece of On-Demand Writing in the Genre You Are About to Teach

The system we have used works as follows:

During the first few days of the school year, every teacher, grades 1–8 (and many kindergarten teachers) are asked to set aside fifty minutes for this assessment. Teachers tell students, "We want to come to understand something about your writing. Will you take the next fifty minutes and write your best personal narrative (that is, your best true story, your best Small Moment story) about one particular time you experienced."

Then children produce their narratives, and teachers gauge the quality of each student's work by measuring the text against a sequence of student-authored narrative texts, ranging from level 1–15. The qualities of those narratives have been described in some detail. The teachers do not look at spelling and punctuation because those are important but separate. This is a measure of a student's ability to write effective narratives.

After Teaching Students to Write in that Genre, Again Ask for an On-Demand Example of What They Can Do

Then, after two units of study in narrative writing (and after two months), there will be an author's celebration to recognize the students' hard work on pieces of writing that they've taken through the entire writing process. After this, the teacher repeats the assessment, using exactly the same words and conditions, looking to see whether the work that the students produce now reflects increased skills. The larger question is whether the work the students did over the intervening two months helped those writers improve not only the drafts that they produced with input from peers and teachers but also the level of what they could do another day, on their own, in a timed assessment. This same assessment is repeated two or three other times throughout the year.

Replicate this Process for the Genre of Responses to Historic Fiction

By all means, we suggest that you replicate some portions of this straight away. Why not read aloud a short historical fiction text—perhaps a picture book—and then ask students to take a set amount of time—perhaps just forty minutes, if time is short—to write an interpretative literary essay about that text, in which they write about a big idea they developed while reading it. If you want to be more directive, you could ask them to write about what the text is really about, about the life lessons the text is teaching.

In this assessment, as in the on-demand writing assessments the Project is already using, it is important for you to be hands-off. Let your students flounder, if that's what they know how to do. In a situation like this, what you want is simply to understand their understandings. If they do not have a way to proceed, document that. You'll have a great "before teaching" to contrast with your "after teaching" story! Then get busy thinking about how you will take your students from where they are to where they need to be.

We aren't able to offer you examples of student writing in this genre along a spectrum of development the way we do with narrative writing, but we may build such a sequence eventually. In the meantime, this would be an important project to take on as a grade level or school! Below I describe some strands along which you may choose to look for development.

A Framework for Assessing Literary Essays: Strands of Development

When you assess your students' work, you'll undoubtedly see strands of development along which students proceed. That is, you'll see that different students are more or less far along in these (and other) lines of development.

Putting Forth an Idea

Students will vary in their abilities to put forth an idea—not a fact, not a retelling, but a claim, a theory, an idea that the student has developed about the text. Sometimes you'll see that students know how to retell a story but not tell an idea. Then you'll know you have some work to do either helping them develop ideas, or helping them capture ideas in written language. It's possible that your students do develop ideas in their conversations, but that they're not used to writing about these ideas. So if your students slip immediately into retelling when they write about reading, remind them to start with what seems particularly important about this text or what the story seems to really be about.

How Well Does the Idea Reflect Knowledge of Literary Scholarship?

The ideas that students put forth will vary in the ways in which they reflect knowledge of literary scholarship. Does the student use literary language, when appropriate, and stay within the conversations of literary scholarship, when appropriate, doing things such as citing the author, genre, and title of the text being discussed? Does the student describe the text briefly, perhaps giving an angled retelling that gets her ready for her idea?

How Much of the Text Does the Idea Take into Account?

The ideas students put forth will vary in their relevance to the entire text (rather than to just one part of it, generally the end). It's not that a literary essay can't be about part of the text, but then the thesis needs to make that part's significance clear, and generally a strong thesis relates not just to a part of the text but to the whole of it as well.

How Well Matched to the Text Is the Idea?

The ideas students put forth will reflect varied amounts of traction in the actual text. That is, to be powerful, a big idea has precision and grounding, so that it feels as if it was tailor made for this occasion, although also relevant beyond this text and this reader.

How Powerful Is the Idea?

The ideas students put forth will vary in the extent to which they are compelling. Usually, for them to be compelling to *readers* of the essay, there needs to be a sense that they are compelling to the *writer* of the essay. One way to convey this is for one idea to give way to a second, dawning idea.

Including Evidence for the Idea

Students will vary in their proclivity to ground their ideas in specific references to the text. Some will tend to do this. Whether they do it well or not is another question, but they will tend to do it, while others will show no uneasiness over conclusions that are unsubstantiated.

How Strong Is the Evidence for the Idea?

When students do ground their ideas in references to the texts, sometimes the references are appropriate and actually do support the ideas, and sometimes they seem somewhat irrelevant or peripheral.

How Well Does the Language Connecting the Idea to the Evidence Clarify the Importance and Relevance of the Evidence?

When students ground their ideas in references to the text, some contextualizing of those passages or references is necessary for readers to follow the argument.

To provide evidence, many children will rely on transitional phrases such as, "For example . . . ," "For instance . . . ," "Also . . . ," "In addition

. . . ," "This was evident when . . . ," and "One time. . . ." Some higher-level transitional phrases include "moreover," "however," and "on the other hand," phrases that mark levels and stages and counterpoints of an idea, rather than simply additional evidence.

How Well Analyzed Is the Evidence?

When students ground their claims in references to the text, they vary in their abilities and proclivities to turn from citation to analysis. Ideally, the reader shows how a reference makes the point the reader has claimed the example makes, using phrases such as "This shows that . . . ," "Notice how . . . ," and "It is important to note that. . . ."

Organizing Ideas

Effective academic essays usually provide the reader with a structure that makes it easier for the reader to read, take notes on, and learn from the text. This is true of expository texts and for effective literary essays. (Although the structure of an essay can be an internal skeleton, as it is on human beings, or an exo-skeleton, as on beetles, when students write essays on standardized tests, those essays are judged by readers who make snap judgments and may not have a great deal of experience structuring essays. The best advice, then, is for students to provide a very clear exoskeleton when writing on standardized tests.)

How Sophisticated Is the Essay's Structure?

Another way to consider students' progress in writing literary essays is to notice what they attempt to do in their essays. Although an essay can be simple in design and sophisticated in content (or vice versa), it is helpful to realize that there are some essays that are fairly accessible for even novice literary essayists, some that are more complicated and demanding by design, and some that are especially sophisticated.

A Continuum of Development Along the Strand of Organizing Ideas

Now let's take one of the above-mentioned strands of development along which children may grow as they strengthen their ability to respond in writing to texts, in this case, to historical fiction. For this strand, I'll offer you a bit more of the detail about what some of the stages along this strand might look like. Together with your colleagues, you may want to

unpack another of the strands in the same fashion that I unpack this one, based on your examination of lots of student work, over time.

Essay Type 1: One Character Trait Through Three Parts of the Text

A format for literary essays that seems to be especially accessible is one in which a person describes a character's traits. For example, if a student were to write about *Number the Stars*, he might organize the essay around the claim, Annemarie is brave. The essay could then provide examples of times when she is brave. The start of the essay might be written in one of these ways:

- In Lois Lowry's novel, *Number the Stars*, the main character, Annemarie, is very brave. For example, she is brave when she stands up to the soldiers on the street corner, she is brave when the soldiers come into her house, and she is brave when she carries the basket past the soldiers to Uncle Henrik.

- In Lois Lowry's historical fiction novel, *Number the Stars*, the protagonist, Annemarie, is brave enough to stand up to the Nazis. She is brave at the beginning of the book, in the middle of the book, and toward the end of the book.

Both of those essays set the reader up to write about passages in the book that illustrate their premise and to proceed chronologically through the book as they do this. The examples are literal. The writer needs to retell or to quote sections of the text that come at these different points and that illustrate the character's bravery. Ideally, the writer will also "unpack" those sections, showing how they illustrate Annemarie's bravery. The writer might pose a contrasting scenario, writing, "She could have . . . , but did she? No! Instead, Annemarie. . . ." The writer could also explore the sources of her courage, of the specific things she did that were brave. But the essence of this essay is that it provides examples to illustrate the one, static, claim.

Essay Type 2: Evolving Character Trait Through Three Parts of the Text

There are several alternative ways for the design of an essay to be more complex. First, the same character trait essay could be written in a way that shows the character's trait in evolution. For example, in the *Number the Stars* essay, the student could write that although at first Annemarie was timid, she became increasingly courageous across the story. Such an essay might start like this:

> *Annemarie learns to be increasingly brave throughout the story of Number the Stars. At first she is nervous even to talk to the soldiers. But by the end, she deliberately tricks the soldiers. She learns to be daring.*

Of course, the same claim could be worded differently. The claim could be that the main character learns or changes. This change over time is still a fairly easy essay to write, because there can be one paragraph about the character demonstrating the absence of the trait early on and one about the character demonstrating the presence of the trait later on. Ideally, there may also be a paragraph about moments of change and growth. It is important in change essays that the writer not simply leap to the finale, bypassing the starting condition.

Essay Type 3: A Lesson the Reader Might Learn from the Text

Another way for essays to be somewhat more complex is for them to explore the lessons that the character learned. Usually these lessons are brought home at the end of the book, so one of the challenges is to teach readers to show how some of the lessons were also learned earlier in the book. In *Number the Stars*, for example, a child structuring an essay in this way might write that the book teaches the lesson that when people band together, they can make a difference. The example that first comes to mind is the way in which the fishermen and villagers combine to help bring the Jews safely to Sweden. Children who are working on this kind of an essay will need to work a bit to find instances of lessons that are taught earlier in the book.

Essay Type 4: An Idea, and Evidence, from the Text, Other Texts, and Life

The design of the most complex essays will tend to be characterized by a few qualities. First, the writer will address an idea that is universal, applying it not only to the text at hand but to other books and to life. For example, such a writer might say of *Number the Stars,* "This book tells that in times of crisis, people find themselves capable of surprising bravery." The basic premise is the same as the essay described earlier—Annemarie is brave—but by wording this in a more abstract way, the essay is pertinent

not only to this text but in a broader context. This also means that evidence is not apt to be drawn from the text alone, but instead may be synthesized from life itself and from other books.

Perhaps the Writer's Thinking About the Text Has Grown

One way to help readers progress from a literal interpretation to a more interpretive and universal one is to suggest that they first write their literal interpretation of the text in the first body paragraph and then try to push themselves to ask, "What life lessons, beyond this text, can be learned?" A form that works well for this is for the writer to write, "When I first read XYZ, I thought it was about . . . , but now, after thinking more deeply, I'm coming to realize that actually, it is about. . . ." Of course, a progression of thinking can be conveyed in lots of ways. "On a literal level, X is the story of . . . , but on a more interpretive level, X is actually the story of. . . ."

Perhaps the Writer Compares to Other Texts

It can also be challenging for students to write across more than one text while still developing a coherent essay. One way to do this is to focus the essay on similarities:

> *In both Rose Blanche and Number the Stars, we learn that children can be heroic.*

Such an essay, of course, would then show examples from both texts of children being heroic. Another way to write an essay that extrapolates from across texts—and this is more challenging—is to write about similarities and also differences.

> *While the children in both Rose Blanche and Number the Stars are heroic, the children are in very different situations because Blanche acts alone and Annemarie has the support of her family.*

This kind of thesis will lead to a more nuanced essay that really delves into similarities and differences that are lodged in the details of the texts.

These are some of the factors that may be helpful for you in assessing your students' literary essay skills, and in helping to develop them. You may find it useful to gather together some student essays and sort through them with your colleagues, making a continuum of ones that you find increasingly strong, and then give some language to what makes those essays strong. Then you'll have some clear stages and qualities, as we've developed for a narrative continuum.

SESSION IX

Making Significance

IN THIS SESSION,
you will teach your students that readers pause to read important passages attentively to grow ideas about our texts.

oming home from a summer vacation, my family and I love to talk through all of the experiences we've had that will now be a part of us forever. It is usually as we head home that we have this conversation in a grand and deliberate way. We mull over our vacation, remembering the time we couldn't get the fire

GETTING READY

- In the connection portion of this minilesson, we again reread the tiny excerpt from Chapter 3 of *Number the Stars* that begins, "Soon we will have to add another blanket to your bed." You could substitute a lot of other passages, so choose a favorite quotation, one that causes you to linger on it.

- During the teaching portion of this minilesson, you'll continue reading *Number the Stars* by starting in Chapter 3 with the line, "Annemarie was almost asleep when there was a light knock on the door," unless you have decided to weave a different text throughout the unit. If you read Lowry's book, you'll read a few pages of the text, up to the part that ends with, "Your mother told me about what happened on Osterbrogade."

- You will also return to a portion of *The Tiger Rising*, Chapter 10, or another favorite read-aloud, reading an excerpt from that book to illustrate what you mean by the passages that an author seems to have written in bold.

- Since this teaching portion switches between reading from the text and asking children to stop and jot, you may want to mark the read-aloud to show places where you'll pause.

- During the active involvement portion of the minilesson, you'll set children up to continue the work you modeled during the teaching section, and to do so, you'll ideally want to distribute copies of *Number the Stars* to each club or copies of a few pages from Chapter 3 to each club. An excerpt from Chapter 3 is available on the *Resources for Teaching Reading* CD-ROM.

- Prepare a chart entitled "Thinking Deeply About Important Passages in a Book," which is detailed in the active involvement of this session. You'll use this chart today and in future sessions.

- During the mid-workshop teaching, you'll create a quick checklist of thought prompts readers use to push their thinking. Or you could prepare it ahead of time.

- Your children will be meeting with their clubs today, but for most of the time, instead of doing their usual work around their club books, they will problem-solve around predictable difficulties.

- During the teaching share, you will add to the chart, "Growing Powerful Book Club Conversations," which was created in Volume 1.

started and had to eat wet peanut butter sandwiches in the rain under the stand of skinny birch trees (how they glowed against the gray sky) and remembering the time we misjudged the distance so that what we thought would be a three-hour hike lasted all day, yet we persevered and as day slipped into evening, stood triumphant on the granite ledge at the top of the mountain. We link each indelible moment to another, threading them like pearls on a necklace. And threading through those memories will be an awareness of

> *Today you will say that it can be not a patch of birch trees but a passage of a text that causes us to gasp and that reorders our internal world.*

how we are the same and not the same on successive visits, across the years.

Sometimes, as we reflect on a summer, we'll even get out a water-stained, peanut buttery, crumpled and sooty map of our journey and pore over it together. That's where we saw the fox. That's where we heard the loon. That's where we had those delicious grilled cheese sandwiches at the diner. As we connect one event to another, we build meaning out of what we've done. We see reoccurring pleasure, we come to understand how these events characterize us as a family and the life we want together, and we realize that we're talking not only about events but also about values. And the remembering and the talking helps bring all that we did into all that we are so that later, once the vacation is over, we go forward differently, bringing all we have expe-

rienced with us. The talking makes it more likely that we are forever people who have seen a moose in the morning drinking deep from a still lake.

Of course, some children have never been invited into conversations like those. Some have never yet stayed up the whole drive home, past the time when littler kids go to sleep and the tones become quieter. Some children haven't been part of the conversations that thread one event with another, through this vacation and the last one, and loop toward next summer, when the kids will be bigger. For those children, the reading workshop is all the more important. The work of interpretation is very much a part of what it means to be a reflective human being.

The question, of course, is, How do we help children do the intimate work that fits so well into those long drives home from a vacation? How do we bring that work into a class full of busy elementary school students, each progressing through books at their own rates? How do we make sure that children pause and think across the terrain of the book they're reading, noticing threads, asking weighty questions, making deep connections, and deriving large meaning, so that in the end, reading leads them to reflect not only on the books but also on their lives? How do we help them go forward, carrying with them all this knowledge, all the ways that they have been moved by their books?

These are big shoes that we're setting out for readers and for us, too, as teachers of reading. Surely this work will require the whole of this unit and the whole of life in our classroom, long after this unit is over. Today is just a start. Today's session asks readers to become deep, thoughtful readers. You will teach readers that the big ideas that make such a difference do not emerge out of looking up in the air and trying to have spiritual, meaningful insights. They emerge from close, attentive readings of texts. For today's session, you will teach children to pause especially at passages that, as you'll put it, "seem to be written in bold letters."

What you will really be saying is similar to the message you conveyed yesterday. Readers pay attention, and to do this, we decide some things matter. We push a metaphorical pause button when things seem laden with meaning, and then we do not simply drink in more, more, more of what the text says, of who is going where and doing what. Instead, we pause to think hard not only about what is happening in the book but also about what it all means.

This is a mental move that people can make in our lives as well as in our reading. So often I rush through my life, not really letting anything I see effect me. I walk through the woods, talking on the cell phone, racing to get home to check more items off my to-do list. John Dewey deplored this way of going through our days, so that "ordinary experience is often infected with apathy, lassitude and stereotype."

In today's session, the message is that it doesn't have to be this way. We can instead live with openness to our own lives, expecting meaning and making meaning. We can walk through the woods, taking in the miracles of this day. The other day I was walking in the woods, making my cell phone call, checking the time, when suddenly I come around a corner into a startling riot of yellow birch leaves and stark, white trunks, and I felt that gasp of recognition and suddenly, reordered my internal world to accommodate this glorious sight. I then moved forward with birch trees inside me forever. Today you will say that it can be not a patch of birch trees but a passage of a text that causes us to gasp and that reorders our internal world.

One of the ways I know a book is a good one—one that will stay with me, change me, teach me, and move me—is that it provides me with many of those stopping places where I feel rung through like a gong with new meaning. It is this that you will bring to your children.

MINILESSON

Making Significance

CONNECTION

Find an anecdote that makes the point that instead of hurrying with blinders on through life, it is important for people to pause to experience our own experiences.

"Readers, you know the poet Naomi Shihab Nye is one of my personal heroes. One day when she visited me, she told me that earlier that day, she had taken her son to see the sights in New York City. She and her son had stood in a long line waiting for the ferry to take them to the Statue of Liberty. Beside their line of people, a couple of gymnasts did tricks—leaping, flipping, standing on each other's shoulders.

"Naomi said that most of the people in the line stood with their eyes glued on the distant dot of the ferry, not even turning their heads to watch the gymnasts. All of a sudden, one of the gymnasts broke ranks from the group and addressed the crowd directly. 'Please pause,' he called. 'The boat will come. I promise you; it will come. Take your mind off what will happen ten minutes from now, an hour from now. Right now, right here, right before your eyes, we are doing something you can't do. It is beautiful. You are missing the show. Pause. Please pause.

Although I am telling about Naomi Shihab Nye's advice to writers, almost any writer who advises aspiring writers gives similar advice. Certainly Byrd Baylor's beautiful book, I'm in Charge of Celebrations *carries the same theme, as does Annie Lamont's* Bird by Bird.

As I help graduate students and teachers design units of study, I find that many of them don't tap into the potential power of these earliest moments in a minilesson. This is a wonderful time to bring to life some of the concepts that you have taught on preceding days. It is possible to simply say, "Yesterday we learned that readers often . . ." and then repeat the teaching point, referencing a chart, but I think it is much more valuable if we can find a way to bring yesterday's work to life, to make it real and important.

Within your own class, moments will happen on any given day that can become touchstone moments, and you'll want to return to those moments, retelling the story of them and making meaning from them. You will probably have stories that you introduced in writing workshop that convey this "please pause" message. Whatever the source of the moment, it is probably important for you to notice the way I've written the minilesson so that it incorporates an anecdote. First I tell a little story. Then I essentially say, "And isn't this true for us all, as readers?"

"Naomi suggested that the gymnast was giving advice not only to sightseers but also to all of us as people, and as readers and writers. In life, we are all of us rushing, rushing, trying to get to the next place. And we do need someone to say, 'Pause. Please pause.' We need someone to help us push the pause button in our lives so that we stop and notice what is right before our eyes."

Suggest that readers, like people in general, need to press the pause button to think deeply. Recall times when reflecting on the read-aloud yielded new meaning.

"We have learned that thoughtful readers don't just focus on what's coming next in a text, reading faster, faster, faster. Instead, we sometimes push the pause button to reflect.

"You'll remember that last time we met, I pushed the pause button when we were reading that rather everyday descriptive passage from *Number the Stars:*"

> "Soon we will have to add another blanket to your bed," Mama said one morning as she and Annemarie tidied the bedroom.

> "Kirsti and I are lucky to have each other for warmth in the winter," Annemarie said. "Poor Ellen, to have no sisters."

You can write a similar connection, situating it in your own classroom. Imagine, for example, that during the preceding day, you all looked at rocks, searching for fossils. Perhaps at first kids all called out, "I don't have any fossils on my rock," but then they looked more closely and suddenly began to see traces of long-gone sea creatures, learning they could read even a rock. Had such a moment happened in your class, you could definitely use it in your minilesson! If it happened three years ago or happened to a friend rather than to you, you can still use it. The anecdote I've told from Naomi Nye must have occurred twenty years ago, and I return to it not only to teach reading but also to teach writing. Of course, it is easier for me to talk about Naomi's life lesson than for me to actually take it to heart. I have so much to do, so much to get to.

You'll no doubt have a gesture that you use to illustrate pressing the pause button. For me, I'm accustomed enough to the old-fashioned tape recorders with pause buttons that one pushed down on, using a thumb, that I always pretend to be pausing one of those tape recorders when I talk about pressing the pause button. You may bring a different image to this. Most of our students are familiar with the pause buttons on DVD players, and iPods. Your classroom may have an old-fashioned VCR, with a Pause button right there. The important thing is to understand that visuals can support your oral language.

"I wasn't quite sure why, but something in me was telling me to pause, to linger here. During yesterday's teaching share, it was *you* who decided when to press the pause button. I've been thinking about it, and I realized that what you did yesterday when you paused to stop and jot is exactly what *really* thoughtful readers do. You read, you paused, you pondered."

Name your teaching point. Specifically, teach children that thoughtful readers expect to pause as we encounter passages that seem laden with significance.

"Today I want to remind you that thoughtful readers sometimes press the pause button, lingering to ponder what we've read and to let a bigger idea begin to grow in our minds. For each reader, there will be passages in a book that seem to be written in bold, parts that just call out to that reader as being important. Often these are passages that harken back to earlier sections in the book and that seem laden with meaning, and we read those passages extra attentively, letting them nudge us to think."

Teaching

Recall times, within the life of the class or of previous read-alouds, when something made us all listen with wider eyes, leaning in.

"Readers, this is something we all already do, in our lives *and* in our reading. When someone, whether it is a friend or an author, says something we know is important, our eyes go wide, we lean in, we drink in each word, we make sure we don't miss anything. If we're reading a story, we let the story cue us so that we know the places in which to do this: to pause, to ponder, and to respond, perhaps even to record ideas in our notebooks.

"I'm sure you remember when we were reading *The Tiger Rising* how certain parts of the book were just begging us to pay really close attention. In certain parts, Kate DiCamillo seemed to give us a window not just on the details of the story, but on a bigger landscape of meaning. Remember this part, when Willie May tells Rob what she thinks his rash is all about?"

Remember that if in the previous session you described pausing with reference to a tape recorder, likening what readers do to "pressing the pause button," then you will need to stay with that metaphor for a bit. It can be very confusing to children when we throw too many metaphors around. The flip side is that it can be very helpful to give children words that allow them to think and talk well about something as invisible as reading.

Later in this minilesson, you will see that one way that authors layer passages with added meaning is by using phrases or objects that are situated in earlier parts of the text. So when Annemarie lies in bed trying to tell herself that she is old enough to rise to the challenge of protecting the Rosens, she says to herself that she is ten, with no more dreams of pink-frosted cupcakes. The reference to the cupcakes brings up the whole story about Kirsti and those cupcakes, so it is more than a word, more even than an object or image. Similarly, when our teaching cites portions of previous lessons, we bring the entire experience of those lessons to bear on whatever we are currently teaching, and this is one way to layer our teaching, to make it deeper, and to keep earlier work alive.

Of course, you'll do all that you describe so that actions accompany your words. Over and over, you are trying to tell readers that reading requires a choice—a choice to let the text in. This is the old curmudgeon minilesson, in a new metaphor! You could also describe how, when you see a movie, there will be parts where the whole audience gets silent, because something really important is happening, or there will be parts where even if you really have to go to the bathroom, you don't even consider leaving the theater, because you don't want to miss one moment of this part.

Reading aloud an excerpt that you and the class have already discussed deeply will get your students on board in an efficient manner because the read-aloud will resurrect the prior conversations, allowing students to remember not only a part in the text but a part in their lives. If necessary, give your students some context for the passage you read so they instantly grasp it. Obviously, there is nothing sacrosanct about this particular passage.

Willie May opened her eyes and looked over the top of her glasses at Rob's legs.

"Mmmm," she said, after a minute. "How long you had that?"

"About six months," said Rob.

"I can tell you how to cure that," said Willie May, pointing with her cigarette at his legs. "I can tell you right now. Don't need to go to no doctor."

"Huh?" said Rob. He stopped chewing his gum and held his breath. What if Willie May healed him and then he had to go back to school?

"Sadness," said Willie May, closing her eyes and nodding her head. "You keeping all that sadness down low, in your legs. You not letting it get up to your heart, where it belongs. You got to let that sadness rise on up."

"We talked a lot about this passage when we were reading this book; don't you agree it's one of those parts that almost seems like the author wrote it in bold so we'd pay close attention? One of the sentences I carry with me is the one when Willy May said, 'You got to let that sadness rise on up.'"

Read aloud an upcoming section of the read-aloud, selected because it is laden with bits that could be regarded as significant. Ask children to signal when the text almost seems to be written in bold, and then ask them to stop and jot.

"Each of our books has parts like this one, parts that are just dying for our undivided attention. Readers are alert to important passages, ones that feel as if they've been written in bold, and we notice them as we read. Let's practice noticing parts that call for attention as we read on in *Number the Stars*. I'm going to read aloud, and let's pay special attention to any part that seems to be just begging for us to pause. Signal with a thumbs up when we get to a part in which you would like to press pause, and at some point I'll pause. It may be a part that harkens back to earlier passages; certainly it will be a part that brims with significance."

Time and again you will want to pass the baton to your children. Earlier this year, when you read aloud, you were probably the one to decide on stopping spots. Yet in life, one of the jobs a reader needs to do is determine thought-worthy passages and to stop after reading them to mull for a moment. How reasonable, then, that you'd be asking your students to identify those stopping spots before asking them to mull.

"Remember, we won't all gesture to pause at the same places in the text, and that's the way reading is. Our decisions about when to pause will be informed partly by who we are as individual readers. Don't worry if the place where you want to pause is not the same place where others want to pause.

"Okay, I'll start reading and I'll go for a page or so before we pause, so that we get into the story and have some text to work with."

> Annemarie was almost asleep when there was a light knock on the bedroom door. Candlelight appeared as the door opened, and her mother stepped in. "Are you asleep, Annemarie?"
>
> "No. Why? Is something wrong?"
>
> "Nothing's wrong. But I'd like you to get up and come out to the living room. Peter's here. Papa and I want to talk to you."
>
> Annemarie jumped out of bed, and Kirsti grunted in her sleep. Peter! She hadn't seen him in a long time. There was something frightening about him being here at night. Copenhagen had a curfew, and no citizens were allowed out after eight o'clock. It was very dangerous, she knew, for Peter to visit at this time. But she was delighted that he was here. Though his visits were always hurried—they almost seemed secret, somehow, in a way she couldn't quite put her finger on—still, it was a treat to see Peter. It brought back memories of happier times. And her parents loved Peter too. They said he was like a son. Barefoot, she ran to the living room and into Peter's arms. He grinned, kissed her cheek, and ruffled her long hair.
>
> "You've grown taller since I saw you last," he told her. "You are all legs!"
>
> Annemarie laughed. "I won the girls' footrace last Friday at school," she told him proudly. "Where have you been? We've missed you!"
>
> "My work takes me all over," Peter explained. "Look, I brought you something. One for Kirsti, too." He reached into his pocket and handed her two seashells.
>
> Annemarie put the smaller one on the table to save it for her sister. She held the other in her hands. Turning it in the light, looking at the ridged, pearly surface. It was so like Peter, to bring just the right gift.

It is crucial to clarify this point for children—and for ourselves. We are not teaching readers to find the particular places we have already marked as especially significant in each book. Instead we are teaching them to read with an open and sensitive mind, to find parts of texts that resonate for them. In life and in reading, no one tells us when to pause and see more, when to think more deeply. When we walk in the woods, nobody says, "Stop and take a good hard look at this particular view." We simply gasp, remember, lean forward, and feel.

Granted, there will be passages in the books we read, of course, that clearly brim with significance, that are multilayered and striking and resonant. But those passages will certainly not resonate in the same way for each reader, and each reader may indeed choose different passages to think deeply about. We are guiding students not toward choosing the "right" passage but toward paying deep attention as they read so that they can identify and then focus deeply on those passages that resonate the most strongly for them. We are also, implicitly, showing our students that they matter—that the curriculum is not something that we will spoon into them, but that they are important in the curriculum. Indeed, they are the curriculum.

I do believe there is enormous significance to the gift of seashells. They are so fragile, as if reminding readers that joys are fragile. The seashells also remind me of Kirsti's longing for summer vacations by the seashore and for pink cupcakes. The mention of seashells reminds me that Copenhagen is near the ocean, with Sweden across the water, and as you can guess, that will become important to this story. Although the seashells merit thought and although a few children lifted their thumbs at this section, I didn't pause here simply because I don't think the children would see the gift of seashells as significant as I do, and I'm not convinced it is relevant at this point to try to teach them otherwise. There is an overwhelming urge to teach students the significance of symbols in the stories they read. But if they have not yet begun to notice these objects, I try to refrain from telling them what to think.

"For your mama and papa, I brought something more practical. Two bottles of beer!"

Mama and Papa smiled and raised their glasses. Papa took a sip and wiped the foam from his upper lip. Then his face became more serious.

"Annemarie," he said. "Peter tells us that the Germans have issued orders closing many stores run by Jews."

"Jews?" Annemarie repeated. "Is Mrs. Hirsch Jewish? Is that why the button shop is closed? Why have they done that?"

Peter leaned forward. "It is their way of tormenting. For some reason, they want to torment Jewish people. It has happened in other countries. They have taken their time here—have let us relax a little. But now it seems to be starting."

"But why the button shop? What harm is a button shop? Mrs. Hirsch is such a nice lady. Even Samuel—he's a dope, but he would never harm anyone. How could he—he can't even see, with his thick glasses!"

Then Annemarie thought of something else. "If they can't sell their buttons, how will they earn a living?"

"Friends will take care of them," Mama said gently. "That's what friends do."

I noticed some children signaling that this is a stopping spot, and I gestured to those signals, and agreed. "Hmm, I know *I* certainly have the feeling that I want to linger here; I can see many of you do, too." I began that lingering by rereading: "'Friends will take care of them. . . . That's what friends do.' This seems like it is a little nugget for readers and for Annemarie to hold onto, to believe in. And it does connect back with things that came earlier in the story, doesn't it? So let's think about why this part seems important. What's it really saying? I'm going to jot for a minute to get my mind going, and you can do the same."

I read this part with great significance, almost imbuing my voice with bolds, knowing that this will channel many readers to signal that this is a good stopping place. Frankly, I've already decided to stop here.

You'll figure out how you want to go about channeling your students to turn and talk or to stop and jot. You could be blunt, saying, "Let's think about what this part is really saying. Stop and jot." And if you say that with energy and meanwhile grab a pen and start scrawling furiously, children will become very good at picking up their pens instantly and writing off from the momentum of what you just said. On the other hand, you may wish to have a more invitational tone, as you see in this example: "What's this part really saying? I'm going to jot for a moment to get my mind going. Will you do the same?"

The only sound was the scratch of pens. Once everyone was writing, I shifted among the children, noticing what they were writing. Aly, Jasmine, and Brianna had all written a short paragraph in their notebooks: *[Figs. IX-1, IX-2, and IX-3]*

Coach into children's thinking and writing about the passage to channel them toward interprettive thinking. Especially nudge them to think, 'How does this one passage connect with earlier ones and with the whole message of the book?'

After children had written for a minute, I said, "Readers, here's a tip. When readers think deeply about one part of the story, it helps to think about how that one part connects with other parts of the story." Again I left time for children to write, write, write.

Continue reading, and again ask children to signal when the text feels so laden with meaning that it requires readers to pause and reflect.

After a minute or two more, I looked up. "Readers, let's keep going. We may find other parts that feel as if they were written in bold font. If so, you can continue scrawling your thoughts if you want." I read.

> Then Annemarie thought of something else. "If they can't sell their buttons, how will they earn a living?"
>
> "Friends will take care of them," Mama said gently. "That's what friends do."
>
> Annemarie nodded. Mama was right, of course. Friends and neighbors would go to the home of the Hirsch family, would take them fish and potatoes and bread and herbs for making tea. Maybe Peter would even take them a beer. They would be comfortable until their shop was allowed to open again.
>
> Then, suddenly, she sat upright, her eyes wide. "Mama!" she said. "Papa! The Rosens are Jewish too!"
>
> Her parents nodded, their faces serious and drawn. "I talked to Sophie Rosen this afternoon, after you told me about the button shop," Mama said. "She knows what is happening. But she doesn't think that it will affect them."
>
> Annemarie thought, and understood. She relaxed. "Mr. Rosen doesn't have a shop. He's a teacher. They can't close a whole school!" She looked at Peter with the question in her eyes. "Can they?"

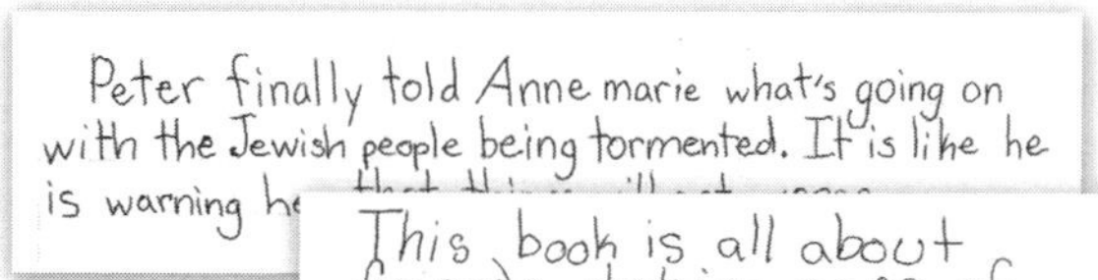

Peter finally told Anne marie what's going on with the Jewish people being tormented. It is like he is warning he[...]

Figure IX-1

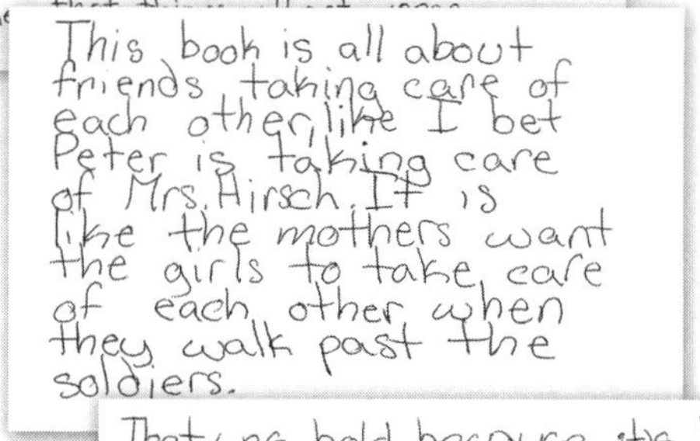

This book is all about friends taking care of each other, like I bet Peter is taking care of Mrs. Hirsch. It is like the mothers want the girls to take care of each other when they walk past the soldiers.

Figure IX-2

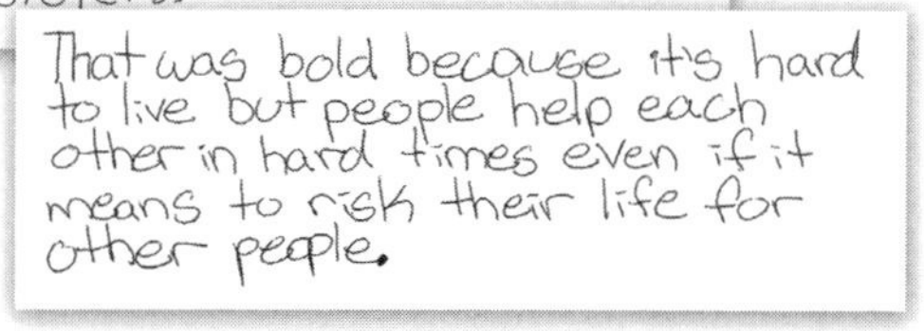

That was bold because it's hard to live but people help each other in hard times even if it means to risk their life for other people.

Figure IX-3

One of the decisions you will want to make is whether you imagine children writing as you read, or whether you want their rapt attention, in which case you may or may not provide them with time to write after you read some more. The more fluent your children are as writers, the more you can encourage them to scrawl as you read. That takes an ability to think and listen, which you'd expect of experienced fifth graders but certainly not of third graders. You might decide, if you are teaching third graders or children who are not fluent as writers, to channel kids to turn and talk, not stop and jot. Of course, this second bit of reading aloud does not need to be processed, necessarily.

"I think the Rosens will be all right," he said. "But you keep an eye on your friend Ellen. And stay away from the soldiers. Your mother told me about what happened on Osterbrogade."

ACTIVE INVOLVEMENT

Coach into children's thinking and jotting, channeling them to explore ways this new passage resonates with previous ones. Then read aloud again, zooming quickly along until you are ready to read another significant part.

"Continue to jot," I said, and I ducked my head to do some writing myself. Once the children had begun writing, I voiced over their work, rereading a sentence or two. [Fig. IX-4]

After a bit, I said, in a quiet voiceover, "I'm remembering back to earlier parts of the book, aren't you?" I left a pool of silence as I started to jot, hoping the children would do the same. I was pleased that the reminder nudged Sam to harken back to earlier parts. He wrote: [Fig. IX-5]

After a minute, I read into that silence, rereading a passage from earlier in the text that seemed relevant. I read it as if I was just casting my eyes backwards and had stumbled on this and was thinking about it now.

Kirsti is so dumb. No one in Copenhagen had taken a vacation at the seashore since the war began. There were no pink-frosted cupcakes; there hadn't been for months.

Then I was silent again, leaving another minute for writing.

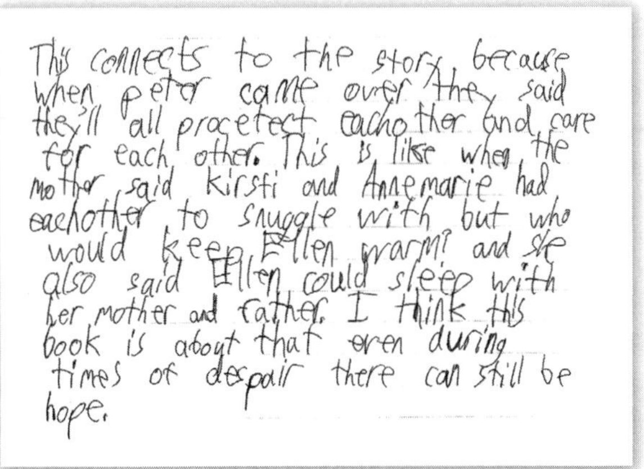

This connects to the story because when peter came over they said they'll all prooetect eachother and care for each other. This is like when the mother said Kirsti and Annemarie had eachother to snuggle with but who would keep Ellen warm? and she also said Ellen could sleep with her mother and father. I think this book is about that even during times of despair there can still be hope.

Figure IX-4

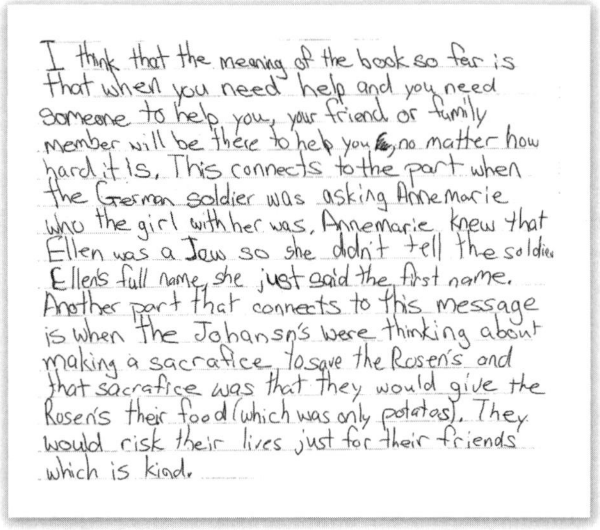

I think that the meaning of the book so far is that when you need help and you need someone to help you, your friend or family member will be there to help you, no matter how hard it is. This connects to the part when the German soldier was asking Annemarie who the girl with her was. Annemarie knew that Ellen was a Jew so she didn't tell the soldier Ellen's full name, she just said the first name. Another part that connects to this message is when the Johansn's were thinking about making a sacrafice, to save the Rosen's and that sacrafice was that they would give the Rosen's their food (which was only potatos). They would risk their lives just for their friends which is kind.

Figure IX-5

If you want children to write in response to a passage that you have read, you can't read the passage and then proceed to give elaborate directions about the work you want children to do, or your instructions will have erased the effect of the literature. For this reason, in the classrooms that I know best, teachers have developed a ritual of reading a passage from a text aloud, and then immediately after reading it, we say "Stop and jot" (nothing more), or we may not even say that, but simply lower our eyes and start writing up a storm. Kids will for a moment look around, startled, as if saying, "Huh? What are we supposed to do?" but they quickly grasp that they are being asked to write in the wake of literature, and they often do this with stunning and surprising power.

Distribute copies (or a few pages) of the book and ask selected children to resume reading aloud where you leave off and to choose a spot in which to say, "Stop and jot" to classmates, inviting reflective writing.

I looked up. "As we continue reading the last page of this chapter, I'm sure we'll come to more passages that almost seem to be written in bold letters, passages that beg for readers to pause and think. I'm going to pass a copy of the book to some of you. Will the person who receives the book begin reading it aloud to whomever is sitting close to you. The rest of you, pull in to hear one reader or another. And readers, when the book reaches a place that feels important, perhaps a place that harkens back to earlier stuff, call, 'Stop and jot.' Then all of you, jot as fast as your fingers can go."

As I distributed the books, each open to the passage I'd been reading, with a Post-it marking the exact place I left off reading, I called their attention to a chart that I had already prepared." If those of you who are jotting need help thinking about how to grow deep ideas, I have some questions written up here that might help. You don't have to answer all these questions, of course, but one of them might stir something up in you as you listen to the passage." I turned the tablet of chart paper to reveal a page on which I'd written:

Thinking Deeply About Passages in a Book

- What is Significant about this part of the story?
- How does this part fit with other parts and relate to what the whole story is really, really about? How do all the parts of the story fit together and contribute to the message of the book?
- Why might the author have written this part in this particular way, including these details, using these words?
- What might the character be learning about life, the world, and what might I be learning about life, about the world?

You should feel as if you are collecting a repertoire of ways for kids to be engaged during whole-class teaching:

- *You can ask them to do whatever you don't want them to do and then to do whatever you do want them to do, as in trying out what it is like to read like a curmudgeon, contrasting that with trying out what it is like to read as if a text is gold.*
- *You can do a symphony share, with you pointing your invisible baton toward kids and one child after another adding his or her contribution into the air.*
- *You can distribute white boards or chart paper to four or five kids and ask those children to write on the chart paper while everyone else jots in notebooks.*
- *You can ask each student to create a Post-it on which he or she does something (say, predicts) and then you can ask them to share their Post-its in groups of four, identifying the best one, then revising the others to make them as good as the best.*
- *You can suggest kids enact a scene, with half the class assuming one character's role, and their partners assuming a second character's role.*
- *You can do the same, suggesting the whole class make their faces or bodies illustrate how someone is acting or feeling.*
- *And now you have another option. You can ask a child to assume your role as the teacher who reads aloud and then ask that child to call for a turn and talk or a stop and jot, just as children have seen you do a million times.*

Pass the book to children who will be able to read clearly and confidently. If there aren't enough children in the class who can do so, you will skip this part of the active involvement, and instead, you can simply continue reading, perhaps asking children to signal when they think you should pause.

Then I listened in to individual children who were still reading, having not yet reached a passage that they believed merited saying, "Stop and jot." In those instances, I did some of that signaling myself, nudging readers to pause and write.

LINK

Send readers off to read, reminding them to pause at passages that seem to have been written in bold.

After a few minutes, long before the previous activity had run its course, I convened the class's attention. "So readers, remember that you are the authors of your reading. As you read today, there will be times when the book nudges you to read on and on, faster and faster, where you have to *find out* what happens rather than *think about* what is happening! And I hope there will also be some places in the book where it is almost as if the text has been written in bold, places where the book seems to be begging you to press the pause button and to think, perhaps even to jot. Later today when you are in your clubs, you can share those passages and your responses to them, remembering that what you notice will come from your whole life.

"There will be a few things that the author does when he or she is nudging you in the ribs—wanting you to take notice—and one of those is that the text will hearken back to an earlier reference, like the references to Kirsti's pink cupcakes or to the fact that all Danish people are bodyguards protecting the king. I'm not sure what the other things are that authors do that nudge us to pause, but it is something we should research together so we can teach each other about how to notice those stopping spots. Spy on yourself so you can help us figure this out.

"Before you disperse, club members, remind each other of the goalpost page for today's reading. I'll give you a signal when it's time for your clubs to meet."

You may think, "These questions seem like the meatiest aspects of the entire minilesson, and that is true. You may wonder, then, why they weren't embedded in the teaching point."

The first answer is that children were not ready for these questions at the start of the minilesson. Readers do first need to select significant passages and to think and write in response to those passages before these prompts can help us do this in ways that are interpretive. The other answer is that talking about these questions before one even tries them on for size may not be all that effective. Perhaps the best way for kids to feel the power of these questions is for them to literally use them to prompt thinking. But you are right that this content will need to be revisited.

You may decide not to mention that one way the author signals she is layering the text with added meaning is by referencing earlier images, ones that tend to weave in and out of the story. You could, instead, leave that for the kids to discover. Earlier you told them that you needed them to invent ideas within this unit, and surely this is one place where their inventive work would be helpful.

# CONFERRING AND SMALL-GROUP WORK

Coach Readers to Think with Reading Friends

During most of the previous units of study, the mid-workshop teaching point was inserted into reading time, with the share session setting up and bringing closure to partnership work at the end of reading time. Now that the reading workshop will sometimes include club meetings and sometimes won't, the mid-workshop teaching point will be used in more flexible ways. Sometimes this will be a voiceover, coaching into children's reading work, and sometimes, like on this day, it will come after a half an hour reading and will launch clubs, marking the transition between independent reading and book club work.

MID-WORKSHOP TEACHING POINT

Readers Prepare for Book Talks Beforehand

"Readers, can I interrupt you? I want to remind you that you're going to be meeting with your club later today, and that should change how you read because you anticipate that conversation. Does that make sense to you? Remember earlier this year when we talked about how important it is to bring something worthy to a potluck feast? Coming to a potluck dinner bringing just a little package of napkins at the bottom of a plastic bag just doesn't make it! Instead, when you go to a potluck dinner, bring a big steaming platter of something. In the same way, you have a responsibility to bring ideas to your club that will help your club have a fantastic literary conversation.

"Here's a tip about how to make sure you are bringing something talk-worthy to your club. Even before you get to your club, start having the club conversation in your mind (or on the page!). So if you have found a passage that feels important, like it was written in bold font, then before you meet with your club, you can write or think about it in a way that lets you talk over in your mind what the passage might be really, really about—using the questions we talked about earlier. (I gestured to the 'Thinking Deeply About Important Passages in a Book' chart.) You can think how the

continued on next page

Some Thought Prompts Readers Use to Push Our Thinking

* I think ...
* This connects to ...
* What's more ...
* This makes me think ...
* I used to think ... but now I'm realizing
* On the other hand ...
* This is important because ...

continued from previous page

passage fits into the whole story and why the author wrote it in that particular way, and about what the characters might be learning.

"Readers, you can also talk back to your own thinking, like I know you are talking back to each other's ideas in your book club and in our read-aloud conversations. To do so, sometimes it's helpful to use some common thought prompts. These are phrases that people often use to move a conversation back and forth. They help us to rev our engines, which is good, but they also help us respond to each other with respect. You've used these before, so I'll just remind you of a few here that are tremendously useful, as a kind of checklist.

"Listen to what Sam just wrote about a bit of his story. He used those prompts to help him take what might have been a little teeny napkins-at-the-bottom-of-the-plastic-bag thought and turn that thought into something worthy of his group. Sam, will you read us what you wrote?" Sam read: [Fig. IX-6]

"Readers, in two or three minutes of scrawling, you can come up with ideas that feel worthy of your group. But part of the challenge is that you want to make sure that you read differently because your group is expecting something grand of you."

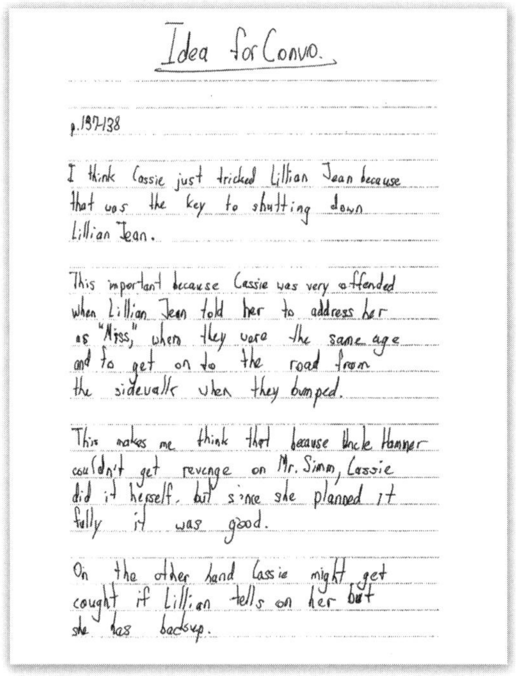

Idea for Convo.

p. 137-138

I think Cassie just tricked Lillian Jean because that was the key to shutting down Lillian Jean.

This important because Cassie was very offended when Lillian Jean told her to address her as "Miss," when they were the same age and to get on to the road from the sidewalk when they bumped.

This makes me think that because Uncle Hammer couldn't get revenge on Mr. Simms, Cassie did it herself. but since she planned it fully it was good.

On the other hand Cassie might get caught if Lillian tells on her but she has backup.

Figure IX-6

I mentioned earlier that when my colleagues and I at the Teachers College Reading and Writing Project began studying reading in earnest about twenty-five years ago, we decided that just as we'd studied what adult *writers* do, developing an understanding of the writing process and then bringing that knowledge to our work with children, so, too, we needed to study what adult *readers* do. We received a grant to support what began as ten and eventually became closer to one hundred adult book clubs. Across the entire city of New York, clusters of teachers and principals met once a week to talk about shared novels.

Meanwhile, we researched the patterns in those adult reading clubs, noticing what worked for us as adults and what did not work. There was one pattern, above all, that emerged. Time and again we found that when we as adults came together to talk about the reading (and the writing about reading) that we'd done, it was as if we arrived at the table with each of us carrying a card or two, an idea or two. As talk began, one person would "play his or her card." Meanwhile, everyone else had cards in our pockets that we were dying to play. So someone else would make a feeble effort at a transition, saying, "That reminds me of an idea I have," and then play her card. That would typically continue, with one idea after another being laid onto the table and with the interaction feeling more like a round-robin report-back session than a conversation.

In some clubs, the entire meeting was devoted to that sort of parallel talk (not parallel *play*, like toddlers do in the sandbox when they talk all the time but never to each other and when they each have one tool—a shovel, a pail—and never dream of sharing it, but parallel *talk*, which is the same thing minus the sand and the tools). But in other clubs, the laying out of one's cards was a preliminary move, and there would come a time when one person's card, one person's idea, moved front and center, with the whole group acknowledging that for a time they'd linger with that idea, talking back and forth about that one idea. The remarkable thing was the total transformation in the group when finally, the presentational talk of premade ideas was over, and real conversation began. Suddenly people would lean forward, listening to each other with minds going a mile a minute. New ideas would be grown—grown out of the intersection of one person's thinking and another's.

We came from this work committed to teaching kids strategies for moving from the presentational talk to real conversations and believing that one portion of this involved helping children learn to focus on a single idea, on, you could say, a single Post-it.

Once Youngsters Focus on a Selected Idea, They Can Begin Developing Ideas Together

Listen to the conversations your clubs are having about books. Start with one group of children, and listen in. Then go to the next and the next. Chances are good that unless you have taught children otherwise, you'll find their conversation jumps from one topic to the next and the next. No one will think anything of this. There won't even be comments such as, "Do you mind if we change the topic?" or "Are we finished with that topic?" Kids will just jump, jump, jump. (Actually, if you listen to conversations at your faculty meeting, you'll probably hear the same thing.)

If you see that your club members are skimming over the surface of lots of topics and rarely delving deeply and collaboratively into any one topic, you can smile to yourself because you will have identified a problem that is fairly easily addressed and that, when addressed, can be transformative. You've got the next step of your teaching cut out for you, and it is sure to pay off!

One way to ready yourself for the teaching you will want to do is to think for just a moment about when you have seen a similar phenomenon in your children's writing. Their talk should remind you of the writing that children do who have had very little instruction in writing. They tackle a subject like "My Summer" and leap from one episode to another to another.

Think for a moment about the techniques you have learned for conferring with writers who jump from one underdeveloped topic to another.

You probably say to those writers, "My goodness! You've addressed so many topics! You've written this, and this, and this, and this. Of all those topics, which is the one that is especially important to you? I'm asking because usually it works best to zoom in on a single subtopic."

Then, when the child locates one subtopic, perhaps with a questioning intonation, unsure whether that topic warrants interest, you throw yourself wholeheartedly behind that topic. "Oh! I was *hoping* you'd say that! It is such an interesting topic. Can you say more about that?" After helping the child find his voice and sense of authority on the one subtopic, and after the child rewrites the draft, this time producing something much more focused and alive, you will name what the child just did in such a way that you help the child extrapolate lessons that can apply to another day, another time.

When you listen to members of a reading club as they tear about among lots and lots of subtopics, your conferring can be almost exactly the same as it has been when writers do the same thing. You can admiringly point out the assortment of subtopics the children have addressed even within just the few minutes while you were nearby, and then you can pop that question: "Of all these subtopics, what is one that seems especially worth addressing?" Once again, you'll probably find that children worry that if they constrain their talk to a single subtopic, they'll quickly run out of things to say, so your job will be to help them realize they have more to say than they'd once thought. Over time, you'll also give kids a host of ways to grow ideas as they talk. On the DVD, you'll see Kathleen lead a conference such as this with a book club, and you'll see lots of examples of kids who have internalized this lesson enough that their conversation mines one subtopic before progressing to another.

There are lots of concrete ways to help a club stay on a topic for a longer time. For starters, it helps enormously to suggest that the members of a club first talk about what they will talk about, deciding together what they will maintain as the focus of their conversation. Sometimes—oftentimes—this means the club decides on one person's Post-it or entry or idea, agreeing to talk at length about that one claim. Sometimes, instead, the club will see a pattern across many of the ideas that people bring to a conversation, but that would probably take some extra teaching, so let's leave it to the side for now.

Helping Children Learn Ways to Focus On Particularly Meaningful Ideas

Let's listen in to one of the clubs and think about the conversation we hear in relation to the ideas I've just summarized. Because these write-ups have kept you especially attuned to the Freedom Fighters Club, let's listen in to their conversations, using this as a case in point. To listen in, we'll sit on the carpet in the meeting area, around the club, creating a sort of fishbowl effect. Such a fishbowl is commonplace in the staff development work that my colleagues and I lead, and I hope it is commonplace in your work with your colleagues as well.

Of course, when a group of us descends around a club, the readers will usually stop their ongoing conversation, and one or more of the children will turn to tell us the narrative of the club. As usual, I motion that instead, it would be good for them to keep talking. This group had been reading *Roll of Thunder, Hear My Cry* for while now, and they were almost halfway through the book.

Aly, who had shown herself to consistently function as a leader within this club, began by talking about a plan of action for the club. I admired her decision to have a procedural conversation before jumping into content and listened while she said, "How about if we begin and everyone says their best idea? Then we can talk? We could go in a circle." When every reader produces an idea, round-robin style, all the ideas tend to glom together, making it hard to select and develop one. Plus, this can eat up time that could be invested in a real conversation, so the specifics of Aly's plan didn't thrill me as much as the fact that she was making a plan, but I wanted to see how this unfolded.

"Okay, so how about if we each say our thought really quickly and then maybe we can choose whose idea we'll discuss today?" Sam said, adding onto Aly's opening salvo. It was clear that Sam had been influenced by instruction. The conversation was off to a good start.

Stepping up to lay his card on the table, Josh said, "Well, I noticed that Cassie stands up for her rights. It's like she isn't aware of how unsafe the world still is for Blacks."

"I noticed something almost the same," Fallon said. "Cassie seems really brave to me. I mean, especially since Whites have so much power and they can get away with seriously hurting Black people. Like when they burned the Berry men and there wasn't one punishment for that. Cassie *still* insists on being treated fairly. It's really strong of her." I was pleased that Fallon had made an effort to link her new comment to Josh's idea, the one that had already been on the table, and I noted that Fallon was right when she said her idea was almost exactly the same as Josh's. Often children *say* "My idea is the same," when actually there are gigantic differences that they're glossing over. I also appreciated that Fallon didn't just say, "I agree with what you said" but that she restated Sam's idea in her own words. I knew the children had been taught this and was glad they were continuing to do as they'd been taught.

Aly piped in, "I noticed that sometimes being quiet is the better way to go. Like Mr. Morrison and Big Ma keep the family safe by kind of hushing people, or taking them away from fights. But Cassie and Uncle Hammer are always ready to fight, and that doesn't work so well." I hadn't read the book in a long while and wondered if Cassie and Uncle Hammer were similar, one to the other, and if so, wondered what that was about.

Isaac said, "The thing I noticed is just how unfair things are for the Logans and all the Black people. I got so angry reading this book. I don't get why the color of your skin matters so much." I was glad to see this emotional response and glad that Isaac had identified with the Logans. It was as if each of these children had, in turn, shown a spotlight on a different character. My mind raced ahead to possible trails of thought they could follow. I could imagine these children making a chart—a grid—on which they recorded the different characters' reactions to the inequities in the story, but I no sooner thought of that idea than I questioned whether it would take the conversation any farther. It could, after all, guarantee that they didn't synthesize their thinking.

"Back then, your color mattered," Sam added, qualifying Isaac's comment. "The book takes place about fifty or sixty years ago. Even though Black people weren't slaves, they *had* been slaves not that long before." I'm always astonished when children act as if all the injustices of history are things of the long-ago distant past, but I kept this thought to myself and continued to listen. Sam had already said, "What I thought about was, was . . . " And he searched for a particular Post-it. Finding it, he read: [Fig. IX-7]

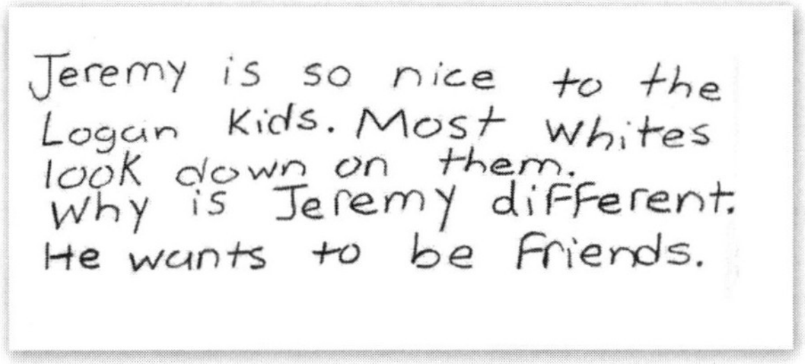

Jeremy is so nice to the Logan kids. Most whites look down on them. Why is Jeremy different. He wants to be friends.

Figure IX-7

The children had now all laid out their ideas. Sam, who had been the one to suggest this would be a quick process, said, "How about if we put our ideas, our Post-its, in a pile and then we can draw one and talk about it?"

The kids had clearly done this before, and they began the familiar process.

At this point I leaned in and said, "I have two tips for you. Do you mind if I jump in?"

The children nodded while continuing to fold their Post-its into little packets for the drawing. Not wanting to continue without their attention, I said, "I'll wait," and this time, they put their folded wads down and looked at me. "You've got the rhythm for how book conversations often go. When I meet with friends to talk about books, we often start the same way that you've started, with each of us bringing out the idea we're most hankering to talk about. And like you, after a bit, we often take a second to say, 'How about if we start by focusing on . . . ,' and then we name an idea that becomes the center of our starting conversation. So I want to congratulate you on a very grown-up conversation, especially because you seemed to listen to each other's ideas and to link your new thought to the ideas that were already on the table, saying things like, 'My idea is sort of the same,' or 'My idea really centers on a different character.'

"But, here's the thing: In conversations, just like in writing, it is important to pick a subject *that matters*. Like in *The Tiger Rising*, Kate DiCamillo didn't tell us that Rob had a collection of whittled animals and then go on and tell about ten other things he had—a deflated basketball, a battered popcorn popper he'd had for three years. Rob had more than just his whittlings, but we didn't hear about those things. That's because none of

them would really matter. Authors make choices. So do book club members.

"After you have laid out possible things to talk about, you have a chance to step back and to think over the possible trails of thought your group could follow, asking yourselves, 'Which of these is going to take us to new and deeper thinking?'

"Can I suggest a process for doing that? It helps to just repeat the ideas that are on the table and then to think, 'Which of these ideas will help us get to new and deeper ideas?' I'll lay the ideas out and you can think about them, okay?" Then I summarized what the children had said, synthesizing the ideas a bit as I did so. "You have the idea that Cassie stands up for her rights as if she's unaware that it is risky for her to do this. And she is brave for doing this. She and Uncle Hammer do this. And you thought that others, like Mr. Morrison, Mama, and Big Ma, believe in quiet protests to keep the family safe. And then—there's the idea that all this is unfair. It is unfair that the Logans are treated in these ways and either need to hush up or be at risk. And how does Jeremy fit into this? Why is he nice to the Logans when others aren't?"

There was silence. "Where do you want to go in your conversation?" I pressed. "Remember that at the start of this unit, your club decided to think more deeply about characters. You are definitely thinking about characters, but now the goal is to do that work of getting deeper. Can I make a suggestion for how, in general, you can usually help your conversation go deeper?" The children nodded. "When we want to deepen our thinking about characters, it usually helps to ask ourselves, '*Why*?' Like that question, *why* did Jeremy treat the Logans differently? But you could also ask, '*Why* is Cassie so brave? *Why* might Mama, Big Ma, and Mr. Morrison hush people—and the others, like Uncle Hammer, handle this differently? What's at stake if they don't hush protests? Could you try taking a why question and thinking about it?"

"Yes," the group answered simultaneously.

Again, Aly took the role of focusing the club. "Does anyone want to discuss their idea, only this time, as a why question?"

"How about if we first talk about Jeremy, and then Cassie," Sam suggested.

The kids all agreed and motioned for Sam to put his Post-it about Jeremy on their club mascot—a Yankees hat that didn't in any way relate to their club theme. Sometimes clubs have a little basket at the center of their meeting area and put the idea under discussion in that basket. Sometimes they make a game board with a square marked off for the conversational focus, peripheral squares for related ideas, and distant squares for the idea dugout.

"So, if we're going to ask why Jeremy's nice to the Logans, my first answer is, Who knows? It makes no sense. His dad is like the worst redneck, and Lillian Jean is beyond horrible," Isaac said. This comment reminded me that often after a group settles upon a topic of discussion, it is helpful for the group to set aside five minutes for everyone to jot some notes on the new focal topic, so no one approaches this new conversation empty handed, as Isaac was doing.

I was glad when Sam jumped in because presumably he'd thought a lot about the idea, because it was his idea in the first place. "Yeah, I mean, the family seems really prejudiced and cruel," Sam said. "That's what makes it so interesting to me that Jeremy is actually looking at Cassie and her brothers like they're humans."

"It seems like he especially wants to be friends with Stacey," Aly added.

"I know, which is funny because Stacey is, like, so not interested in being Jeremy's friend," Josh said.

"Well, it's kind of understandable. I mean, why would you trust someone in that family?" Fallon said. "That family is full of hatred."

"Yeah, but not all family members are alike," Aly interjected.

"You still haven't thought a lot about your initial question of why Jeremy might want to be Stacey's friend," I pointed out. Then, hoping to not just support this conversation but to help in ways that might effect another day's conversation, I added, "That happens in a conversation. When the question is puzzling, we circle around it. One thing that works is to try saying, 'Could it be . . .' and throwing out ideas.

"Could it be that Jeremy just knows that Stacey's a really good guy? Stacey's protective of his family and looks out for everyone," Josh said.

"Yeah, I mean, when I was reading, I kind of thought Stacey would make a good friend," Sam said. "But why Jeremy would be his friend . . . I don't know if it says."

I coached into what the kids were doing, saying, "Remember earlier, when you were trying to figure out whether the family in *The Gold Cadillac*

is poor or not? We talked about how the author doesn't always tell you things right out. She doesn't tell you what the details add up to, either, but she does give you the details. They're on the page, waiting for you to take note."

Sam, recalling that work, said, "I have an idea. Let's reread and see if we can find out why Jeremy would be Stacy's friend, other than 'cause he'd be a good friend." At this point, I gave Sam (and the club) a thumbs up gesture (one done deliberately and with great significance) and moved on to another group.

I could have stopped this conference much earlier, of course, and just picked an idea that would pay off, channeling them to discuss that idea. It is tempting to try to get something done fast, fast, fast by bypassing the kids' muddled efforts. It is invaluable, when we can make time to show members of a club that by continuing to question, what may at first have seemed like a meager idea emerges as an interesting one.

As I left this club, I considered whether one or two club members, or the whole club, could coach another club on how to settle on a topic and stay with it. There were some strong leaders in this club, and I knew that if they were called upon to demonstrate this work, they would all probably get better at it fast. Also, learning to do this to teach it to another club would be another way to honor their voices and their intellectual growth. I made a note to prepare these club members for a possible teaching opportunity, perhaps with the American Dreamers (the immigration group).

TEACHING SHARE

Readers Can Use an Artifact to Provide a Focal Point for Conversation

Remind readers of earlier goals that club members aspired to, and ask them to use this chart to make personal resolutions for themselves.

"Readers, time for your book club. Before you get started, look over our chart of ways to make your book club conversation powerful. Think of this as a checklist for yourself, the kind that pilots use when they get ready to fly the plane. How can you use it to be ready to be your best self?" I gestured to the "Growing Powerful Book Club Conversations" chart from earlier in the unit.

Add another item to the list, talking up the value of putting an artifact at the center of the conversation and using it to weld ideas together.

"Today, I want to add one more thing to our list, and it is this: Conversations go better if you put an artifact in the middle of the table, and the whole group looks really closely at that one thing. Let me suggest a few artifacts that could be really powerful. You all just did some writing about reading. You took an idea you had about a powerful passage, and you wrote long about that passage. You could put the original passage from your club's book at the center of your club. You could each annotate that one copy of the passage with Post-its that hold your various ideas about it. And then you, as a club, could talk for your whole meeting about that one passage, remembering to think how it fits with earlier parts of the book and to think about the craft decisions the author has made.

"You might decide to put something different at the center of your conversation. A timeline, with notes about turning points. A map."

"The Allies, for instance, decided to put one child's notebook entry in the middle, and they all did another round of jotting in response to their club mate's writing. Kadija had written: [Fig. IX-8]

"Kadija's club looked at her writing, jotted thoughts in response, and then talked off of Kadija's entry."

After a bit, I closed the workshop, saying, "Readers, from now on, remember that using an artifact really helps readers to ground their thinking."

COACHING TIPS

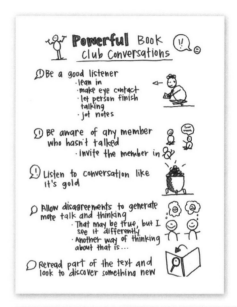

Figure IX-8
Kadija compares the protagonist from *Autumn Street* with one from *Number the Stars.*

Seeing Big Ideas in Small Details

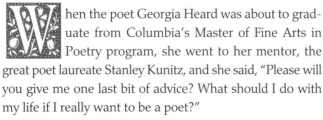

When the poet Georgia Heard was about to graduate from Columbia's Master of Fine Arts in Poetry program, she went to her mentor, the great poet laureate Stanley Kunitz, and she said, "Please will you give me one last bit of advice? What should I do with my life if I really want to be a poet?"

Stanley looked at Georgia for a long moment, thinking. Then he gave her advice. "Go be a rock hound, a star gazer, a pastry chef. Listen to the rocks, the stars, the pastries. From them, you'll get your metaphor."

So often, the biggest meanings in life are conveyed through metaphor. In weddings, two people join hands and join their lives. They exchange rings to further symbolize a never-ending commitment to each other.

I remember the day, a long while ago, that I found a small box in my mother's top dresser drawer. In it, I found the tiniest strip of slim plastic with my name printed in fading type. I realized this had been the bracelet worn on my wrist when I was released from the hospital as a newborn. I was surprised that my unsentimental mother had kept such a useless memento. Of course, I now realize the tenderness with which a mother looks upon that strip of "useless" plastic. My own child's hospital bracelet symbolizes both my child's entry into the world and my connection to my mother, a connection that is not only that of mother to child but also that of mother to mother.

The first apartment key means so much more than unlocking the door to a building; it unlocks the door to a world of adult independence. Picking raspberries off a bush is about more than just fruit; those berries hold summer afternoons, lying in the meadow with my sisters, the grasshoppers springing among us.

I will never forget listening to Ellin Keene, author of *Mosaic of Thought* and a friend of mine, talk about the importance of inviting kids to think about big ideas. She said something to the effect of "My teacher once said to me,

GETTING READY

- Prior to teaching today's minilesson, you should have finished reading aloud Chapter 4 of *Number the Stars*.

- Today's connection marks a departure from other connections. You will read all of Chapter 5. This means that the minilesson will run longer than usual.

- During the teaching portion of today's minilesson, you will be referring to the chart from the previous session, "Thinking Deeply About Important Passages in a Book." During the link, you will refer to a chart from Volume 1, "Making Our Way Through Historical Fiction."

'Ellin, there are two kinds of people in this world. There are the people who think about the *things*, and there are the people who think about *ideas*. You need to choose which kind of person you want to be.'" Ellin went on to describe the heady, intoxicating experience she had when she first realized that she, Ellin Keene, could be a person who thought about ideas, who lived the life of the intellect.

> *Reading—like love and loss—depends upon ordinary words and defies them at the same time.*

How important it is to make sure we give ourselves, and our children, the time to have ideas! I have come to believe, though, that we human beings don't choose between thinking about things and thinking about ideas. *The most powerful ideas are embedded in things*, in the grit of life. In a plastic bracelet, bearing a newborn's name. In a bear, dressed in green corduroy overalls with one button missing—a bear who is nonetheless adopted and loved. In a woman knitting in the crowds, her eyes riveted to a blood-stained guillotine. I believe that reading literature is all about understanding that we human beings do not need to choose between thinking about things, about the grit of life, and

thinking about ideas, because the biggest and most complex ideas in the world are just that—lodged *in the world*.

So, too, the pink cupcakes that Kirsti longs for (*Number the Stars*) are not just pink cupcakes, and the star necklace, its imprint imprinted on Annemarie's hand, is not just a necklace. Reading—like love and loss—depends upon ordinary words and defies them at the same time. We hope our students will enter the mood and pulse of their book's world and feel the unspoken words—to sense, for example, that red ink splattering across the newly whitewashed wall from an accidentally dropped pen in this story could be suggestive of impending doom. Or that a brief encounter with a soldier that makes our heroine uncomfortable in the first chapter suggests that this soldier—or the source of this discomfort—will resurface in a later chapter.

This session helps readers talk about the meanings in a text by using the specific details and objects in which those meanings are lodged. In doing so, it helps children understand the concept of representation and begin to experience the power of symbols. The emphasis is not on using the terminology of symbolism or even of metaphor. In fact, the terms hardly surface at all. Instead, the emphasis is on the child coming to understand that when a person has something huge and complex and rich and deep to say, often the most powerful way to convey that meaning is through tiny concrete specifics. The Star of David, imprinted on Annemarie's hand, is a tiny thing—so small, so big. Exploring the meaning of that imprint on her hand will be a way to bring children toward an exploration into representation, symbolism, abstraction—and into the relationship between gritty specifics and big ideas.

MINILESSON

Seeing Big Ideas in Small Details

CONNECTION

Tell children that today's minilesson will proceed differently than usual. Then read an intense section of the read-aloud book, pausing at a passage that gives readers pause.

"Readers, the next part of *Number the Stars* is special, so I'm going to start our mini-lesson simply by reading to you. Perhaps we'll come to a place in the text that makes us pause, but then again, perhaps the text will be written in ways that say, 'Don't stop! Read on, read on.' Let's read." I opened *Number the Stars*, paused while the children settled themselves, then leaned in and began reading.

Chapter 5: Who Is the Dark-Haired One?

Annemarie eased the bedroom door open quietly, only a crack, and peeked out. Behind her, Ellen was sitting up, her eyes wide.

She could see Mama and Papa in their night-clothes, moving about. Mama held a lighted candle, but as Annemarie watched, she went to a lamp and switched it on. It was so long a time since they had dared to use the strictly rationed electricity after dark that the light in the room seemed startling to Annemarie, watching through the slightly opened bedroom door. She saw her mother look automatically to the blackout curtains, making certain that they were tightly drawn.

Papa opened the front door to the soldiers.

"This is the Johansen apartment?" A deep voice asked the question loudly, in the terribly accented Danish.

COACHING TIPS

You'll want to read this chapter swiftly and dramatically, demonstrating for children the sort of passionate, fast and furious reading we do when we encounter a part that begs us to read quickly, not pausing until you reach a natural ending.

I own a book called Remarkable Reads, *edited by J. Peder Zane, which contains essays that a score of people have written about the books that have meant the most to them. To me, these essays remind me that when I want to read a book aloud really well, I am aspiring for that book to be the greatest book in my students' lives. It is worth noting, then, that the books that people recall as their most remarkable are books that sizzle with intensity.*

Anatole France says that it is the reader's response that makes words "dull or brilliant, hot with passion or cold as ice." When she was young, Denise Gess stole a copy of Camus's The Stranger *from the library, riding her bike home faster than she thought possible, her sneakered feet slipping off the pedals. "I had broken one of the Ten Commandments. I was in mortal sin territory. I'd stolen with full knowledge and intent. If a car hit me and hurtled me into the air to certain death before I reached home, I was going straight to Hell unless I could find the wherewithal to murmur an 'I'm sorry' before my body crashed, broken, to the ground. Still, it hardly mattered. I had the book I needed."*

"Our name is on the door, and I see you have a flashlight," Papa answered. "What do you want? Is something wrong?"

"I understand you are a friend of your neighbors the Rosens, Mrs. Johansen," the soldier said.

"Sophie Rosen is my friend, that is true," Mama said quietly. "Please, could you speak more softly? My children are asleep."

"Then you will be so kind as to tell me where the Rosens are." He made no effort to lower his voice.

"I assume they are at home, sleeping. It is four in the morning, after all," Mama said.

Annemarie heard the soldier stalk across the living room toward the kitchen. From her hiding place in the narrow sliver of open doorway, she could see the heavy uniformed man, a holstered pistol at his waist, in the entrance to the kitchen, peering in toward the sink.

Another German voice said, "The Rosens' apartment is empty. We are wondering if they might be visiting their good friends the Johansens."

"Well," said Papa, moving slightly so that he was standing in front of Annemarie's bedroom door, and she could see nothing except the dark blur of his back, "as you can see, you are mistaken. There is no one here but my family."

"You will not object if we look around." The voice was harsh, and it was not a question.

"It seems we have no choice," Papa replied.

"Please don't wake my children," Mama requested again. "There is no need to frighten little ones."

The heavy, booted feet moved across the floor again and into the other bedroom. A closet door opened and closed with a bang.

Annemarie eased her bedroom door closed silently. She stumbled through the darkness to the bed.

"Ellen," she whispered urgently, "take your necklace off!"

Denise Gess described reading that book. "How telling that I took it to the basement, descending to the underworld of the house to read it. I can still hear the initial soft crack, feel the pop of air that accompanies the opening of any book. 'Mother dies today. Or maybe, yesterday; I can't be sure.' I reread those opening words at least a dozen times, I read them aloud, hearing both the strangeness and the utter beauty of a voice so detached from a mother's death."

In Remarkable Reads, *Scott Weidensaul wrote that when he read a passage of the book he now identified as his most remarkable book—A Sand Country Almanac by Aldo Leopold, he looked up and thought, "Dang. That's me." He adds, "A Sand Country Almanac remains the most resolute book I've read. I hold it close because it seems to have arms wide enough to take in the entire world, it blends an unabashed passion for natural places and wild animals with a simple, clear logic that argues for a more balanced relationship with the natural world." What beautiful reverence toward this book.*

Reading those passages helps me remember that the work of reading aloud is nothing less than giving the breath of life to a book.

In The Child That Books Built, *Francis Spufford describes the experience of coming to understand the nature of stories through the voice of a teacher: "It isn't the page that teaches us that story is language . . . through which you see visions. That comes after. The medium of the first encounter is an adult voice speaking. . . . The voice that tells us a story aloud is always more than a carrier wave bringing us the meaning; it's a companion through the events of the story, ensuring that the feelings it stirs in us are held within the circle of attachment connecting the adult reading and the child listening. . . . Yeshiva students turning the dangerous pages of the kabala would do so in groups, around their rabbi, so that the authority of the rabbi entered into the reading, and each was protected from the intensity of a solitary encounter with wild knowledge."*

Ellen's hands flew to her neck. Desperately, she began trying to unhook the tiny clasp. Outside the bedroom door, the harsh voices and heavy footsteps continued.

"I can't get it open!" Ellen said frantically! "I never take it off—I can't even remember how to open it!"

Annemarie heard a voice just outside the door. "What is here?"

"Shhh," her mother replied. "My daughters' bedroom. They are sound asleep."

"Hold still," Annemarie commanded. "This will hurt." She grabbed the little gold chain, yanked with all her strength, and broke it. As the door opened and light flooded into the bedroom, she crumpled it into her hand and closed her fingers tightly.

Terrified, both girls looked up at the three Nazi officers who entered the room. One of the men aimed a flashlight around the bedroom. He went to the closet and looked inside. Then with a sweep of his gloved hand he pushed to the floor several coats and a bathrobe that hung from pegs on the wall.

There was nothing else in the room except a chest of drawers, the blue decorated trunk in the corner, and a heap of Kirsti's dolls piled in a small rocking chair. The flashlight beam touched each thing in turn. Angrily the officer turned toward the bed.

"Get up!" he ordered. "Come out here!"

Trembling, the two girls rose from the bed and followed him, brushing past the two remaining officers in the doorway, to the living room.

Annemarie looked around. These three uniformed men were different from the ones on the street corners. The street soldiers were often young, sometimes ill at ease, and Annemarie remembered how the Giraffe had, for a moment, let his harsh pose slip and had smiled at Kirsti.

But these men were older and their faces were set with anger. Her parents were standing beside each other, their faces tense, but Kirsti was nowhere in sight. Thank goodness that Kirsti had slept through almost everything. If they had wakened her, she would be wailing—or worse, she would be angry, and her fists would fly.

We don't want to talk about powerful, interpretive reading experiences. We want to orchestrate them.

"Your names?" the officer barked.

"Annemarie Johansen. And this is my sister—"

"Quiet! Let her speak for herself. Your name?" He was glaring at Ellen.

Ellen swallowed. "Lise," she said, and cleared her throat. "Lise Johansen."

The officer glared at them grimly.

"Now," Mama said in a strong voice, "you have seen that we are not hiding anything. May my children go back to bed?"

The officer ignored her. Suddenly he grabbed a handful of Ellen's hair. Ellen winced.

He laughed scornfully. "You have a blond child sleeping in the other room. And you have this blond daughter—" He gestured toward Annemarie with his head. "Where did you get the dark-haired one?" He twisted the lock of Ellen's hair. "From a different father? From the milkman?"

Papa stepped forward. "Don't speak to my wife in such a way. Let go of my daughter or I will report you for such treatment."

"Or maybe you got her someplace else?" the officer continued with a sneer. "From the Rosens?"

For a moment no one spoke. Then Annemarie, watching in a panic, saw her father move swiftly to the small bookcase and take out a book. She saw that he was holding the family photograph album. Very quickly he searched through its pages, found what he was looking for, and tore out three pictures from three separate pages.

He handed them to the German officer, who released Ellen's hair.

"You will see each of my daughters, each with her name written on the photograph," Papa said.

Annemarie knew instantly which photographs he had chosen. The album had many snapshots—all the poorly focused pictures of school events and birthday parties. But it also contained a portrait, taken by a photographer, of each girl as a tiny infant. Mama had written, in her delicate handwriting, the name of each baby daughter across the bottom of those photographs.

In Better Than Life, Daniel Pennac ends the book with a climactic call to invite children to read aloud to themselves and each other. He writes, "The mute page is comfortable, I agree...the page and the self, muzzled in the cozy rooms of our intelligence, with commentary working its silent knitting needles. When we judge a book outside ourselves, there's no danger of it judging us. But once the human voice is engaged, the book begins to comment on its reader. The book says it all. . . .

If he really reads, if he adds all his understanding to the act and masters his pleasure, if his reading becomes an act of empathy, with the audience and the book and its author, if he can communicate the necessity of writing by touching our deepest need for stories, then books will open their doors, and those who felt excluded from reading will follow him inside." (204–205)

She realized too, with an icy feeling, why Papa had torn them from the book. At the bottom of each page, below the photograph itself, was written the date. And the real Lise Johansen had been born twenty-one years earlier.

"Kirsten Elisabeth," the officer read, looking at Kirsti's baby picture. He let the photograph fall to the floor.

"Annemarie," he read next, glanced at her, and dropped the second photograph.

"Lise Margrete," he read finally, and stared at Ellen for a long, unwavering moment. In her mind, Annemarie pictured the photograph that he held: the baby, wide-eyed, propped against a pillow, her tiny hand holding a silver teething ring, her bare feet visible below the hem of an embroidered dress. The wispy curls. Dark.

The officer tore the photograph in half and dropped the pieces on the floor. Then he turned, the heels of his shiny boots grinding into the pictures, and left the apartment. Without a word, the other two officers followed. Papa stepped forward and closed the door behind him.

Annemarie relaxed the clenched fingers of her right hand, which still clutched Ellen's necklace. She looked down, and saw that she had imprinted the Star of David into her palm.

Conclude that you've just encountered a passage that makes readers pause to think, "What's important about this part? How does it fit with the whole text?" Prompt kids to freewrite quickly, capturing their thoughts on this excerpt.

I looked up from the book. Kids were on their knees, leaning in toward the story. "Whoa! This is certainly one of those important passages that feels written in bold, doesn't it?" I said, pointing to a chart that channeled children to see this as an invitation to think deeply about this important passage. The kids nodded their heads.

Don't stop reading, but do notice the intensity of this section. Notice that there is a way in which Lise had to die that Ellen might live.

"So let's pause and think about those huge questions that readers ask when we get to really important parts of a book," I said, and gestured to the chart from yesterday's minilesson. "That list is a useful checklist for thinkers. It can't tell you which part is your starting point. Only you can do that, because what's important to you may be different from what's important to another reader. But right now, we all have this beautiful session, and brave Annemarie with that Star of David imprinted on her hand."

Thinking Deeply About Important Passages in a Book

- What is significant about this part of the story?

- How does this part fit with other parts and relate to what the whole story is really, really about? How do all the parts of the story fit together and contribute to the message of the book?

- Why might the author have written this part in this particular way, including these details, using these words?

- What might the character be learning about life and the world, and what might I be learning about life and about the world?

"Take a few minutes now and write whatever you are thinking. What *is* significant about this chapter so far? What stands out for you and why?" I signaled for one child to write on chart paper at the easel and distributed white boards so that a few children, dispersed among the group, could write on them while the rest of us wrote in our reading notebooks. I wrote for a minute as well, helping channel everyone's energy through their hands onto their pages. Then I crawled among the children, noticing some of what they'd written. I noticed that Lily had written: *[Fig. X-1]*

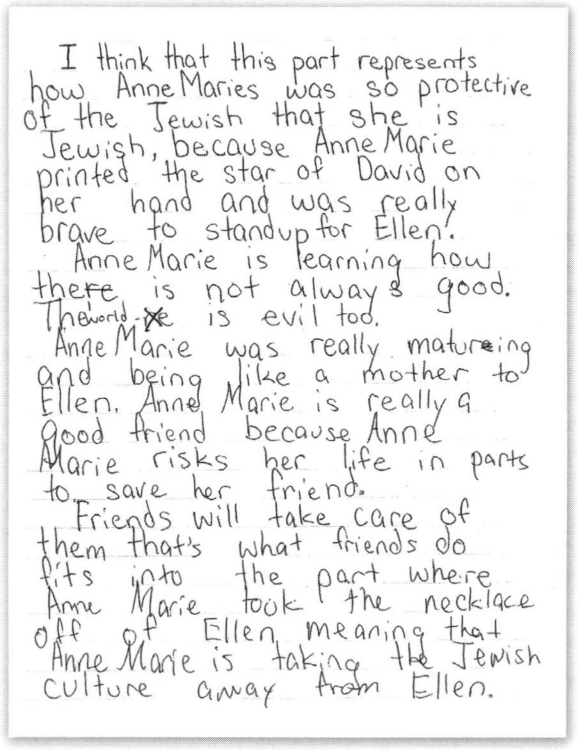

You'll see that time and again in this unit, I use writing as a tool for growing meaning. Always know that talking and writing are interchangeable, and you could decide to instead ask kids to turn and talk. If your kids' writing is slow as molasses, I would definitely substitute talking for writing much of the time. There are many classrooms, however, in which you can ask kids to jot, and within two minutes, every child will have written a third of a page, and many will have written more. In those classrooms, channeling kids to do a quick stop and jot can be very powerful.

I think that this part represents how Anne Maries was so protective of the Jewish that she is Jewish, because Anne Marie printed the star of David on her hand and was really brave to standup for Ellen!
Anne Marie is learning how there is not always good. The world is evil too.
Anne Marie was really matureing and being like a mother to Ellen. Anne Marie is really a good friend because Anne Marie risks her life in parts to save her friend.
Friends will take care of them that's what friends do fits into the part where Anne Marie took the necklace off of Ellen meaning that Anne Marie is taking the Jewish culture away from Ellen.

Figure X-1
Lily's response to Chapter 5

After a few minutes, I convened their attention.

Name your teaching point. Specifically, teach readers that when we write or think about big ideas, it helps to lodge those thoughts in concrete details.

"Readers, you are all writing about big ideas and big questions. And today I want to teach you one incredibly important bit of advice. The writer Richard Price has said, 'The bigger the issue, the smaller you write.' He means that when you are writing, or thinking, about big ideas, you lodge your ideas in the smallest details and objects from the story."

Teaching and Active Involvement

Offer students examples of ways that big ideas from the year's read-aloud books are captured in concrete specifics.

"Let me show you something. Think about *The Tiger Rising,* right now. Think about the big ideas you learned from that book." I gave children a minute of silence to do this. Now let me ask you something. As you think about those ideas, are they lodged in small, concrete details, objects—in a suitcase, or a tiger, or a cage, or a rash? My hunch is that for most of us, the biggest ideas from that book *are* crystallized into concrete specifics, like a suitcase that's so full of pain that it can't be zipped closed, or a tiger that's caged in the woods, or a boy named Rob who's caged into loneliness.

"Let's think if this is true also for *Number the Stars.* Are the biggest ideas conveyed in small details in this book as well? Let me think. Let's say I wanted to talk about the children missing their pre-war lives, for example. I wonder if we could lodge that idea in something concrete and specific. Hmm . . ."

On cue, the kids burst out with "Oh, oh, I know, the pink cupcakes."

Teachers, you'll want to be alert for signs that your children are growing as readers and thinkers. I'm pleased, as I look at their writing, that when the children respond to parts of the story, they are doing so at a much higher level than they did at the beginning of the unit. You can see these children using details from the story, not just to make sense of what is happening, but to imbue the event with significance. They are also gathering up parts of the story that seem related.

Roy Peter Clark recently led a sequence of conference days at the Teachers College Reading and Writing Project. Academic Dean of the Poynter Institute, an institute that supports journalists, Roy has taught a number of journalists who are winners of Pulitzer Prizes. When he was with us, his job was to teach us how to help kids write essays. He said that one of the most important skills that he teaches writers of all ages is that one can think about a ladder of abstraction. On the top rung of that ladder, there are abstract terms such as "enduring grief." Then at the far end, the bottom rung of that ladder, there are concrete specifics. For example, a journalist traveled to Utah to visit a family whose daughter was brutally murdered eighteen years earlier by a man who was finally being put to death. The journalist went to leave the home and noticed that although it was midday, the light was burning on the porch. He reached to turn off the switch and saw it was taped on. He looked at the girl's father, as if to ask, "Huh?" and the father explained that when the children were young, it had always been tradition that the porch light was left on until the last of the children was home, and they would turn off the light, signaling, "We're all home." For eighteen years now, that light has still been on. Roy Peter Clark's point was that writers and readers, too, need to work between the two levels of abstraction, and to work especially with the concrete.

I nodded. "Oh my gosh, you are right. It is almost as if those cupcakes represent everything they can't have anymore, don't they? Wow!"

I paused, as if thinking hard, then went on: "And if we want to talk and think about people taking care of someone else, we can lodge that idea in the anecdote about . . . what, I wonder?"

Again the children stepped up to assume the lead role. "How people will take care of the button shop?" "How the Danish people are bodyguards for the king?"

Channel students to continue writing about the big ideas conveyed in the passage you just read aloud, crystallizing their big ideas through tiny concrete details.

"Go back and continue writing and thinking about the big ideas you were coming to during today's read-aloud, and this time remember, 'The bigger the idea, the smaller you write.' If you feel that you are onto a big idea, push yourself to think, 'Is this lodged in any of the concrete details, or even objects, of the story?' and weave those details into what you think and write. You will find that some small objects start to have bigger and bigger meanings."

Scaffold your children's work by reading aloud some of the small details they might incorporate into their writing about the passage.

After a minute, I said quietly, as children continued to work, "If you had copies of the book in your hands, you'd skim back over the book to keep the images and details from earlier sections in your mind. I can't give each of you a copy of the book, so I'll skim back over it, as I imagine you'd each do, dipping in to reread some passages aloud. Here's a hint, too, readers. The author wouldn't put details in unless they were meaningful in some way, and you wouldn't notice them unless something in your heart or mind was saying, 'This matters!'"

Okay, I confess to some deceptiveness here. It is not the case that I actually couldn't think of the concrete detail that has been used to capture pre-war life. So when I said, "Hmm, I wonder if the book uses a detail to convey pre-war life?" I was really being a bit manipulative.

I was glad children remembered the episode when Annemarie and her father talked about the whole country of Denmark being bodyguards for the king, because I know this becomes an important metaphor. By the end of the story, Annemarie steps into the role of bodyguard for Ellen and for others, too. If your children do not mention this, it is not essential, and you do not want to do all the work for your kids. It's so important (and so much better for our students) that we take a breath and remember that teaching our students to make meaning on their own is more valuable in the long run than making sure they know about every potentially symbolic detail in a text.

Teachers, we decided to simply use the words details *and* objects, *to downplay the idea that some objects start to have symbolic value in a story. We will be getting to symbolism, but we prefer to first make sure students are accustomed to exploring ways in which concrete specifics represent something bigger. The reason we are doing this is that sometimes young readers become obsessed with finding and defining symbols, as if doing so is somehow interpretation. The stories the children are reading are, in fact, laden with symbols, ordinary objects that come to have significance. But what matters, for now, is that our readers can begin to edge toward this kind of thinking, and the first step is to realize that if the author puts a detail into a story, it's in the story because it matters. If it's there more than once, it really* matters. *In good stories, details matter.*

This way, as children write about their big ideas, the details from earlier sections of the story will be in the air. If you have had excerpts of the book up on chart paper, children could also look at those or at duplicated copies.

Whenever you have asked children to write within a minilesson, you can signal to a child or two to write on the easel or on a white board that others can read. This provides demonstrations for children needing more support.

I read:

> Mama held a lighted candle . . . it was so long a time since they had dared to use electricity.
>
> She saw her mother look automatically to the blackout curtains, making certain that they were tightly drawn.
>
> His face was set in anger.
>
> There was nothing else in the room except a chest of drawers, the blue decorated trunk in the corner, and a heap of Kirsti's dolls.

I paused and read another line.

> "I can't open it," said Ellen frantically.
>
> "This will hurt." She grabbed the little gold chain, yanked with all her strength, and broke it.

And finally, I read:

> Annemarie relaxed the clenched fingers of her right hand, which still clutched Ellen's necklace. She looked down, and saw that she had imprinted the Star of David into her palm.

Then I was silent and let children continue to write.

Looking over her shoulder, I saw that Jasmine had written: [Fig. X-2]

I noticed Grace biting her lip in concentration, and looked over her shoulder. She had written: [Fig. X-3]

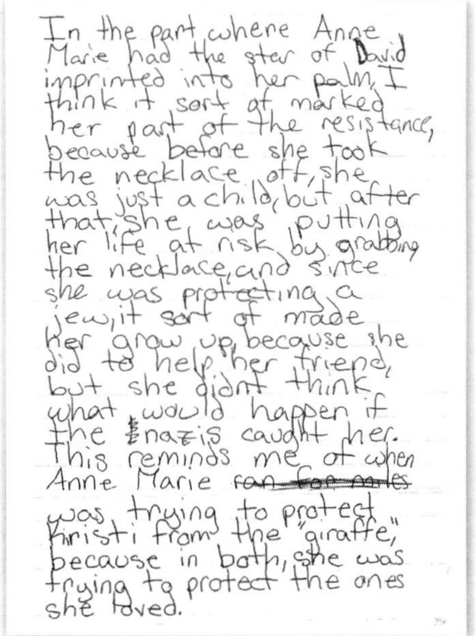

I could also have read:

> *He laughed scornfully. . . . "Where did you get the dark-haired one?" He twisted the lock of Ellen's hair. "From a different father? From the milkman?"*
>
> *In her mind, Annemarie pictured the photograph he held: the baby, wide-eyed, propped against a pillow, her tiny hand holding a silver teething ring, her bare feet visible below the hem of an embroidered dress. The wispy curls. Dark.*

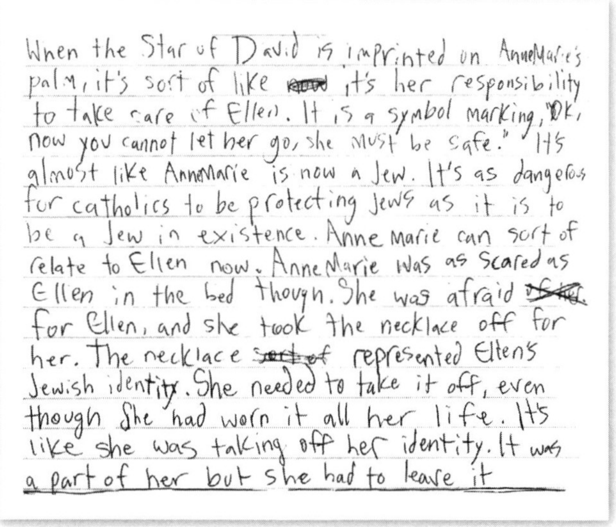

In the part where Anne Marie had the star of David imprinted into her palm, I think it sort of marked her part of the resistance, because before she took the necklace off, she was just a child, but after that, she was putting her life at risk by grabbing the necklace, and since she was protecting a Jew, it sort of made her grow up because she did to help her friend, but she didn't think what would happen if the Nazis caught her. This reminds me of when Anne Marie ran for miles was trying to protect Kirsti from the "giraffe," because in both, she was trying to protect the ones she loved.

Figure X-2

When the Star of David is imprinted on AnneMarie's palm, it's sort of like it's her responsibility to take care of Ellen. It is a symbol marking, "OK, now you cannot let her go, she must be safe." It's almost like AnneMarie is now a Jew. It's as dangerous for catholics to be protecting Jews as it is to be a Jew in existence. Anne Marie can sort of relate to Ellen now. AnneMarie was as scared as Ellen in the bed though. She was afraid for Ellen, and she took the necklace off for her. The necklace sort of represented Ellen's Jewish identity. She needed to take it off, even though she had worn it all her life. It's like she was taking off her identity. It was a part of her but she had to leave it

Figure X-3

Convene a brief share, harvesting some of the insights children have developed in response to the questions on the "Thinking Deeply" chart.

Although many students were still writing, I said, "All right, everyone. Let's start with a couple of the questions from our chart and talk as a group for a few minutes." Gesturing to the chart, I threw one question into the air. "What is significant about that part we just read? How does it fit with other parts?"

Sarah started us off. She read: *[Fig. X-4]*

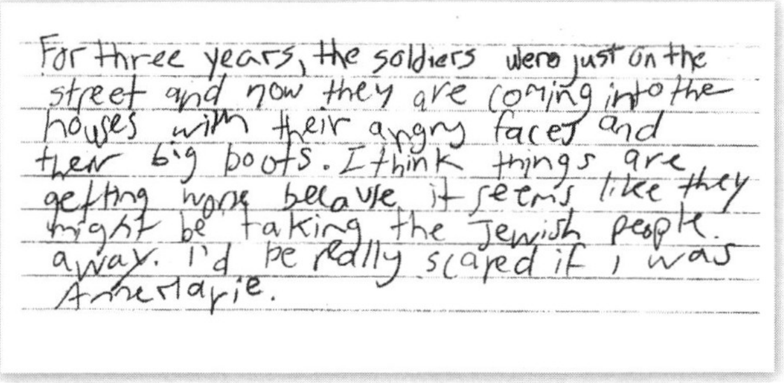

For three years, the soldiers were just on the street and now they are coming into the houses with their angry faces and their big boots. I think things are getting worse because it seems like they might be taking the Jewish people away. I'd be really scared if i was Annemarie.

Figure X-4

I nodded. "Wow." I let the room take in that comment. "Let's talk back to what Sarah, Grace, Jasmine, and the rest of you have been thinking. What's on your mind?"

Jasmine raised her hand and said, "I would have been terrified . . . like . . . (she imitated a shivering, paralyzed-by-fear little girl)."

"Would you have been scared like that only if you were Ellen—or if you were Annemarie, too?" I asked, knowing full well that my question would channel children

When you launch a whole-class discussion by raising something worth discussing and then sending kids to talk in pairs, this allows you to listen in on students' conversations, so that when you later ask one child to share her thinking with the whole class, with the expectation that the whole class will extend what the one child says, you'll have selected a good starting point.

Teachers, it is worth thinking a bit about the passage yourself before launching this discussion. There is a lot here worth noticing. For me it is really important to see that it is now not only Annemarie's parents who are protecting Ellen. It's Annemarie who does this, too, when she removes the Star of David necklace from Ellen's neck. Up until now Annemarie has had a vague sense that the soldiers pose a threat to her friend; this is the first time she shows that she grasps just how serious that threat is. She shows bravery and quick thinking by pulling that necklace off of her friend. Of course, our goal here is not to teach students to see what we see in the text but to see things themselves, and to make connections themselves.

When you want to have a little bit of whole-class discussion embedded into a minilesson, these embedded conversations are so short that it takes a bit of maneuvering to be sure they pack a punch. I'd already heard the children I'm calling upon talking to their partners, so I knew their ideas would help the class.

toward talking about the great risk that the Johansens were taking on their friends' behalf.

"Either!" Kobe said. "Both."

Gabe added, "Annemarie and her family could get in big trouble for hiding the Rosens. It is not just the Jews who are in trouble."

"Yeah, and it is not just the parents who are looking out for the Rosens. It's the kids, too. Like Annemarie was the one to jerk the star necklace off Ellen," Lily piped in. "Me and Jasmine were saying that Annemarie is really brave and smart, too, 'cause when the soldiers are coming to her room, she must be scared stiff but still she remembers about the necklace. And when Ellen can't undo it 'cause her fingers are probably frozen up with fear, Annemarie is brave to rip the necklace off really hard; it must have hurt Ellen, but she was saving her."

Emma said, "We agree with Lily, and we found other places where Annemarie was brave and where Ellen was, like, paralyzed, 'cause when the soldiers stopped them from running, it was Annemarie who talked to them. Ellen was frozen then, too. Ellen is probably scared for her life."

When children identify a pattern in a book—even a fairly simple one—push for them to explore the significance of the pattern. One way to do this is to teach readers to ask themselves, "What is the author teaching about this?"

"Readers, you have made an idea: Annemarie is brave. You have lodged your idea in specific details, like the time Annemarie pulled off the Star of David necklace and the time she handled the German soldiers who stopped her on the street. Annemarie is brave not just one time but several times.

"It is wise of you to look for specifics that can be evidence for your idea. As you do this, though, you may also want to talk and think about the big ideas. One way to do that is to ask yourself, 'What might the author be trying to teach me about this idea? Annemarie is brave, not just once but more than once. So what is the book teaching about being brave?' You have your own questions you've been asking as well. Keep

Although the children have not pointed this out yet and may not have thought about it, by holding that necklace in her hand, Annemarie risks the possibility that the soldiers will mistake her for the Jewish one, so she is risking her own safety to protect her friend. I'm not going to add this in because I know the class will come back to this passage often, rereading it, and I'm just as glad that this particular reading is leaving some important work still undone.

Notice that when I want to keep the discussion from veering off in all sorts of new (and potentially promising) directions, I reiterate the ideas that have the floor now and ask if others have anything to add to those specific ideas. In quiet ways, it is not hard to steer children's responses to a text so those responses cut a deep furrow.

asking, 'What is the book saying about my idea so far?'" I let the room fall silent, and I thought about that question, too. I noticed both Jasmine and Grace added on to what they'd written before: [Figs. X-5 and X-6]

LINK

Send children off to continue reading their club book, reminding them to pause at sections that seem to be written in bold, to ask questions that get them to think deeply, and to think (and write) in ways that link big ideas and specific details.

"So readers, it is past time to get going on your own reading. You might think for a moment about where you are in your book and remind yourself of the different sorts of work that readers of historical fiction are apt to do at the start of a book, in the middle of a book, and at the end of a book. You'll notice I added some of our new work to the chart. Let's try together to keep this chart updated so you can use it as a checklist as you read. "

I gestured to the chart that we'd made earlier in the unit, to which I had added our most recent strategies.

"Club members, remember to set up your reading work for your club. At the end of today, you and your club mates will do something special together, but you won't continue your regular club conversation 'til tomorrow."

As children compared notes on their end-goals, I voiced over, saying, "By the time you meet with your club, you'll be like a soda bottle that has built up quite a fizz! When you and your club mates get a chance to talk, ideas are definitely going to spurt out. Let's take a moment to consider some of the choices you might be making about your reading work. Remember that now and always, if you come to a part that feels important, in bold even, you're going to want to mark that passage and think really hard about it. You can ask yourself questions. (I gestured to the 'Thinking Deeply About Important Passages' chart.) Remember to think in big ideas *and small concrete specifics* including details and objects. I can't wait to see the work you do. Off you go. Get to reading."

This is a big move for young readers, who often state their idea as simply one word. Friendship. Courage. Here, you coach them to illuminate their idea through a specific part of the story and then to elaborate it by saying what the author teaches about their idea.

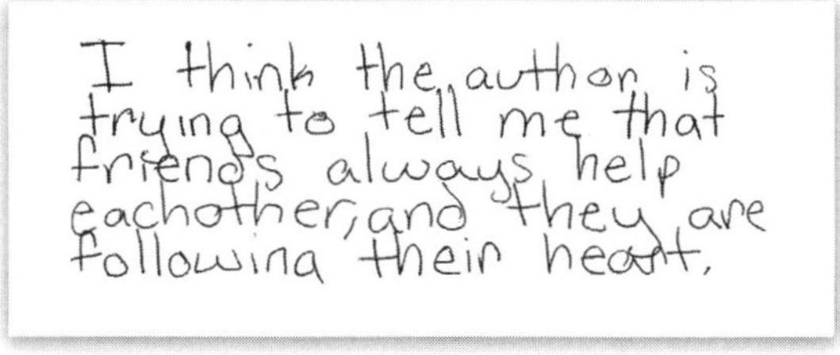

> I think the author is trying to tell me that friends always help eachother, and they are following their heart.

Figure X-5

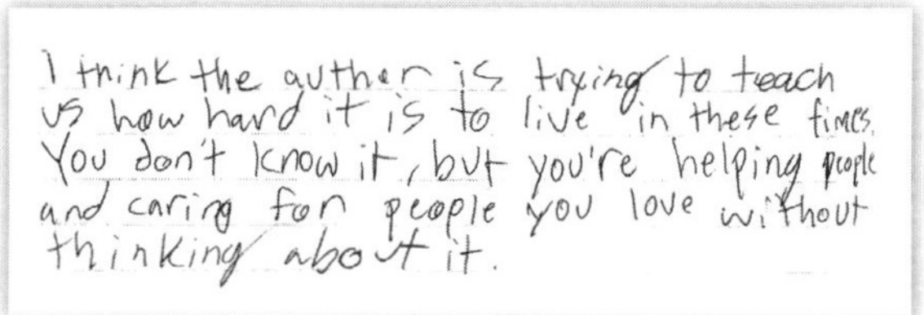

> I think the author is trying to teach us how hard it is to live in these times. You don't know it, but you're helping people and caring for people you love without thinking about it.

Figure X-6

CONFERRING AND SMALL-GROUP WORK

Coach Readers Who Need Help Seeing Fine-Grained Detail

When I work with teachers, trying to help people become stronger at conferring, one of the ways I sometimes begin our work together is by asking, "What are you learning as you confer with individuals and small groups?" The question sometimes catches people off guard because, of course, we think of our conferences and small groups as times for *teaching* more than for *learning*. But I do think one of the most important ways to dramatically raise the level of our conferring and small-group work is to address the question, "What are we studying as we confer with individuals and small groups of readers?"

It is very easy to answer, "I'm studying my children," but I want to suggest that to really truly take on that project would be the most transformative, beautiful work that you could possibly do. It would mean studying not just what a reader is doing right now but what the patterns have been in this child's reading development, and the phases and the turning points and the obstacles. What a wonderful thing it would be if you could really story-tell the narrative of each of your children's development as a reader, telling not just the titles and levels but the insights, the ahas, the strategies, the tools, the goals that comprise the

---

MID-WORKSHOP TEACHING POINT

Readers Imbue Details with Significance

"Readers, eyes up here." I waited until I had everyone's attention. "What many of you are noticing as you read is that when you approach a page, knowing that it's all really meaningful, then *everything* in a story—the words, the people's gestures, the objects—can have profound meanings. This requires a way of thinking that is so much more than thinking just about the who, what, where, when, and how of a story!

"Here's a quick example. Right now, think about a time when you were with someone you really cared about, and you knew this was probably your last time together. Or think about a time you were in a place that really mattered to you, and you knew you were leaving it, so you just had a minute to see things one last time. Have you ever had one of those times? You can imagine it. It is the last day before your best friend is going to move away. You always have snack together, always share your snacks. And on this day, she opens her bag of chips, the same bag as always, and . . . what? The chips fall onto the floor so no one can eat them? The chips turn out to have mold on them? If something happens to those chips, on that day, it will all seem so huge, like it is an omen or something, like it is saying something about the friendship.

"The same thing happens when you are reading. Once a book becomes meaningful to you—which usually happens after you pause, after you ask questions like, 'What's this really about?'—then nothing is just what it literally is. The brown leaf that Annemarie finds floating in the sea near Uncle Henrik's house. It is more than what it at first seems to be. Maybe that leaf has bopped

continued on next page

---

story of each child as a reader. If you truly are doing this work as you confer, then you'll be carrying your own big-idea Post-its (I'll call them pink Post-its to the kids soon) with you as you pull your chair up alongside a reader. You'll have a theory going about the reader's trajectory as a reader, and you'll see what this reader and that one does through the lens of your current big idea about the person. How important this would be for you—and for the field as a whole!

My entry into the field of writing came when I left classroom teaching to spend two years sitting alongside four youngsters, studying their every decision and action as writers, trying to let them teach me how kids develop as writers. The work that my co-researcher, Don Graves, and I did then has been credited with transforming the field of writing instruction. I do believe that if one of you truly studied your children's progress as readers and then taught the world what you discovered, this could transform the field of reading instruction in a similar fashion. There have been quite a few studies of emergent readers becoming beginning readers, but few people have really created detailed maps of the reading development that occurs once kids can read.

I am convinced, however, that truly studying the whole story of each of your readers would be the most ambitious undertaking of your life, and that most of us need to tackle smaller bits of that work. And I think one way to do this is to allow yourself to become interested in some thread of reading development—and then take that interest of yours and let it become a personal project as you study your children's work.

For me, the power of informal assessments is that they invite my colleagues and me to press the pause button in our teaching in ways that help us to think not just about the plotline of our teaching—the unit, the minilessons—but about some of the deeper meanings. When we assessed scores of children who'd been assessed as being children who could read level S texts (or texts that were in that band of text difficulty) and found that a large percentage of these children seemed to read without attending to the fine-grained details that we felt were critically important to the books they were reading, this gave my colleagues and me a learning project that could invigorate a good deal of what we did in our conferences. Recently, then, if you'd asked me, "What are you learning during your conferences and small-group work?" one of my answers would be, "I'm learning ways to help children pay more attention to the fine-grained details in stories, and I'm learning about how and why they often don't notice those details."

MID-WORKSHOP TEACHING POINT

continued from previous page

on the water, coming from across the sea, from Sweden, where Jews are free. In the same way, the Star of David necklace that Annemarie has hidden in a safe place until it is time for Ellen to wear it again—it is not just a necklace that she has hidden. What is it? Where is it hidden and what does that mean?

"So today, readers, as you read, think about the meanings that you are finding—no, the meanings you are *making*. You have another ten minutes to read, and then you can meet with your clubs, and I know you'll be saying to each other, 'I've found something that I think is more than what it at first seems to be.'

"I've created a little guide sheet from our 'Growing Powerful Book Club Conversations' chart (I handed each child a copy). Most of you have gotten really good at things like listening without interrupting and working through disagreements, but all of us sink into counterproductive behavior now and then during especially animated talks. You might want to put this sheet in the center of your conversations to help keep you on track."

It so happened that one of our reading clubs was actually reading *Skylark*, so although the assessment we'd done that had revolved around that book used it simply as an example of a level S text, we couldn't help but be especially fascinated by the way that readers constructed meaning from this specific book. I already knew that 80% of the readers we'd assessed had barely noticed, and certainly not seen any significance, in the passage in *Skylark* in which Sarah, the new bride, stares for a long while at Seal, the cat, after learning that Seal is pregnant with her first litter of kittens. Papa smiles at Sarah's look, as Sarah gazes meaningfully at Seal and then breaks into a smile, saying, "Kittens" with a smile, "Kittens," And the chapter ends.

Because I was focusing on the whole question of how to help readers pay attention to the fine-grained detail in their stories, when I pulled my chair alongside Lily as she read *Skylark*, I asked if she'd mind a question or two. I took her back to the passage about the pregnant cat and asked her what she thought was going on. She looked at me blankly and retold the sequential plotline. I tried to push a bit, asking, "What's really, *really* going on here?" but Lily looked at me curiously. "Sarah is happy for the cat. She probably likes kittens." I tried again. "Lily, here is the thing. In the books you are reading now, every detail matters. The author doesn't put details into a scene unless there is some bigger message hiding behind the detail. So think again about why the pregnant cat is in this story. There's Sarah, she's newly married to Papa. She's looking at the cat, who is going to have kittens, and Sarah starts smiling. Now, what might this all mean?"

Almost at once, Lily started to jump around in her chair. "She's going to have a baby, too!" she shouted. "Or she thinks she is. She's definitely happy about it."

The important thing to realize is that I do not care a bit whether Lily picks up on this particular detail or not. But it matters very much to me that Lily and other readers like her assume that details are in their stories for reasons. As it turned out, Lily and some of her club mates ended up becoming enthralled at the idea that they could figure out parts of the story that the main character hadn't yet figured out. (The narrator in this story—the little girl, Anna—didn't realize that when Sarah looked in that way at the cat, this was because Sarah was having a baby, but Lily and some of her club mates did realize this, which added another layer to all that we were teaching and learning.)

Helping Readers Connect Details to Big Ideas

You may discover children who, instead of overlooking details entirely and hence missing deeper meanings, tend to latch onto one or two particularly riveting details at the expense of the story's larger ideas. They may become so focused on particularly silly or quirky bits of information that they aren't taking in the big picture. Gabe tended to be one of those readers, and I knew I hadn't addressed the issue with him directly yet, so it was in my mind as I approached him.

Gabe was nose-deep in *Civil War on Sunday*, which his club had just started, when I pulled up next to him. I knew that this would be a simpler read for him (and for his club mates) than some of the other books his club had read or would read, such as *Nettie's Trip South* and *Freedom's Wings*, but I liked the idea of them having something they could zip through relatively quickly before getting back to something a bit more challenging. I also liked the fact that the book gets closer into the actual Civil War battlefield, something that many of the other books they were reading mention only peripherally.

"Gabe, how's it going? You are really cruising through that book! Didn't you just start it yesterday?"

"Yeah, it's really good. It's more about the fighting part than the other books we've read. Well, they were good, too, but they weren't really about the war so much, they were before."

"True, but I bet that reading about slavery and the Underground Railroad really helped you get a sense of some of the reasons for the war, right?" Gabe nodded his assent and opened his book again. He was clearly itching to get back into it. "I know you want to find out what happens, Gabe, but I'm wondering if first you could just retell a little of the story for me. I've read this one, but a really long time ago."

"Sure. Well, you know, like from the last books, Annie and Jack are trying to find some writing to bring to Camelot, to save Camelot, and they have to get some paper or something from the Civil War times, and the tree house takes them there. And it's so gross! There are, like, guys bleeding everywhere. And there are cannons, and shells, and the soldiers are just in the trenches shooting muskets at each other all day. And this one kid is a drummer, and he has heat stroke, and he keeps fainting. . . ."

Gabe was clearly absorbing lots of details from the book. I noticed, in particular, his use of some of the military terms: musket, shells, trenches, and so on. I also noticed the recurrence of something I'd noticed in him earlier in the year as well: a propensity for focusing on the things that particularly fascinated him, like the names of weapons and the gory details of battle. *Magic Tree House* books don't head too far into gory territory, but Gabe was certainly soaking up whatever he could—it seemed, at the expense of not only a coherent retelling but also an understanding of the book's larger ideas.

This resonated for me as a fairly big problem because I'd recently studied scores of informal assessments in which children who constructed very problematic understandings of *Amber Brown is not a Crayon* often did so in just this same fashion. In the Amber Brown work, more than one child had seemed to focus above all on a few details related to toilets (there'd been, in the book, a passing reference to flushing a turtle down the toilet), and when details that were inconsequential to the narrative through line of the book were foremost in a reader's efforts to retell and reconstruct the book, this proved very problematic. Something similar was showing up in our assessments of these children's nonfiction reading as well. The example that had become emblematic for my colleagues and me was an article about the threat to the habitats of several animals;

at one point the article mentioned that the endangered habitats had meant that food sources were at risk, and as a case in point, the article had mentioned that prairie dogs—the food for one of these animal species—were less plentiful now. Countless readers reconstructed the entire article around that one detail, in a way that involved letting go of any grasp of the actual big ideas in the text. So when Gabe showed even just small signs of perhaps doing this same thing, I wanted to investigate more. I wondered if Gabe's fascination with the gory details was the whole picture, or if he was just most excited by those particular details and was actually absorbing on a deeper level. Before jumping into teaching, I decided to probe a little deeper.

"Wow, Gabe, I'm not surprised that you remember all of those details. It reminds me of when we were in our nonfiction unit, how you just seemed to absorb all of the details about the manta ray and other creatures you were learning about. It sounds like life on the battlefield was pretty awful during the Civil War."

"Yeah. But it's kind of cool, too."

"You sound like Jack! I think he thought it would be cool to visit a battlefield, too, didn't he? At least at first." I was trying to see, with this comment, if Gabe would bring up the fact that once Jack actually visited the battlefields and field hospitals of the Civil War, he was horrified and frightened and quickly decided that war was not at all "cool."

"I guess," Gabe said, noncommittally. I decided to forge ahead with my teaching point, because it seemed that Gabe really *was* letting his interest in the details drive the way he was taking in and interpreting the text. I knew that in fact, Jack's revulsion and struggle with mastering his fear so that he could help Clara Barton and the soldiers was a prominent through line in the book, and I wanted to remind Gabe of some work we'd previously done about noticing and remembering the *important* details as we retell, not just the ones that might stick the most easily in our minds. For Gabe to move from retelling a hodge podge of details into a more sophisticated summary, he'd need to first isolate the details that are central to the book from those that aren't, and then link the more essential details with bigger ideas.

"Gabe, I'm noticing that while you're certainly remembering lots of details from the book, it seems like your mind has kind of a mish mash of details and some of them might seem sort of cool but aren't necessarily all that important to the book. This can happen sometimes when you're reading pretty fast. And I bet you're reading this book pretty fast, right, since it's a quicker and easier one than some of the other books you've been reading?" Gabe nodded sheepishly.

I saw Gabe had also written some entries in his notebook. A quick glance suggested they followed along the same theme as his oral work on the book, but it was a step ahead for him to choose sometimes to write entries rather than simply Post-its. One entry looked like this: *[Fig. X-7]*

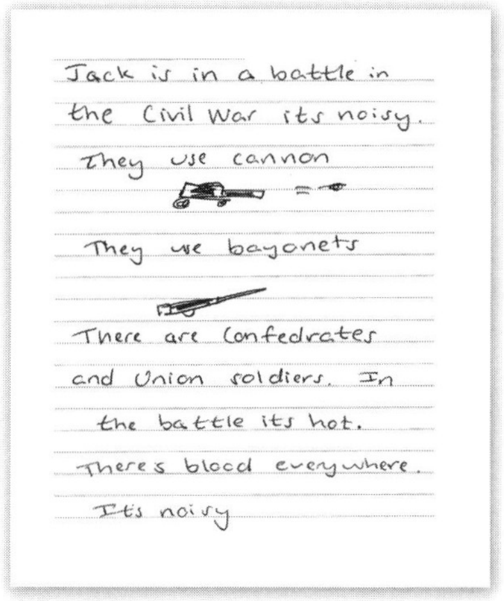

Figure X-7

"Don't get me wrong, it's great that you're motoring through this book! But I'm a little bit worried that what you are holding onto in your mind are the gory details, the gross details, and that your mind is so latched onto them that you might not be really taking in the main story line of this book. Let me show you what I mean. Pretend you were reading my story and it goes like this:

My dog was missing. I ran outside, calling and calling her, but I couldn't find her. I even checked along the sides of the road to see if she had been hit by a car. I saw my neighbor's polka-dot underwear hanging out on her clothesline. We had ten people searching for Emma. Then, walking across our driveway, I saw something move in the car and realized she'd been shut in it all along.

"Pretend I asked you what my story was all about and you said, 'Polka dot underwear.' Do you see that although it is true they were there—sort of stuck onto the story—they weren't the main thing, and that retelling the story in that way will seem like you missed the main thing. This is a really extreme example, and your reading of *Civil War on Sunday* is not close to as problematic as that, but I saw a hint of you having the polka dot underwear problem, when your retelling focused on the weapons and blood, because they aren't the main thing, any more than polka dot underwear is the main thing in my story.

"I'm going to go work with another reader, and then I'm going to come back. Before I come back, reread this book, or scan it anyhow, and get ready to do another retelling, this time one that goes over the main things in the book."

Gabe was game. As I headed off, I wondered to myself whether Gabe might actually have an easier time finding and holding onto the big ideas in books that were a bit more developed. Could harder books actually be easier for him? In any case, though, I was quite sure he hadn't picked up on the important themes that did exist in this book and that he could do so.

A few minutes later when I returned, Gabe was ready for me. Before I said anything, he started in on a new retelling. "So Jack and Annie are going to the Civil War times, and Jack is really excited to see the cannons and the battlefields, and they have to find something to bring back for that quest they're on, a piece of paper or something . . ."

Gabe's voice trailed off and he looked up at me, clearly trying to judge from my expression whether he was on the right track or not. I said, "You said Jack is really excited to see the cannons and the battlefields. Does he stay that way throughout the book?" I hoped that my leading question would nudge Gabe toward the through line of Jack's changing feelings about war.

"Oh, no, actually, not at all." Gabe said, excited to be catching on. "At *first* Jack is super excited because he thinks the war is going to be fun, kind of like a game. And Annie doesn't really want to go. But it's funny, when they get there, Annie is the one who isn't grossed out or scared, and Jack is! He just wants to go home at first."

"That's a great start. You're including really important parts in your retelling. Keep going!"

"Well, they get the paper they were looking for that I told you about before, to help Camelot, and Jack wants to go home, but Annie says they have to stay and help and follow the things on the list that someone gave them when they decided to help at the field hospital, which are like, 'be cheerful' and 'be brave' and 'don't give up.' And so they stay, and they meet Clara Barton, this nurse that was a real lady I think, and they end up helping these boys, one that was a Confederate soldier and one that was a Union soldier, a drummer boy, and he looks like Jack. And that's where I'm up to now."

"That's so interesting, Gabe. Jack really goes through a lot of changes in the book. It's interesting to me that they end up helping a Confederate soldier *and* a Union soldier at the same time. What do you make of that? Which were the good guys and which the bad guys to them?" Gabe was now retelling using important details, and I wanted to nudge him a bit toward making something bigger of those details.

"Well, it's like, like, really when you are at the hospital it's not divided into sides, into our side and your side. The actual people, they aren't really any different from one side or the other. I think Jack is thinking it's more complicated than he thought before, war, and less fun."

"Gabe, that's magnificent thinking! You caught on really fast to what I meant when I asked you to retell the important parts. Rereading helped, didn't it? If you ever feel like this is happening again, where you are focusing so much on the polka dot underwear that you don't take in the main story line, remember that rereading is a way for you to fix that up. Okay, you can get back to reading now. I know you're dying to find out what happens!"

TEACHING SHARE

Readers Learn that Ordinary Objects Can Symbolize Big Ideas

Share a few examples of student writing in which the student used an object from the story to represent a big and abstract idea, and explain that this is symbolic thinking.

"Readers, as I've been peeking over your shoulders, reading your big ideas grounded in tiny details, you've surprised me once again! I knew you would come up with great ideas—you always do—but I had no idea that you'd take this work to the next step.

"Many of you are discovering something that really sophisticated, usually *older*, readers tend to notice. That something is called *symbolism*. I hadn't planned to talk to you about symbolism because it is usually taught in high school, but because you're already gesturing toward it, I've changed my mind. Listen to a few entries some of you wrote. Then I'll explain. Emma, who has been reading *Letters from Rifka* with her club, wrote: *[Fig. X-8]*

I paused, then picked up a second notebook and said, "Josh wrote this next one. He found himself thinking back to a book he and his club mates finished a while ago, *The Gold Cadillac*. He wrote, 'It seems like the mom wants the family to stick together so she is giving riding in the Cadillac a try. It's no longer about the Cadillac, it's about safety, putting family first . . . . It's about the safety of who she loves.' *[Fig. X-9]*

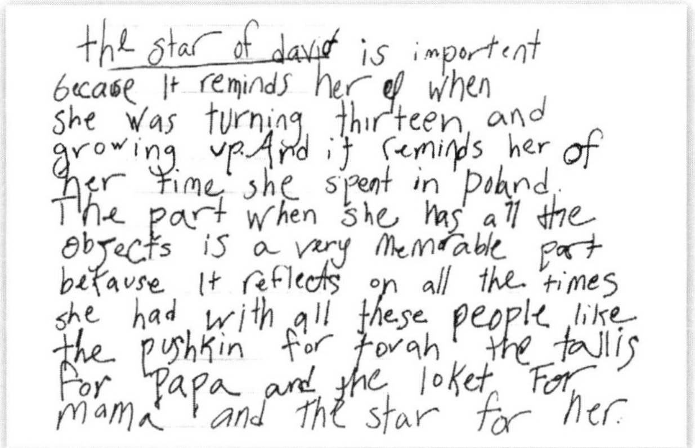

I know, I know. Earlier in this session I wrote that we made a deliberate decision not to use the word symbolism just yet. Instead, we would speak to children about "details that represent big ideas" and "objects that carry meaning," hoping to convey simply that concrete specifics in stories can be imbued with significance. But teaching, as you well know, is full of surprising turns in the road, and often your children themselves will lead you toward teaching moves you hadn't anticipated making even minutes earlier. In this instance, the children have shown me that they are ready to learn the word symbolism because they are all but saying it themselves. For another group of children, I might make a different choice.

> the star of david is importent because It reminds her of when she was turning thirteen, and growing up. And it reminds her of her time she spent in Poland. The part when she has all the objects is a very memorable part because It reflects on all the times she had with all these people like the pushkin for torah the tallis for Papa and the loket For mama and the star for her.

Figure X-8
Emma's thoughts about objects that matter in *Letters from Rifka*

> • It seems like the mom wants the family to stick together so she is going riding in the cadillac a try
>
> • No longer about Cadillac but about safety
>
> • Putting her family first
>
> • Trying to prove a point
>
> • For her, It's about safety and who she loves.

Figure X-9

"Readers, although Emma and Josh didn't write, 'The locket symbolizes X, and 'The Cadillac symbolizes Y,' each of them, in their own way, named what those objects symbolize, what they represent. Earlier I told you that big ideas are often lodged in details. Symbolism is an extension of this. It means simply that objects represent, or stand for, a bigger idea. So, for example, earlier we decided that the cupcakes in *Number the Stars* represent everything the kids can't have anymore. If we take that a step further, we might say that those cupcakes, which remind the kids of a simpler, easier life when little pleasures were easy to come by, symbolize, for the children in this book, a loss of early, carefree times."

Ask students to think about what the objects referenced in the students' writing symbolized.

"So let's return to what Emma and Josh wrote, and I'm going to give all of you the chance to think about what these two were imagining the objects they wrote about symbolized, or represented."

I showed the class Emma's entry. [Fig. X-10] She had done some sketching about Mama's locket, which plays an important role in the novel, and then she had described why objects are so important in the book. I said to the class. "So, these various objects each remind Rifka of someone in her life, including herself. And they all remind Rifka of times when she was with these people and of a time when she was younger. So what might these objects symbolize?"

Predictably, Lily was already up on her knees vying for my attention. I gestured for her to speak. "It's like all those objects, they're her memories!"

"Beautiful, Lily! So those objects *symbolize* Rifka's memories. Does anyone else have another take?"

Gabe looked like he might have a thought, but he seemed less certain than Lily. "Gabe, what do you think?" I nudged him.

"Well-l-l-l," he drawled, scratching his forehead, "maybe all those things are for the people that she's thinking about. It sounds like they're not around anymore. So, like, the tallis is her dad, and the locket is her mom, and the pushkin is Tovah?" Gabe asked.

"So you're thinking that each of those objects *symbolizes* the people she loves and misses. They're little reminders of those people, those loved ones she has left behind. So maybe the objects *symbolize* family for Rifka."

"Yeah," Gabe said, grinning.

"Nice work, Gabe. Okay, let's think about Josh's entry now." I reread his entry out loud. Then I said, "So what do you think Josh is getting at here? What does this Cadillac

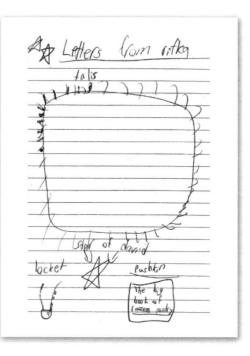

Figure X-10

Literary scholars might say that the cupcakes symbolize innocence, lost innocence in this case, but this seems to me to be over the top for nine-year-olds!

You've no doubt noticed that I rephrase what each child says to incorporate the word symbolize *into what they have said. This is intentional. I'm hoping that children will begin to try out this word themselves. Even if they don't say it, I know that hearing it over and over will help crystallize the word's meaning for them.*

symbolize?" Fallon waved her arm dramatically. "Fallon," I said smiling, "I know you have a terrific idea about Josh's thinking since you're in his club, but let's give someone who is in another club a go. Let's see . . . Sarah?"

"I haven't read this book," Sarah said, "But it seems like this mother has had something against the car up until this point, but now she's rethinking that because the car will keep the family together somehow. So maybe the Cadillac represents unity."

At this point, Josh jumped in. "Actually, it's funny 'cause the car at first makes the family kind of fall apart. The mom is really mad and she refuses to drive in it. But later, when she puts her family first, and she rides in the car, the family kind of comes together. I mean, it's slow, but I think they're stronger for it. So maybe the car kind of represents different things at different times?"

"Josh, I'm so glad you said that. The truth is that objects in stories can symbolize one thing to one reader and something else to another, or they can symbolize one thing at one part of the story and something else later. And sometimes an object is just that. No hidden meaning. Just a spoon, just a toothbrush, just a comb."

Those of you who have read The Gold Cadillac *may argue that the car represents anything but* unity, *or for that matter,* safety, *as Josh wrote. If anything, you may argue, the car represents* dis-unity. *That's okay. What Josh is onto here is that the mother has chosen to put her love for her family and concern for their safety above her own feelings. The truth is that the car represents different things to different characters, which is what makes it such a fascinating object to analyze—and why I chose to spotlight Josh's insight. A reader could say the car symbolizes pride and freedom and a realized dream to the father; it is a sign of success and status to the envious neighbors and a sign of a squandered dream to the mother. Arguably, it becomes a symbol of racism later in the story. Then, too, the mother's decision to ride in the car marks an important shift in the story, and while the car itself is not what unifies the family, the mother's decision to place her family above her own distaste for what the car represents to her is significant. In that moment, perhaps, in some sort of way, the car does unite the family. Of course, this is all too sophisticated for these children at this stage, and I won't share it with them, but it is interesting to consider that when we note the symbols children find, we need to resist the urge to correct them. Often they are onto something big even if it doesn't ring exactly true for us.*

Again, I can sense the concern you're feeling. What if my kids start to see meaning where there is none? What if every little object becomes significant to them? I worried about this, too, but let's relax. It's bound to happen, just as kids will mix up metaphor and simile, make "allusions" that are in fact connections, and overuse ellipses and exclamation points when they first learn these. Overusing, and using and confusing, are a natural part of learning. And besides, we should be so lucky that our kids find too much, not too little, significance in their books!

Forging Trails of Thought as We Read

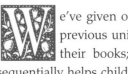

IN THIS SESSION,
you will teach your students that readers keep our big ideas in mind, allowing them to shape our thinking as we read on.

We've given our kids plenty of opportunities in previous units of study to retell the stories in their books; we know that retelling a plot sequentially helps children see one event's connection to the next, and retelling helps children develop a strong sense of where they are within the trajectory of story structure.

As the year progresses, our teaching has progressed as well. The skills we taught in previous units will, time and again, prove to be fundamental stepping stones to more complex work. In this unit, we have helped young people know that although, yes, reading is all about holding tight to the often hair-raising, death-defying dramas of historical fiction books, reading is not only about following the literal action of the story. Reading is also about coming away from reading with deeper thoughts about what bravery or friendship is, or about how loss and defeat can be handled, or what compassion can feel like. In other words, this unit aims to help young people read between the lines so they come away with bigger ideas about their lives and their world.

All good stories are really about ideas, but these are rarely presented to the reader on a plate. Sometimes, teachers have resorted to simply doling out to children the "right interpretations" of texts. When I was in school, my teachers used to tell me the theme of each story that the class studied. I studiously recorded their words in my spiral notebooks, writing, "*To Kill a Mockingbird* is a coming-of-age story," or "*To Build a Fire* addresses the theme of 'man versus nature.'" When exam time came, I could parrot back what my teachers had taught me. For the stories we studied, I had the right answer. But I had no way to produce an interpretation of any text that hadn't been predigested for me and stuffed down my throat as if I were a baby bird.

GETTING READY

- In tomorrow's session, you will read part of Chapter 8 of *Number the Stars*, so you'll want to do some reading aloud of that book outside of the reading workshop. Do not read aloud past page 70, however. You'll see why if you look ahead.

- For the teaching component of this minilesson, you'll want to find a student who can share a fresh, big idea generated by his or her writing about reading.

- For the link, you'll add on to the chart "Making Our Way Through Historical Fiction."

- Your children will be meeting with their clubs today, so be sure the work you do in the link and mid-workshop teaching helps to set them up.

Since then, the nation has learned the importance of a process approach. In the writing workshop, we no longer simply show children stellar works of literature, saying, "Go and do likewise." Instead, we pull back the curtain that hides the writer working at his magic and show children the concrete, replicable strategies that the writer uses, and we help children use those same strategies.

> *How important it is to remind ourselves, then, that the goal is not for children to parrot back our grown-up interpretations of a text, but, instead, the goal is truly to teach kids the process that they can use to grow their own big ideas.*

In reading workshops, we rely on the same process approach. Nowhere is this more important than when teaching interpretation. This is an area of reading instruction in which educators are especially eager for children to pro- duce the "right answer," to cite themes that feel literary and mature and sophisticated. How important it is to remind ourselves, then, that the goal is not for children to parrot back our grown-up interpretations of a text, but, instead, the goal is truly to teach kids the process that they can use to grow their own big ideas.

So the challenge that we face as teachers and designers of curriculum is that we need to spy on ourselves when we're engaged in the interpretive work we hope our kids will learn to do, and we need to take note of the specific strategies we use that pay off for us, that yield new insights.

This session comes from teachers, researchers, and me doing just that. We've spied on our own reading and found that once we have a big idea or two in our head, it is impor- tant for us to read forward in a way that involves more than just tracing the chronology of an action-driven plot. Instead, reading forward becomes a way to grow the nascent ideas that we've found lurking beneath the plot. We grow those ideas until we have much larger ideas—of the kind that become big enough to apply not just to this one book bu,t possibly, to other books, to our lives, and to our world.

Once readers have a big idea or two in mind, with parts of the story to support it, then readers have a way of gath- ering more parts, revising that idea, as we read on. This early interpretive work, connecting parts of the text under a big- ger meaning, makes the process of reading more challeng- ing. Sometimes two moments in the text that are intimately connected will be physically separated by not just a few, but by dozens or even hundreds of pages. Powerful readers encounter a passage that strikes a chord, and soon we are turning back to details and phrases and incidents from ear- lier parts of texts to make our idea one of significance.

ESSON

Forging Trails of Thought As We Read

CONNECTION

Share examples of a few readers from the class who have generated provocative, important ideas as they read.

"Readers, I've been thinking about the big ideas that you and your clubs have already started to grow in this unit, and I just need to share with you some of the amazing thinking you've been doing. When the Pioneer Club read *Dandelions*, a picture book about Westward Expansion and living out on the prairie, Kobe came up with this idea: [Fig. XI-1]

"Izzy also pushed the pause button as she was reading. I watched her reading *Letters from Rifka*, and at one point she looked up. And it looked like she was going to explode with an idea that she just *had* to talk about, but it was reading time and not club time, so instead of talking, she wrote this entry: [Fig. XI-2]

"And *then* do you know what Izzy did? She reread the entry and added more onto it. She added:"

> It's like the book is about Rifka **keeping herself**, from when she was in Russia, but also finding a way to get to America and become a new person.

"We know that when we press the pause button to stop and think, we come up with bigger meanings. There are big ideas hiding in our books, but to find them, we need to pause and think. And often, that thinking involves reading backward, doesn't it, and thinking backward."

COACHING TIPS

> The dandelions are having a hard time moving from one place to another just like Bolton family.

Figure XI-1
Kobe imbues small details with big meanings.

> The stuff that Rifka carries with her that she got from her parents and family is almost like having family with her. It's like those things are her parents and help her remember to keep going so she can get to them.

Figure XI-2
Izzy has recorded her big ideas onto Post-its.

Tell readers that you want to talk about what new happens after readers pause to think. As we read upcoming texts, we look at that new text through the lens of our big ideas.

"Readers, yesterday we didn't really talk about what happens *after* you hit that pause button. Today I want to tell you that when we press Play again and get back to reading, we carry our big idea forward as we read on. We look at the rest of our book through the lens of the idea, asking ourselves questions such as, 'How does the rest of the book support this big idea?'

"Take Kobe's idea that the dandelions are struggling to take root in a new place just like the family in *Dandelions*. He's not done with that interpretation; now, he'll look for more about that idea as he reads on. He'll look through the idea as if it's a lens.

"And when Izzy continues to read *Letters from Rifka*, she will read with her idea in mind: 'How is Rifka holding on to her old self while finding ways into her new life?' She will look through each event or struggle through the lens of this idea, asking, 'How does Rifka hang on to her old self while in this situation? And what about that one?'"

Name your teaching point. Specifically tell kids that once we have a big idea, an interpretation, we hold onto that big idea as we read, letting it shape the way we think about the rest of the book.

"So, readers, today I want to teach you that once a reader has paused to think deeply about a book, and developed an idea that seems true, from that point on, the reader wears special glasses, special lenses, and looks at the upcoming text through those lenses. We read on with our interpretation in mind, and say, 'Ah yes!' or 'Huh? That doesn't fit!' Doing this is one way that we continue to develop our ideas."

TEACHING

Tell about some readers who developed an idea about their book (one that will later prove applicable to the read-aloud) and then put that idea aside, finding new ideas.

"Readers, yesterday the Allies were reading *The House of Sixty Fathers*. Even though they had only read a bit of the book, they found passages that seemed to be written in bold, and they paused to grow big ideas about the portion of the book they'd read.

I actually wear reading glasses so I have a built-in prop for this session. You may decide to forage around for a pair of glasses you can borrow so that you, too, can ground the crucial portion of this teaching point in visual supports. In any case, do what you can to actually communicate with your readers, because the idea of the session is a big one—that readers take in text through the lens of a big idea, or an interpretation, we have already developed. It's not a totally new idea, of course, because we taught this same teaching point in Following Characters into Meaning. *But it's not the sort of thing one can say and kids instantly master. The complex part of this, of course, is understanding what it means to see a text through the lens of a big idea, and I hope this helps people understand that work.*

With younger readers, I'm apt to stick with the language of "big ideas." With more sophisticated readers, I might choose to move to the language of "interpretation," or I might introduce the term theme. *When a reader starts to see an idea appear in more than one story, then it is a particularly good time to introduce the notion of theme. You'll know your students and can decide how much literary language you want to bring into your teaching at this point.*

They kept returning to the idea that the little boy, Tien Pao, has to be so responsible at such a young age, and to the idea that war makes children grow up before their time."

I held up one of Brandon's Post-its and read: [Figs. XI-3 and XI-4]

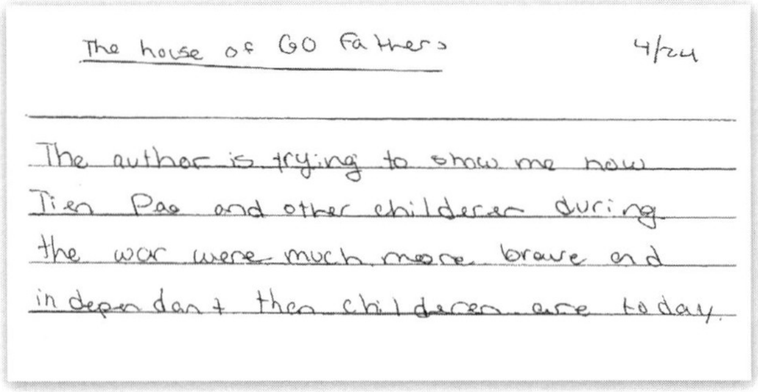

The house of 60 Fathers   4/24

The author is trying to show me how
Tien Pao and other childeren during
the war were much more brave and
independant then childeren are today.

Figure XI-3

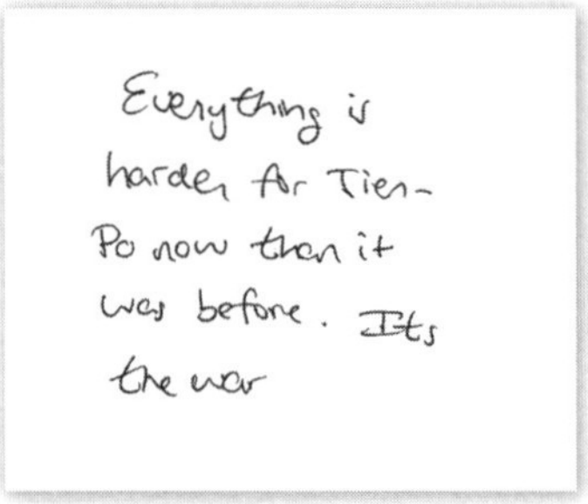

Everything is
harder for Tien-
Po now than it
was before. Its
the war

Figure XI-4

"What you need to realize is that Brandon and the other Allies *created* these ideas. The book doesn't come out and say, 'Tien Pao has to be so responsible.' Or 'Tien Pao has to be so grown up.' But reading about all the things Tien Pao went through led the members of that club to create this idea.

"So, anyhow, after the Allies Club came up with their initial interpretation—that war makes children grow up quickly, making them more responsible—they then gathered evidence for this idea. Then, they put the idea in their 'Finished Work' pile, and they read on, coming up with new ideas."

It is great that those readers came up with new ideas. Sometimes a story seems to suggest idea after idea. I wrote today's teaching point with the Allies in mind because it is important to remember that once a reader has developed an idea that seems true, from that point on, the reader wears the idea as if it is a pair of special glasses and looks at the upcoming text through those lenses, thinking "Ah, yes!" or "Huh, that doesn't fit with what I was thinking. . . .' So once your group comes up with a new idea, let's not put it aside. Readers hold onto those good ideas, and when more ideas come up, we connect them into the first good idea, if we can.

The interesting thing to note is that especially in some of the lower levels of text difficulty, the ideas (like the character traits) are actually explicitly addressed in a book, The reader's challenge is actually mostly to notice the idea once it is addressed and to recognize it as important, carrying that idea as the reader reads on and applying it to sections of the text. I still talk about the reader's job as authoring ideas because I think that even when ideas are explicitly stated, readers often think that they deduced them themselves. So the experience of reading feels as if it involves making ideas even when sometimes readers actually collect, apply, and combine more than make ideas.

Recruit the class to join you in seeing one club's newest idea through the lens of their original idea, helping the members of the class practice synthesizing ideas.

"Let's do this together. First, we need to put that idea on as our glasses: Tien Pao has to be so responsible at a young age; war makes kids grow up before their time."

I pretended the idea was a pair of glasses, put them on, and added, as a rueful aside, "You wouldn't want to leave an idea like theirs just left lying beside the road of the book! No way. Let's keep that idea in mind as we move on. We could read more of the story now, but let's instead hear an idea that Kadija came up with for the next part of the story, seeing that idea through the lens of the existing idea." I then took up Kadija's new idea, and looked at Kadija, standing beside me, who read: *[Fig. XI-5]*

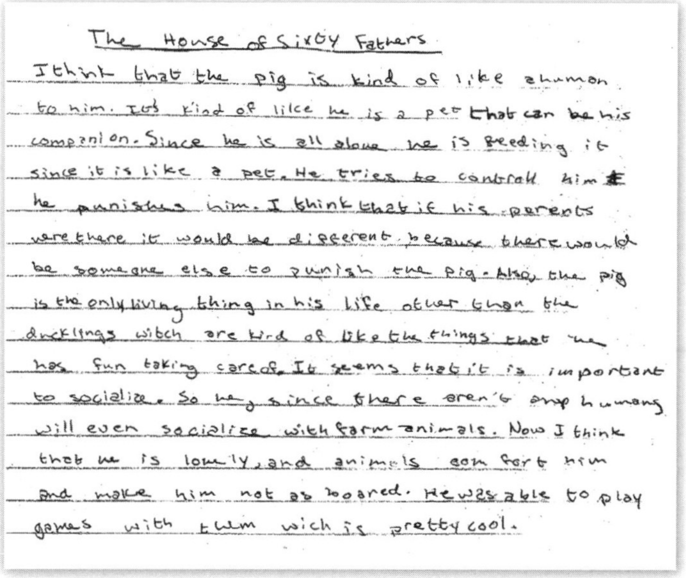

"So class, remember that the job is to look at the new thinking through the lens of the first idea." Picking up my glasses in a way that suggested the kids do the same, with imaginary glasses, I repeated the initial idea (the lens): "War makes kids grow up before their time, Tien Pao needs to be so responsible at a young age," and I looked at what Kadija read about the pig (if his parents were there, someone else could punish the pig). After pausing for a moment, I continued. "Okay, so we are thinking about the new ideas—that the pig is like a friend when Tien Pao is all alone, and that Tien Pao *has to act like a grown-up to discipline the pig*—through the lens of the initial idea about war making kids grow up too quickly."

Triumphant, Kadija said, "The ideas go together! 'Cause war has made Tien Pao grow up early, acting like an adult when he is still a kid. Even with his pig, he has to be the parent and tell the pig how to behave."

"Yeah, he has to act like a parent because his parents aren't there," added Brandon.

Name the work this child is doing that you hope others can do, in other texts. In this case, point out that the original idea can be the lens through which the reader can read the text and make new ideas.

"So what I'm hearing is this: You took away from Chapter 1 that Tien Pao has to be a grown-up before his time. And that big idea lasts, but changes a little, in Chapter 2

Notice that I say, "Let's do this together," as if this was the active involvement section of the minilesson. Actually I am continuing to demonstrate. But I know my demonstration will be most effective if the kids are working alongside me, trying to do what I am doing, so that my work becomes a relevant model for them. The truth is, though, that although I say, "Let's do this together," I haven't yet turned this over to them.

Of course, I am making this pretty obvious. Think of what I am doing as providing training wheels, scaffolds. This is an important way to teach. Over time, children will be invited to do similar work with less scaffolding.

The House of Sixty Fathers
I think that the pig is kind of like a human to him. It's kind of like he is a pet that can be his companion. Since he is all alone he is feeding it since it is like a pet. He tries to control him & he punishes him. I think that if his parents were there it would be different because there would be someone else to punish the pig. Also the pig is the only living thing in his life other than the ducklings witch are kind of like the things that he has fun taking care of. It seems that it is important to socialize. So hey, since there aren't any humans will even socialize with farm animals. Now I think that he is lonely, and animals comfort him and make him not as boored. He was able to play games with them wich is pretty cool.

Figure XI-5

because even when working with the pig, Tien Pao has to be a grown-up, stepping into the role of a parent. Good work! You didn't just drop the big idea about war making people grow up, leaving it by the side of the road of your book (I acted out what that travesty would have been like). You instead read Chapter 2 through the lens of your initial idea. And look at how your idea has developed! You're extending your interpretation!"

ACTIVE INVOLVEMENT

Give children practice taking in text through the lens of a preexisting idea by asking them to borrow the idea cited earlier and then reread the read-aloud book, seeing it through the lens of that idea.

"So before we move on, I'm going to ask you to try something a little unexpected. Pretend that the Allies' idea (about war making children grow up before their time) is an idea *your* club came up with when reading the early chapters of *Number the Stars.*" I jotted this idea up on chart paper to help them remember it:

War makes children grow up before their time.

"So now, hold this idea and turn, in your mind, back to *Number the Stars*. Imagine that you're reading the part we heard the other day in which the soldiers break into the Johansen's house at night to search for Ellen and her family. Now hold the idea up, 'War makes children responsible, children have to grow up fast' and look through it as a lens, and recall that moment in *Number the Stars*, with the soldiers banging on the door in the night, saying, 'Let us in. . . .' Recall how Annemarie reached for the necklace around her friend's neck; 'Hold still' she said and jerked it off. Then she held that Star of David necklace pressed into her hand as the soldiers interrogated her."

A word of advice: As some children gather up parts of the story to support their ideas, they will ignore all the parts of the story that don't support that idea. This means that sometimes, in trying to illuminate the text, young readers actually end up with a more partial understanding. Don't fret about this right now. We'll address that in the next session. Keep in mind that as children add a new reading practice, they'll often run with it, sometimes seeming to have forgotten all the other work they've done as readers so far. It's okay; their enthusiasm is actually a good force. Recall how, as young writers, they started to splatter exclamation marks across the page once they discovered this punctuation mark? In a way, we should consider ourselves lucky that they take a strategy so seriously that we have to curb their enthusiasm. So, expect that your students may strain to make parts of the story fit their idea. They may gather up what seem like remote parts of the text, all in support of an idea to which they are fiercely committed.

It may seem like an amazing coincidence that the idea children had developed for their book, The House of Sixty Fathers, *is applicable also to* Number the Stars, *but in fact you'll come to see later that many big ideas are in fact broadly applicable. Even if your children aren't reading those two books, this will be true for whatever they are reading. That is, you'll find that the theme in one of their books probably pertains to other books—hence the label "universal themes." A word of caution: Don't point this out to children yet because this will be one of the special realizations that provides new energy toward the end of this unit.*

If you opt to do this quick sort of guided remembering instead of actually reading an excerpt, be sure the episode you ask children to remember is one that most will recall.

Scaffold your children's thinking about the text so they grasp what is entailed in synthesizing new text into an overarching idea.

"Remember, you are thinking about the soldiers coming into the apartment not to find new ideas but to see this text through (or you could say, as related to) the lens of the idea that war makes children grow up before their time. When we read that passage earlier, we all thought, 'Annemarie's brave.' So now, tell each other what comes to mind as you look *instead* through the lens of the idea that war makes children grow up before their time. What happens in this part that supports or adds to or changes that idea? Turn and talk."

As the children talked, I crouched alongside them and listened in. After a bit, I reconvened the class to crystallize what I'd heard: "Most of you said that kids have to grow up during war because grown-ups can't protect children like Annemarie from having to act in grown-up and brave ways."

Then I said, "So readers, we carried that idea that war makes children grow up before their time along as we thought about *Number the Stars,* and now we have this more developed idea. That's how readers grow our thinking."

LINK

Recap what you hope readers have learned that is transferable to other texts.

"So readers, always remember that after you have paused to grow big ideas about texts, then when you read on, if your book continues to give off lots of ideas, like a sparkler on the Fourth of July, one of your jobs will be to examine those new ideas through the lens of your initial ideas as we just did."

Teach one more thing, pointing out that it's not just the *plot* of a book that can be put on a timeline, but also the evolution of ideas.

"Readers, before you leave to carry your own ideas forward, can I teach you one more thing about reading forward, carrying ideas? Do you remember that earlier we talked about how our stories unfurl, not just along one but along several timelines: the plot timeline and the timeline of the historical context? Well, I also want to point out that *ideas* develop in a way that can be time-lined. So far, we've said that *The House of Sixty Fathers* goes like this:" [Fig. XI-6]

There will be lots of instances like this one where you are called upon to paraphrase what you've just heard a child or two say. You'll "round up," but don't replace what the children said with what you wish they had said. You are helping them progress along the pathway toward learning to interpret, and you have a lot more teaching to do, and that teaching will lead them to revisit their interpretations, ratcheting them up bit by bit.

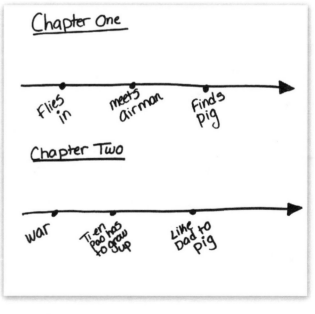

Figure XI-6

"Do you see how we took the big idea from Chapter 1 and wove it into the way we read Chapter 2? And when the Allies read Chapters 3, 4, and 5, you can be sure that they'll follow the ideas that Tien Pao needs to act grown-up before his time, and that the pig functions as family for him.

"So, now you realize that we have a new strategy for our chart, 'Making Our Way Through Historical Fiction.' Stories are about ideas, and we need to answer the question, 'What idea is coming across to me in this story?' I'll write this here on our chart, and as you read, remember that along with all the other work you are doing, you can ask, 'What idea is coming across to me in this story?' 'What big idea am I carrying forward as I read?' You may want to create a timeline of these ideas."

You will want to add this one bullet to "Making Our Way Through Historical Fiction." It is easy to launch an anchor chart and then to forget it, and best if you remind yourself to keep those charts alive in your teaching. You can't expect children to recall the charts from earlier in the year (or the unit) if you and I don't recall them as well!

Summarize what you hope readers have learned about reading onward, taking in the new text through the lens of an idea.

"Today, I hope I've reminded you that when we read on, we don't just drop our first big idea in the ditch alongside the road of the story. If we're in the midst of the story, we first think back to see if there were other parts of the story that would support this idea. And then, as we read, we keep looking through that idea, using it like a lens through which we view the rest of the book. In doing this, we develop our big idea further. You could say that with each upcoming chapter, it is not just the plotline that unfolds, not just the historical timeline that unfolds, but ideas, too, that unfold.

So often we see kids come up with an unbelievably dazzling idea about a book they are reading, and then they seem to completely forget about that idea when they pick up the book to begin the next day's reading. It's as if coming up with an idea is something they do in the moment, which generates a temporary thrill. We need to teach them that holding onto an idea while reading forward in a book is as essential as holding onto who is in the story or what the problems are. Most children are in the midst of texts, so we will need, in conferences, to show them how to first think back, and to then move forward, carrying meaning.

"You'll all have time to read now. Before you get started, look back on your jottings and think, 'What big idea or two am I carrying forward as I read?' I've put a brilliant pink Post-it on each of your reading spots. Write your big idea on that Post-it, and leave it out where you and I can see it. Then read on. And I'll leave some extra pink Post-its because I'm pretty sure your idea might change as you keep reading on."

This pink Post-it will become central to the ongoing unit, so I encourage you to actually do this. Of course, it need not be that color, but this is a good time to nudge readers to commit themselves to an idea related to the text they are reading.

In the mid-workshop teaching point for this session, I address an issue that you can expect will come up for your students during this session. Just as most students don't write a strong, clear thesis statement on their first attempt at an essay, most students grapple with developing a big idea about their stories. If you want, you could attempt to weave this teaching point into the lesson itself. I chose not to do so because the lesson seemed already packed full of material. If you find that only a handful of your students struggle with this, possibly because your students have prior experience with this unit, you might choose to teach this only to that small group and address some other teaching point in the mid-workshop teaching point.

Teach Readers that by Collaborating, We Can Build Towering Ideas

Sometimes I'll notice that my sons, both of whom are becoming young men who tower over me, are, in uncanny ways, very much the same now as they were when they were four years old. Miles has always built forts for himself—for several summers, his greatest joy was to add pulleys, mailboxes, and escape routes from the tree fort he built in the branches of a tree that leaned out over the lake where we spent all those summers. And late August was always a time for him to remake his entire bedroom in preparation for a new school year. There would be special files, shelves, pencil containers—the works. Now Miles has just moved to the West Coast to set up his first adult apartment; he is again building a fort for himself and redefining himself in the process. "Golly," I think, "he's the same kid as ever."

I find it helpful to notice ways in which my sons remain so much the same across the years, the decades, because this makes me more patient when I try, as a teacher, to snap my fingers and, presto, to have kids magically change before my eyes. When teaching involves telling, it can happen quickly. But when teaching involves helping young people to outgrow themselves, to draw on a broader skill set, then it can take a remarkable amount of time.

Teaching Reading Is Nothing Less than Teaching Thinking

One of the enduring challenges that all of us face when teaching reading is that we are teaching nothing less than thinking. And most of us find that many students struggle to develop ideas. One sees those struggles in all sorts of ways. When we nudge children to grow theories about their characters, we've seen some children sum up an entire character in a single generic term. Kirsti is happy; Annemarie is kind. For those readers, it is a big step ahead for them to reach toward more specific terms. Kirsti is childish or naive or unaware; Annemarie is responsible, determined, protective. We can coach children by saying, "Can you be more specific? What exactly is she like?" and we can give children bookmarks or miniature word walls to help them internalize the work of taking a millisecond to think, "Wait. I don't want to use just any word. What is the precisely true word?" We can teach readers that one makes a theory— "Kirsti is nice."—and then reads with that theory in hand, revising it to make it more specific: "Kirsti is always cheerful." We remind readers that often it helps to use lots of words to say

---

MID-WORKSHOP TEACHING POINT

Readers Enlarge Our Claims About Our Texts

I stood in the center of the room. "Readers," I said softly, "when you come to the end of the sentence you're reading right now, mark your spot and give me your attention so I know I can continue." I waited patiently for a few moments. "I just finished reading all the big ideas you had written on your pink Post-its. First of all, I congratulate you on developing an idea through which you can examine your characters, your story, and even other stories. This is a huge step for each of you as a reader. Reading through the lens of a big idea helps to make your thinking deeper and richer."

"I know I told you to write down your big idea right away, and I think a few of you felt rushed, and perhaps even weren't sure exactly what was expected. That's why I asked each of you to put your idea in writing, so that I could get a sense of where you all were in the process. Now I want to teach you a few ways to make sure that your big ideas really are big—that they're ideas that will pay off for you, that have room to grow and change, and that will push you to think about things in new ways. You can make sure your big ideas are really big by taking your time to develop them, by pushing yourself to make a claim that is more than just one thought, and by saying your idea with words that help you see more than just one character or story through the lens."

continued on next page

---

what you mean, not just one: "Kirsti is always cheerful even when the world around her is full of depressing things and her sister and her parents leave her out of things." That is, simply helping readers to go from thinking that a character is nice, mean, friendly to thinking more precisely requires not just that the teacher says this, but that we organize repeated opportunities for children to receive scaffolded practice.

Then, of course, children will no sooner begin to characterize people with more precise terms than we'll have new horizons for them. That's how teaching goes. And so we help these readers know that it would be a really great thing if they were able to cite multiple instances from the text to illustrate the trait they've fastened onto each character. You'll recall that when readers are reading books in the K/L/M band of text difficulty, our record-keeping sheets nudge us to channel students toward this work. Those record-keeping sheets also remind us that even in the straightforward books in that band of text difficulty, the characters go through emotional highs and lows, and helping readers track changes in the characters' feelings, if not their traits, can be good work.

But if we want to help children learn to think more deeply about texts, it is important that we anticipate an instructional pathway along which children can travel, so that when we see children doing one sort of thinking, we can imagine what a next step for them might be. Once children are growing theories about characters that are somewhat precise and can be substantiated through

text references, then there are a few possible next steps that people thinking about books are apt to take. For one thing, it is helpful to notice that characters are not just one way. A person can be different in one situation or another—in one place from another, one relationship from another, one time of the book from another. To notice this, readers often need to generate their own generalizations for how a character is acting in different situations—and that takes thinking. When Rifka was first in Belgium, she was lonely and timid—then she became engaged, interested, enterprising. Once a reader distinguishes what a character is like in one situation and another, this opens worlds of space for thinking, "Why is she different in different contexts?"

It is helpful for teachers to carry record-keeping sheets that nudge us to channel readers (especially those reading in the N-Q band of text difficulty) to develop more complex ideas about characters, perhaps by taking on language such as this: "Sometimes my character is. . . . For example, ... But other times, he or she. . . . For example. . . . This makes me think. . . ."

Another way to do similar work is to think, "The main character has different sides to him or her. When he or she is . . . , he or she is. . . . Then when he or she is . . . , he or she. . . ."

MID-WORKSHOP TEACHING POINT

continued from previous page

"Most of the time, you will not need to decide on an idea in just a few moments, as you did today. Developing a big idea takes time, just as it did when we were developing our theses for the essay in our writing workshop. As you read a story, you'll be asking yourself, 'What idea is coming across in this story?' You might even try out one or two, but then change your mind as different ideas come to the forefront of your mind as the story progresses.

"A big idea is not just one word. Grace had written 'homesickness' on her pink Post-it about *Letters from Rifka*. It's true that Rifka is homesick in this story, and that homesickness is a theme that comes up in this book and in many of your books. But homesickness is not a big idea, not a claim. Think of a claim as a statement that you make based on what you're thinking, just as the thesis of an essay is. Brandon didn't just jot, 'growing up' when he was writing about Tien Pao. He wrote that Tien Pao was forced to grow up too fast because of the war. I went back and asked Grace to expand her idea just like Brandon did, to ask herself, 'What is this story making me think *about* homesickness?' She jotted, 'Rifka feels homesick for the place she lived, and also for the life she had before all of this started.' By pushing herself to elaborate on what she was thinking *about* homesickness, Grace has now developed a claim that's going to pay off as she uses it as a lens through which to consider this story and others. It's much more sophisticated than just saying 'homesickness,' and since it is a claim, Grace can actually find evidence that supports it—or not—as she reads.

"Lastly, remember that theses of our essays, in writing workshop, had more power when we framed them as claims about the world, rather than simply ideas about ourselves. The same is true about these big ideas about your texts. If you can use words like *kids* or *people* rather than specific characters' names, it sort of cracks open your claim, and suddenly you'll more easily see how it applies to other characters. So, when we began to say Brandon's claim, 'War makes kids grow up too fast,' instead of 'War makes *Tien Pao* grow up too fast,' we could see how the same

continued on next page

Another thought frame that can help readers, again one that can be included on a record-keeping sheet, is this: "In the beginning, my character was . . . , but as the story continues, I think my character could be changing. By the end, the character is. . . .

Of course, we'll be helping children think not only about characters but also about the messages and meanings contained in their books as wholes. And here again, it is helpful if we, as teachers, can watch young people do this work, and watch ourselves do it as well, and begin to develop a sense for the instructional pathways along which children travel. Early on, it is probably the case that whatever the main character learns, whatever meaning she or he comes to, is going to be the meaning that the reader comes to as well. Rifka learns that even when she is alone, she can make a life for herself. A more proficient reader might see lessons that apply not only to Rifka but to other characters. When challenges are put in front of people, we often find resources inside ourselves and within our relationships that we didn't even know were there. It is important for teachers to have a sense of pathways such as this so that we can help children travel them.

We can help children become more proficient thinkers not only by ratcheting up the sorts of thinking they take on—progressing from thinking about what one character learns to thinking about what several characters learn, for example—but also by teaching them to talk and write in ways that help them create their own "journeys of thoughts." Again, it helps if the teacher has an instructional and learning pathway in mind. The first step in that pathway is to teach children to talk in ways that support thinking, and then, once they can do this, we can teach them to write in these same ways.

Certainly it's helpful if a club or a partnership or a reader takes the time to decide upon an idea to develop, creating some boundaries so that the reader's thinking doesn't jump along the surface of a dozen ideas. Conversational prompts help, and it helps even more if those are strung along together as in this example: "'One example. . . . Another example. . . . This shows. . . . This is important because. . . . What I hope you notice about this is. . . .'"

MID-WORKSHOP TEACHING POINT

continued from previous page

big idea is true of Annemarie in *Number the Stars*. In fact, now this claim is truly a lens through which we can examine any story, and even real stories that we find in the world. For example, as we discussed Brandon's claim, my mind began to turn toward parts of our world that have been touched by wars recently, and think about how the lives of children in those places must have been affected.

"So, everyone, look at your big idea right now and make sure, first of all, that it is a claim, a statement of something you think, not just one word or idea. You might have to try different ways of saying it, just like we did with our essays. If you need help, turn to someone in your book club and work together to fashion your claims. Whenever you are stating the big idea you're on about in a text, you'll want to make sure it's a big idea, a claim. With practice, this will get easier and easier."

Sometimes it can help to use some concrete physical way to maintain a focus: Putting a single Post-it (or two related Post-its) at the center of a conversation does this job. A "conversation board" with a blank space at the center for children to put the idea that is in play in a discussion can help, especially if there is a bench for ideas one might put into play later. Giving children blocks (or an image of blocks) that get piled on top of one another can help. It can help to teach children that in a conversation, speakers almost ask permission to change the topic of conversation. "Are we done with that topic? Can we shift?"

None of this work is inconsequential, nor can it be done once and then regarded as finished. Learning to talk and think together is challenging work, but it is an essential part of the life of the mind.

Teaching Readers to Sustain a Line of Thinking

The Dust Bowl members were clutching their copies of *Out of the Dust*, talking somber-faced among themselves when I dragged my chair over to join them. The group had recently finished reading *Bud, Not Buddy* and was now reading Hesse's rich and challenging text. It is not a long book, but it is beautifully crafted, highly charged with emotions, and layered with metaphor and meaning. It's also slower-moving than most of the books that children tend to choose to read on their own. I'd channeled this club toward the book because they'd taken on the goal, at the start of the unit, of reading more slowly and thinking more deeply. You'll want to watch a club working with this book on the DVD.

Pulling out a notepad, I began quietly transcribing in shorthand the conversation the children were having. Clubs are accustomed to me doing this. Not only is this my way of compiling notes for future teaching, but it also keeps me in an observer/researcher role, which is crucial to my understanding of how a club is functioning. On occasion, particularly if I feel that a club conversation is developing momentum, I choose not to interrupt the club at all, keeping myself and my notepad out of their way. On this particular day, I had lots to record. As I started listening, one of the club members, Sarah, was busy trying to get a point across to the rest of the group.

Listen As Club Members Find, Develop, and Lose Focus

"Well, she only learned to love her mom *after* her mom died," Sarah said. "I mean, before her mom died, she was full of 'maggoty stew' looks for her. It's kind of like when her mom was alive, Billie Jo resented that her mom was so strict. And she's not liking her dad now either. She said he has these sad songs coming out of him. She doesn't see how sad *he* must be, losing his wife—'cause she's too mad at him."

After a pause, Kwami said, "Well I don't think it's that important that she thought her mom was so strict. I mean, we all hate it when our moms are strict. We could all give our moms those looks. But I disagree when you say that this means we don't love them."

"Yes, but we don't *know* it (that we love them) 'til they're gone. That's what I'm saying," Sarah countered. "Like in the songs, you don't know what you've got 'til it's gone."

"But her dad isn't gone anywhere," José pointed out.

Growing more excited, Sarah continued, "That's my point. He's still there, so she can't forgive him. Like, it's only after she runs away from her dad ('cause I read on, past our goalpost) that she feels that she can forgive her dad. Like she needs space before she appreciates people."

As I sat scribbling, ears tuned like radars to the work this club was doing, I admired that Sarah had come up with a sound idea that she'd managed to successfully defend when Kwami and José challenged the idea. I was wondering at this point if her club members would acknowledge what she was saying—if they would pick up her idea that in several instances, Billie Jo only appreciated people whom she'd lost.

Out of nowhere, Jack asked, "Kerosene is like oil, right? Maybe they used kerosene for fuel." That comment didn't just represent a non sequitur from Sarah's idea, it seemed to come totally out of the blue! In my notes, I made an exclamation mark next to Jack's contribution. I stayed silent, pen in hand, waiting to see how the group would react.

Ignoring Jack's question, José said, "Billie Jo says she's a lot like her dad. Maybe *that's* why she's mad at him. You know, like she sees herself in her dad and she's mad at herself for her mom's death, so she's mad at him, too."

I smiled to myself, recounting the one-on-one conference I'd had with José just a day ago, during which he'd shown me some jottings he'd made about Billie Jo's dad that read "Her dad's really stubborn" and "The dad's an idiot." I was pleased to see that he'd moved beyond that rather reductive idea to a more complex view of this character's relationship to his daughter.

Looking down at the book cover, Kwami added, "I feel sorry for her being an only child. It's like there's no one to talk to about her parents because no one is going through what she is. She's kind of alone." His comment, like Jack's, felt as if it came out of the blue.

At this point I felt like I had picked up a pattern of club members adding new ideas to the discussion without acknowledging, much less seriously considering, anything that had been said before. "The dad's basically an alcoholic, I think," Jack said, shaking his head. Jack's announcement regarding the dad's alcoholism only confirmed my decision to intervene, and I did so, transcribed notes in hand.

Help Readers Recognize When Their Ideas Become Scattered

"May I stop you a second? You are all digging deeper under the plot of the story to come up with bigger ideas, which is great. You are talking about patterns in actions, reasons for action. Those are ways to dig under the plot, so nicely done. But as I sit outside your club just listening, I want to point out that when we're having a book talk, we need to take up each other's ideas. Remember earlier, I taught you that we take our current theory in hand and read on in the book, thinking between the old idea and the new content? In the same way, we can take up a classmate's idea and see the book through the lens of that idea—like we did earlier when we thought about the book through the lens of Kadija's idea about war making people grow up. Just as we don't leave *our own* ideas by the roadside, we also don't leave each other's ideas in the ditch either! And you have left some amazing ideas just lying beside the road of your conversation."

I placed the paper on which I had just scribbled a rough transcript of their conversation on the table before them. "Okay, I'm going to read back just the first few minutes of what you just said, and as I do so, help me keep track of how many times a whole new idea is brought up. Each time one of you introduces a new idea into the conversation, let's raise a finger."

I began reading the start of their conversation back to them quickly, and together we raised a finger at three points: first, at Sarah's point about Billie Jo only appreciating people once they were gone, then at José's idea that Billie Jo is mad at her dad because she's mad at herself, and then at Jack's point about alcoholism. As the group looked at me expectantly, I put down my notes and said, "You know, if the three of you decided to build a tower of blocks, there are two ways you could go about it. One of you could lay a block here," I pointed to a spot before me. "Another one of you could decide, 'Why—over there, in *that* corner, is another really great location for a tower,' and you could go place a block *there*," I pointed to a distant corner of the room. "And a third one of you could look at the rug way over on the other side," I signaled in the opposite direction, "and think, 'Wow, a tower in the center of the room would look so cool,' and place a block there. Pretty soon, what you would have is a room full of blocks lying all over the place—but no tower.

"To build a tower, the second person has to place another block *on top of* the first block, and the third person has to place his or her block on top of the first two. Do you see where I'm going with this block analogy? Your ideas are great on their own, but I don't really see you building a towering idea through your talk. It's like each of you comes in and scatters a new thought that no one takes hold of. There's no connection, no *buildup*.

"So, today I want to teach you that the great thing about having a reading club is that this gives you the opportunity to really grow a *small* idea into a *tower* of an idea. And we do that when we take in another person's idea and almost pretend that that idea is our own and think about the book and our own ideas through the lens of that first idea.

Channel Readers to Resume Work, and Then Coach As a Way to Scaffold

"Sarah began our conversation with a thought that she defended for a while. Sarah, can you get us started? Sarah picked up her writing and read her idea aloud: *[Fig. XI-7]*

Billie Joe resented that her mom was so strict when she was alive. And although she sees that her dad has these sad songs coming out of him, she's full of resentment against him. There's all this blame getting in the way of her seeing how sad he must be

Figure XI-7

"Running away from her home put all this space between Billie Jo and her dad. And the space helped change her feelings toward her dad."

José added, "Well, talking to that guy on the train also helped her forgive her dad."

I intervened again, feeling the need to name what José had just done. "Great, José. You just added to Sarah's idea. She said space helped change her feelings toward her dad, and you're adding that talking to someone helped, too. Your idea builds on Sarah's idea."

A small lull in the conversation followed this. I wondered if the club members were now nervously trying to think of "the correct" thing to say next. Sensing the group's uncertainty, I prompted them in a quieter voice, almost subvocalizing, "Take what Sarah and José just said and pretend *you* thought of it. Then think about the rest of the story through the lens of that idea."

Finally, Kwami bravely began, "But she came back, didn't she? Because she knew it wasn't solving anything to run away. And she said that thing about him being the sod and her being the wheat. She needed her father, leaving helped her figure that out."

Jack added, "It's like you can't run away from your problems. You've got to come back to face them." Noting with satisfaction that Kwami and Jack were now tuned to listening in a way that they hadn't been previously, I made a thumbs up sign and then motioned with my hands as though I was laying one block delicately over another before leaving this group.

It is interesting to note that many of the teaching points for book clubs arrive at the same conclusion: enabling club members to develop collaborative thinking as opposed to talking and thinking in isolation. Often, even under the guise of deceptive opening words such as, "I agree with you because . . ." or "To extend that point further . . . ," we note that children don't always respond to, much less develop, an idea that a previous speaker has made. This is not surprising; such collaborative idea-building is rare even among adults. It requires practice and conscientiousness to develop a culture in which such conversations can flourish.

Many of our teaching points for conversations among partnerships and book clubs, therefore, return through various channels to the same goal of collaborative thinking. In this case, I've just taught a group that to develop a towering idea, they need to build on what the previous speaker has said.

THING SHARE

Readers Learn that Your Idea and Mine Can Fit Under the Tent of a Theme

Convene the class and tell them about a club that thought across the big ideas individual members were pursuing, generating an overarching club idea.

"Readers, I have something enormously important to teach you, so I'm going to need you to come together in the meeting area. Bring your books and your pink Post-its." I waited until the children had all settled down. "Here's my idea. Reading together is a lot like playing cards. Not really—it's not really like playing Go Fish, or Gin Rummy, but what is the same is that you and the other members of your club do each bring your card (I gestured toward the pink Post-it, the one I'd suggested would hold each person's idea about a story) and lay your ideas out. Let me tell you about what another club did with their cards, their ideas, and see if this gives you ideas for something you could do.

"This club had been reading *Sarah, Plain and Tall*, like our Pioneers did earlier. It is the story of a father and his two children, Anna and Caleb, who lived during the time of Westward Expansion, way in the middle of the country, where things were very rural—lots of stretches of farmland, fields of wheat. The children's mother (and the father's wife) had died before the story began. In the story, the father found a catalog through which you could order yourself a new bride, so Sarah traveled halfway across the country to live with this family and decide if she'd marry the father and become part of the family.

"Like you all, these readers had paused to grow ideas and put their big ideas on pink Post-its. Then they got the idea to come together as a club and to try to grow one really huge, really important idea, an idea they could all develop together. I'm going to ask all of your clubs to try to do this as well, so listen really carefully."

Engage children in doing the work the club in your story did. Then show how the club did the work.

"These readers got a big sheet of construction paper—some of you may do that as well—and they laid their pink Post-its out on it. As I do this, see if you can think about how

The story I'm telling actually comes from some work Kathleen did with another class. One of the reasons that collaboration among teachers is so incredibly important is that this way, we merge files. We share examples. The work I describe is far better work than one usually encounters, so the example serves as a marvelous mentor text for kids. And children enjoy hearing what other kids have done even if the stories are borrowed examples, passed from one classroom and one year to another.

these ideas might go together." As I talked, I stuck big pink Post-its on different corners of the chart paper on my easel, saying as I did it, "One person's idea was this and another person's idea was this (and this):"

The father isn't the way he used to be because he used to like to play the fiddle and make music, but he changed after the death of Anna and Caleb's mother. He became more serious.

Anna is resistant to Sarah's mothering her because she is used to her real mother.

Caleb is getting close to Sarah but feels Anna doesn't like want that.

Sarah misses home, but she is learning bit by bit to care for this new family.

Teachers, it is challenging and important to try your own hand at the work that you ask kids to do. In this instance, for example, it's a great exercise to try imagining alternate suggestions you could make for an overarching idea that might function as a big tent idea, broad enough to pull these disparate ideas together. "Learning to love isn't easy—this often involves struggling with resistance." "Loving one person often feels like it's part and parcel of losing another person." "Families become families slowly, over time."

"Right now, talk with each other about how these ideas might go together into one bigger idea. I know you don't all know the book (though many of you do), but you can still think about how these go together. It is really hard intellectual work, so turn your brains up really high."

After a bit, I stopped the buzz of talk. "I heard some of you say that it is not just Sarah, the mail-order bride, who has to decide if this new family is going to work out but *everyone* who has to decide this. And I heard some of you say that these ideas show that you can't just order a new family out of a catalog—that it is hard to bring a new family together. And you had other ideas as well—really smart ones.

"What that group of kids ended up coming to was the idea that *Sarah, Plain and Tall* is a story that shows how different people deal with loss. The father has stopped fiddling because he lost his first wife, and maybe he is having a hard time loving Sarah, too, because he already lost one wife. And Anna doesn't want to fill the hole from the loss of her first mother. And Sarah is homesick for her lost home, so she is dealing with loss, too. So, really the whole book is about how different people deal with loss.

"So club members, get together with the others from your club. Bring your pink Post-its and try to figure out an idea that is almost like a big tent of an idea because there is room for all your thoughts under it. I'll be around to help."

As children put their Post-its and heads together, I listened in and peeked at their work, offering coaching tips as needed: "How might that idea fit with this one? What's the connection? That's a good start. Now push yourselves to come up with a really big idea (I made my arms into a tent shape above my head) that encompasses all your ideas."

After a stretch of time had passed and it was clear that all the clubs at least thought they had landed on big tent ideas, I convened the class.

"Readers, you've done a stupendous job coming up with a big tent idea—and in a short amount of time! The Pioneers, who just recently finished rethinking parts of *Skylark* (that's the sequel to *Sarah, Plain and Tall*), laid their thinking out on Post-its, and eventually they came up with this tent idea 'Even though you love an old place, you can still find a way to love a new place because of the people who are in your family. *[Fig. XI-8]*

"The American Dreamers, who have finished *Letters From Rifka* and are now reading *Maggie's Door*, came up with this big tent idea: 'As people move to new places, they hold onto things that remind them of their old home and the people they love.' I know all of you will be carrying your ideas forward as you read on."

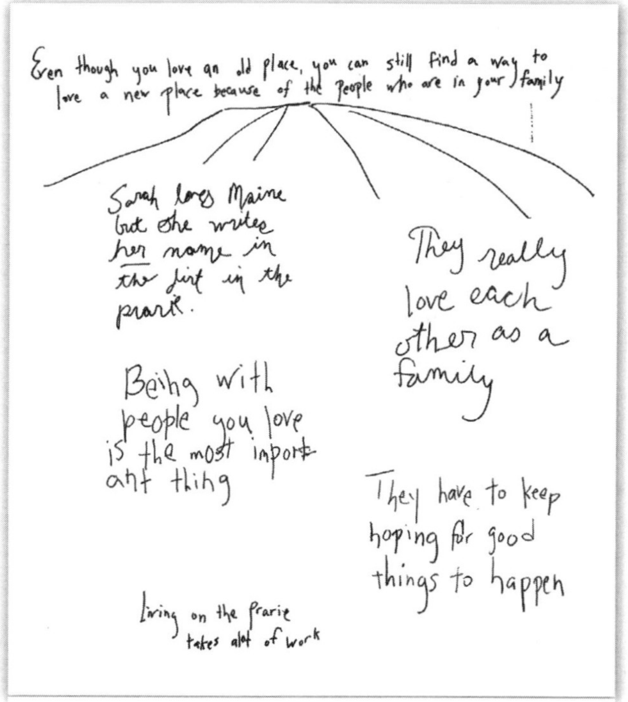

Figure XI-8
This is the theory chart that the Pioneers created, to bring their pink Post-its together under one overarching idea.

Widening the Horizons of Our Thinking

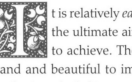t is relatively *easy* to name "lifelong learning" as the ultimate aim of what we want our students to achieve. The concept of lifelong learning is grand and beautiful to imagine. It is deeply satisfying. It emphasizes the loftiness and heft of our very profession. At the very least, it alliterates nicely and sounds wonderful rolling off our tongues.

But then we enter our classrooms. Amid the chattering children and never-enough time, amid the forgot-it-at-home homework and the new troublesome clique, amid the supervisor's visit and the missing books, we shove our grand aims aside, sighing privately at the futility of our best intentions. And we compromise.

It needn't be this way. If lifelong learning seems too idealistic a goal to implement in our very real classrooms, neither the children's chatter nor the supervisor's visit is to blame. The fact is, until we can take lofty ideals and break them down to examine exactly what they entail, they will remain forever elusive. If we want lifelong learning or higher-level thinking to be the goals of our teaching, then our curricula must be structured in ways that support such goals in realistic ways—through piecemeal, teachable habits and strategies that cumulate across levels and across time.

Let's try. Imagine that you and I are having this conversation about what it means to be a lifelong learner. We'd probably agree that a lifelong learner will continue to read even when reading workshop ends, that a lifelong learner would take our teaching and use it as a point of departure, adapting to the requirements of this changing world by constantly adding to and developing what he has already learned, what he already knows. We'd probably agree that a lifelong learner might look at people and listen to their conversations with curiosity and wonder, learning not just from these but also from all sorts of other unlikely teachers: An apple falling off a tree might teach our lifelong learner about gravity; flying a kite during a thunderstorm might teach our lifelong learner about electricity. Even after we set luck and genius aside, the habits of mind that lifelong learn-

GETTING READY

- Find an example of an interpretation you've gradually changed your mind about, through conversation with someone else. We've used an interpretation of the movie *Up*.

- Prepare to add one bullet to the chart "Making Our Way Through Historical Fiction."

- Prepare a list of thought prompts to help students push their thinking in writing and in talking. You might use the list we've used in the share.

ing entail include all the verbs we've just described: continuing to learn after departing from one position, adapting, curiously listening or watching, and wondering.

We must teach these habits of mind even as we teach children math, science, writing, and reading. If we aren't modeling and teaching that readers depart from one thought or point or position to consider another—if we aren't coaching our children into listening to their books and

> *The fact is, until we can take lofty ideals and break them down to examine exactly what they entail, they will remain forever elusive.*

to each other with curiosity and wonder—then our teaching has little chance of rising above the assigning of small forgettable tasks meant to maintain order among twenty-five children on a "busy" workday. In other words, to instill the habits of learning life-long, we have to keep up a continuing conversation of what lasting "things" to teach.

From such conversations, about what it means to have lifelong readers and lifelong learners, emerge many of the teaching points that pepper these units of study. "See if while talking to your partners you can change your mind," we urge readers, teaching them to revise their initial theories about a book or a book's character. "Listen to what your club member says—and try to build off of this," we advise, not *just* because we want courteous conversations, but because listening is a higher-level skill. "Characters aren't just one way," we add, nudging readers out of seeing their world in black or white, good or evil. "Examine the perspective this book has been written from," we advise, pushing readers into wondering about the behind-the-scenes drama of their books.

This session revisits—and deepens—our previous teaching, this time teaching a habit of mind that also helps readers interpret stories in deeper and more meaningful ways. In teaching children to revise their initial sense of what a story might be "really about," and in teaching also, that a way to do this revision is through collaboration, by listening to others' take on this book, we're doing something significant and quite deliberate. We're putting revision and conversation at the heart of interpretation because although we want children to be able to articulate what a story is "really about," we also want children to *revise* initial ideas, to *listen* to alternate perspectives, and to *adapt* their ideas to another person's. By literally readjusting children's stances and posture, we're practically coaching them into an attitude of receptivity. Rather than stressing the product, the importance of a deep, literary interpretation, we're actually stressing enriching the *process* readers might go through to arrive at this product. Since it is "habits of mind" we're after, we must do no less.

MINILESSON

Widening the Horizons of Our Thinking

CONNECTION

Ask readers to recall an unhelpful conversation they've been in, reenacting their posture and expressions during each.

"Readers, I'm going to ask you to do something you'll think is strange at first. Take a moment now to try to remember a frustrating, unhelpful, useless conversation you've been in. (I don't mean that the content of the conversation was of no use. I mean a time when the exchange between you and the other person—the conversation itself—went very badly.) Can you remember a time like that? I had a horrible conversation just yesterday when I was trying to get a refund for a jacket with a broken zipper. The clerk and I talked and talked, but we got nowhere! The conversation ended just like it began. Right now, remember a useless conversation you've had, and make your face, your body, your arms look like you are back in that terrible conversation you remember." I gave people a moment to do this and then made myself look like I would have looked if I was in a talk in which there was no way I was going to budge one inch from my initial stance—arms crossed, leaning back, looking away from everyone.

"Now think about one of the best conversations you've ever been in, one where it's working, and make your face, your eyes, your arms, your body posture look like you are still in that conversation." The children and I looked around, noting the open, receptive postures, the expressions of interest and generosity.

"When you look around at what messages people are sending with their bodies in good and bad conversations, does it remind you of what makes a conversation work? In an unhelpful conversation people are set on one idea, and they are unwilling to change, right? Chances are, people held the same idea at the end of the conversation as they held when the conversation began.

This minilesson should feel reminiscent of the early minilesson in which I suggested readers need to choose whether we'll take on books like we're curmudgeons—or like they're gold. In both instances, I allowed children to role-play the negative stance. I want them to see themselves in my description of curmudgeons and in my depiction of conversationalists who refuse to budge. Each of us has been a curmudgeon at times, and we've each participated in a conversation in which we were dead set against budging from our initial ideas. Neither position is a helpful one!

"On the other hand, in helpful conversations, people listen to each other and are ready to change their ideas, right? They say things to each other like, 'That's interesting. I want to hear more about that,' or 'That's a new thought for me. I'd never thought about it like that before. Can you show me how that works?' People were still connected to their initial ideas. They didn't just drop every idea and go with whatever was being said, but ideas changed, new ideas came up.

"I'm telling you this because sometimes we forget that the reason to have a conversation is to be changed by it. A conversation—like any other life experience—ought to have an effect on the participants. When it's done, our ideas should be different."

Name your teaching point. Specifically, tell readers that an important reason to be in a conversation is to have the chance to broaden our ideas and perhaps even change our minds.

"I want to teach you that although it is really important to fashion ideas and to care about them, it's also important to be open to new ideas. You don't want to read, or to talk, like you are determined to not let your mind budge even an inch. One reason to talk and to read, both, is to learn. In a good book, as in a good conversation, you can feel your thinking being changed."

Teaching

Tell students about a time when you crystallized what a text was really saying, found support for that interpretation, and then revised your initial idea.

"I want to tell you one thing about myself that I am not sure you know. I love to go on journeys. And I'm not talking about journeys to new places. I'm talking about journeys of thought. I absolutely love to have one idea—a really good one, that I'm excited about—and then to find that the one idea allows me to see further than I've seen before, so I end up having another idea—an even better one. And then sometimes *that* idea lets me see even further, so I keep going and going, with one idea leading to the next. That's what I call a *journey of thought*.

"For me, this happened when I went to see the movie *Up*. How many of you saw it? Well, I had some ideas about the movie even before I saw it, because I'd read a lot about it. I knew it was a story about a man, Mr. Muntz, who had been living in his house for a long time. He learned that his house would be taken over by a

Our students, like us, hold tight to their opinions. This happens for a variety of reasons. For one, people like to be right; we get attached to our ideas and feel satisfied when we are right. It can be even more satisfying to persuade others of our ideas. Sometimes, students hold fast to ideas because they feel that strong students develop ideas that everyone agrees are correct. We can help children develop a new sense of what it means to be a strong participant in a conversation by teaching them that deep thinkers are people whose ideas change through conversations. It will help to highlight the fact that we like nothing better than to have our ideas changed through a conversation. You might ask a child, "How is your thinking different now because you all have talked?" And if the child says, "My ideas are the same. I was right," we can express sympathy and console the child, saying, "Oh well, too bad. That's sad when it happens, isn't it? Maybe next time you'll have one of those great conversations where your mind is on fire with new thinking."

When teaching students to write essays, my colleagues and I have found that it helps to give them a set of thought prompts that support them in going on a journey of thought as they write. "I used to think . . . , but now I realize . . ." is one of those thought prompts, as is, "When I first read this I thought . . . , but now, after rereading it, I realize. . . ." Another variation on this is, "Some people might think this is the story of . . . , but I think, deep down, it is really the story of. . . ." These are all scaffolds to help children progress from one thought to another, to learn this sort of flexibility of thinking.

construction company, and he had to get his house out of there. He ended up attaching a huge bunch of balloons to his house and flying to South America. I knew all of this before I went to the movie. Even before I went, I had this idea—that it was a movie about a man who solved his problem by going on a wonderful adventure. If I'd had one of those pink Post-its, I could have written that big idea on it: '*Up* is about a man who solves his problems by going on a great adventure.'

"But I bet you can guess what happened to my idea! As the movie unfolded, I thought about what I knew about the story, and I started to develop a different idea—not altogether different, but more specific, more detailed. I think ideas, like stories, are stronger when they are more detailed. This time my idea was '*Up* is a movie about a man who escapes from his sadness.'

When I say, "I bet you can guess what happened to my idea!" I encourage children to listen actively and to predict what I am going to say. Then when I do say more, they are able to think, "Yes, I was right," or, "Oh, that's surprising."

"Because I had that idea in mind, as I watched the movie, I looked for parts that went with my idea. There were a lot of them! After the movie was over, I thought about how that movie could help me with my life, too. That old man could decide to put the sad or hard situation behind him, to do something to move on—and that could be a lesson to me in my life."

Tell children that you brought your idea to a conversation in which you allowed yourself to go on a journey of thought.

"But then I talked to my sister who had seen the movie, too. She listened to my idea, and she said, 'I don't really see it that way.' At first I was annoyed (I acted the part of someone who didn't intend to move an inch in the conversation), but then I remembered that the best conversations are the ones where people listen to each other and say, 'Tell me more,' and 'That's interesting.'

I could have summarized this, saying, "Later I talked to my sister and she convinced me eventually that my interpretation only accounted for part of the movie," but instead I told the conversation with my sister like a story. I used her exact words, my response, and the progression of actions and reactions that form the plotline of this little story. Usually storytelling will be more compelling than summarizing.

"Anyhow, my sister explained her idea. She helped me to think more about the little boy, Russell, who shows up unexpectedly on the man's porch when the house is flying through the air. I realized that a lot of the movie is about Mr. Muntz developing a relationship with Russell. Although the start of the movie is about Mr. Muntz moving on, the idea that it is okay to leave your sadness behind is not what the whole movie is about, really. When Mr. Muntz goes back to where he started from, he is different because he has learned to open up his heart and to care about someone else. He has learned to let go of his sadness. So instead of thinking that the movie was just

One of the interesting things about the sequence of interpretations described here is that it is not until this third interpretation that I come to an idea that accounts for the beginning, middle, and end of the story. Later you'll see I explicitly teach kids that a good interpretation can't leave out half the text. I could have referred back to my ideas about Up *to illustrate that.*

about a man moving on from sadness, listening to my sister's idea helped me deepen my theory. After talking to her, I thought that it was about the man moving on from sadness *by opening himself up and caring about someone else*. This is just one example of what's true in life: When we think and talk with an open mind, our ideas evolve."

Name what you've done in a way that is transferable to other days, other texts.

"Readers, although I've been talking about the movie *Up*, what I hope you are learning is not just about *Up*. It can be easy to hold on tight to an idea, especially one we're proud of. But we can learn so much more by being willing to outgrow our own best ideas. One of the best ways to do that is to be in conversations with others who think differently than we do.

"Mr. Muntz went on a journey because he opened himself up to someone else, and I've ended up going on a journey of thought for the same reason. Because I let my sister's thinking about that movie change my mind, I've gone on a journey of thought. I could have steeled my face and folded my arms and refused to budge away from my first idea. It was a good idea! I would not necessarily have been wrong. I just would have been missing out on an even better idea."

Active Involvement

Ask students to discuss a recent event that the whole class experienced, focusing on speaking and listening in ways that create an environment of idea sharing. Coach into the small-group conversations.

"Any day, in any subject that you are learning about, you can make a choice. You can have ideas and hold on to them tight. Or you can have ideas and share them, give them, lend them. And you can borrow other people's ideas as well. If you are generous with your thinking and open to new ideas, you end up learning more.

"Let's practice having a conversation where we are open to changing our minds. When I tell you to start, I will be asking you to discuss the nutrition video that you watched in science class yesterday. Take a moment to think back to that video and decide quickly on something that was interesting to you. You don't have to think of something earth-shattering, just something that struck you as worth talking about,

In this minilesson, I've modeled a journey of thought that takes me from a simple to a much more detailed and elaborate idea.

You can choose anything for the class to talk about, but I recommend something that is not part of the reading or writing classroom.

perhaps surprising. Maybe it was the fact that nutrition can affect your mood as well as your health, or the fact that most people in our country don't eat very healthy diets." I paused for children to collect their thoughts. "Okay, now turn your bodies so you're facing the readers in your clubs. Remember, at the beginning of the minilesson, you showed the way you'd communicate with your body when you are part of a good conversation. Okay, now in this conversation, try to help the other people lay out their ideas, and try to have what they are thinking change what you were thinking, even a little bit. Go ahead."

I crouched alongside one club and then another as they talked in small circles on the rug. The interesting thing to me was that many of the clubs continued to repeat their problematic habits. They were trying to listen, but many were having a hard time connecting a classmate's ideas with their own. For example, as I listened in to the Civil War book club, I noticed that physically, they looked collaborative; they'd pulled in close enough so they could make eye contact with each other. Max started off: "I remember from the video that people need lots more fruit and vegetables than I thought. That was surprising. I realized that maybe I eat too much junk food."

Tyrell immediately responded, "I don't. I eat lots of vegetables. But I eat junk food, too. It balances out." The conversation floundered a bit, with other club members basically weighing in on the question of whether or not they eat enough vegetables.

I said, "Your response showed you were listening to Max because what you said was a connected idea. But you sort of said your thought in an 'I'm not budging' sort of a way. How can you show Tyrell that you want to learn more from him even if you don't eat like he does?"

Max said, "Um, okay, well . . . *why* do you eat junk food?"

Max looked at me, and I motioned that the group ought to continue for a bit. Then, I asked, "Did you see how different that felt? Remember this technique when you are talking about books. Try to use words and questions to bring more thinking out so it can connect and so that the conversation, the thinking, can grow."

Making Our Way Through Historical Fiction

- *Collect setting details. What kind of place is this? What does it feel like?*

- *Is trouble brewing? How is it changing? What feels important?*

- *Collect vital data about characters. Traits? Pressures on them? Problems they face? What drives them?*

- *What new understanding and historical information do you have?*

- *What is the sequence of events in the story, including jumps in time?*

- *Notice what's changing in the book. How are the characters' problems escalating? Has the setting or the mood shifted?*

- *Think about how characters are reacting differently to big events and what we can learn from this.*

- *Pause at passages that seem written in bold and ask, "What is significant here?" and "How does it fit with what the whole story is really about?"*

- *Think about big ideas and the little details that hold those ideas*

- *As you read on, carry your theory with you, but be open to new information that might change your theory. Expect to be surprised!*

Convene your students and help them to think about ways to make a productive, collaborative conversation.

"Throughout this unit, we have been saying that for a club to go well, the members need to take care of it. A big part of this involves making a commitment to really listening to each other and building from what each other says, not starting on a new train of thought every time a new person speaks. Now that you are working on such important thinking, I'm going to ask you to make a renewed commitment to doing that. You can shift now to talking about your books, but before you do, make sure your club is positioned for collaboration. You may need to get rid of the table in the middle of your conversation or to pull in much closer, perhaps even sitting up on your knees. You may decide you'll listen better if you have one white board in the middle of your group and all four or five of you take notes on that one board.

"Of course, positioning for collaboration is only a tiny part of truly collaborating. Make sure that today you try focusing on someone else's idea for some of the time, helping that person spin the idea out, even before you try adding that idea to your own. Let yourself go on a journey of thought with the other people in your conversation."

LINK

Freeze the class and ask them to look at their body postures, to note what the conversations look and feel like, and to draw on this image often in the future.

After a few minutes, I said, in a stage whisper, "Readers, freeze just where you are. I don't want to mess up a bit of this. It is so beautiful. Right now, without turning your heads, shift just your eyes a tiny bit so you see what this room looks like. It is so beautiful. And the ways you have started talking to each other is beautiful, too—so collaborative. Let's remember this sort of listening, this sort of talking, this sort of positioning when we are in our clubs which won't be until tomorrow. It's this kind of intense respect and interest that you'll need to grow ideas together.

"You entered today with an idea that is important to you. I'm pretty sure that you've already started to add to that idea or to make another idea or to change your idea. Finish up your conversations in a couple of minutes and shift from talking to reading. And when you read, read the way you've been listening, really listening to the text and also seeing ways the text relates to your idea."

Teachers, there has been a lot of research that shows that you can change your emotions and even the chemicals that are released in your body by changing your facial expressions or body posture. In Blink, Gladwell quotes studies where subjects literally put their mouth in the shape of a frown and then found themselves starting to feel unhappy! And the contrary is true as well. Try it. Lift up the corners of your mouth. Make the smile. You do feel better. For book club conversations to go well, the same holds true. They'll talk better, and think better, when they look like engaged readers.

Sometimes, just calling attention to posture will make everyone sit up a bit taller. If almost all of your students are demonstrating wonderful listening postures, go ahead and tell them to look around. When students know that their peers' eyes are on their bodies or their work, they will want to lift the level of that work. If, on the other hand, you find that most groups have devolved into a kind of messy, distracted posture, then only ask those groups to freeze who are demonstrating what you are trying to teach, asking the others to look at those particular clubs for ideas for their own clubs.

CONFERRING AND SMALL-GROUP WORK

Teach Readers Ways to Pay Attention to Mood and Atmosphere

Even though the children weren't in clubs today, I wanted to convene the Pioneers because although I'd conferred with a few of them individually, I hadn't spent time with the club since they started their new book, the third book in the *Sarah, Plain and Tall* series, *Caleb's Story*. I was curious to see how they were approaching it. At the very start of the unit, this club had taken on the goal of working on fluency, and I'd helped them to select key passages from *Sarah, Plain and Tall* to read aloud to each other. They'd been whole-heartedly invested in that work—choosing key scenes with care and reenacting the scenes several times, imbuing the characters with various emotions.

When they'd finished reading *Skylark*, the club had again chosen a few key passages in the story to reenact as a way to reflect on the story as a whole. In one, Sarah had gotten a letter from her family back in Maine, and the children had role-played this scene with attention to the bleak mood of the scene. I'd celebrated their growing knowledge that the tone and mood of a place are critical to a story.

I asked them to put aside their reading of *Caleb's Story* for a few minutes to have a book talk, so I could hear their thinking so far. The club started their discussion by coming to a quick consensus that Papa's emotional response to his father arriving seemed out of character. This led the children to question what might have transpired to make the grandfather pick up and leave when Papa was only a boy, and why Papa thought he'd been dead for all these years.

"Well, when Papa says, 'This is my father. This is John Witting!' it's like boom! I don't know, I think that is a big deal," Brianna said.

"It's like a huge weight dropping down or something. You know what I mean?" "Yeah, Lily said. I mean I can't imagine seeing my dad after so many years and then finding out he was alive after I thought he was dead," Malik added.

I intervened. "Readers, when you said that all of a sudden, it's like 'Boom' a big weight is dropped, are you saying the event changed the mood? I ask 'cause I know you have been following the mood in your books."

Jasmine said, "Well, I think the mood gets sort of, bad or heavy, you know, because Papa is so upset about his dad coming home." Thinking a bit more, she continued, "Papa's voice kind of changes, and it kind of scares everyone a little bit."

"Even the animals, I think. Like, it says Seal ran up the stairs because she was so upset when Papa burst out like that," added Lily.

"Yeah, it says even the cat was startled by Papa's voice," Jasmine confirmed.

> ## MID-WORKSHOP TEACHING POINT
>
> ### Readers Remember to Keep Up Our Reading Pace
>
> "Readers, can I have your eyes?" I waited. "We're not going to meet in clubs today, because some of you have been doing so much talking and writing that you're falling a bit behind in your reading. So you'll have extra time to read, read, read. Be sure you keep an eye on your pace. I've seen that some of you are inching through your books. I know I've emphasized pausing to think, but a pause is a little stop in the midst of forward movement. Look, for example, at how many pages you've read so far today. You've been reading for fifteen minutes, so you should have read at least twelve pages so far. If you haven't read that much, you may want to pick up your pace.
>
> "You're going to have twenty more minutes to read, so put a Post-it or a bookmark at your goal post, and see if you can step up your speed, get lost in the story, and read, read, read. I know you're thinking as you read. You have your own big idea, and you might be changing it, or growing another. That can happen in your mind, and it needn't slow you down. So get back to your reading."

"Well, it wasn't bad the whole time. I mean I did think that part of the scene was bad when Papa got so upset. But before that, it was . . ." Malik stopped, trying to find the precise word. I was impressed that Malik was aiming for precision and continuing the work they'd been doing, noticing more fine-grained elements of the story's tone.

"I thought it was kind of weird, because you didn't know really who this guy was or why he was there. And he was being a little strange," Kobe said.

The students paused, and I tried to give them words for what they were saying. "It sounds like you are saying that the scene started out with one kind of tone and then it changed. Is that it?"

"Yeah, it started mysterious because he doesn't tell them about these pills. It's like he's hiding something. And he doesn't say who he is or where his home is," Jasmine said.

"It's like he's keeping a secret or something," Brianna said.

"That does sound like it is pretty mysterious in the beginning. Is it mysterious the whole time?" I asked.

"Um, I don't think so. Because then Cassie comes in, and she is funny, and then everyone is happy to see Papa when he comes home," Lily said.

"So the mood kind of brightens, because of Cassie's arrival," I reiterated.

"Yeah. But, it's still a little mysterious because Papa's dad is still there and we don't really know who he is or anything—how he got there," Jasmine said. She added, "I agree with what Lily wrote," gesturing to Lily's Post-it: [Fig. XII-1]

> I cant deleive how mad Pa is. I think hes shocked. Its weird to think that the dad would be away for so long.

Figure XII-1
Lily's response to *Caleb's Story*.

"Hmm, I love that you guys are working on seeing that scenes aren't always all one way. You have been doing such great work paying attention to the way scenes sound and feel in your work, rereading them together dramatically, and you've been finding different kinds of scenes with different moods. Maybe now you could investigate the way one scene can have all different kinds of textures, or feelings, or hints at mood. Remember before, when I suggested that sometimes it helps to put one thing in the middle of a conversation and to talk off that one thing? This would be a great time to turn to specific passages from the book and spend some time looking at them. It's almost like you'll be trying to figure out the kind of music that you hear in the beginning of this chapter, in the middle, and as the scene 'crescendos,' or increases in intensity, when Papa realizes his father is standing there in front of him after all these years."

To get the students started, I directed them to the beginning of the chapter, had them reread a little bit, and then stop and discuss what kind of "music" they were hearing. The chapter begins, "The morning was bright and clear when I woke, no snow or wind. I could smell coffee," and they decided that the mood was bright, that the music was light and happy. I suspected they'd discover the mood changing quickly!

Readers Expect to Go on Journeys of Thought

Ask readers to take three minutes for a quick write, using thought prompts that support writing that will take them on a journey of thought.

"Readers, we have just three more minutes before reading time is over. In that time, I'm going to ask you to write about how your thinking is changing. Start with the idea that you and your club developed during yesterday's share session. For some of you it was, 'As people move to new places, they hold on to things that remind them of their old homes and the people they love.' For some it was, 'Even though you love an old place, you can still find a way to love a new place because of the people who are in your new family,' and for another group it was, 'Even in the face of destruction, it's possible to have hope and find beauty.' Write about that idea, and then about whatever your new thinking is on that idea. To get you going, try using one of these thought prompts:"

Thought Prompts for Generating Quick Writes

- I used to think . . . , but now I realize. . . .

- When I first read this, I thought . . . , but now, rereading it, I realize. . . .

- On the surface, this is the story of. . . . But when you look deeper, it's really about. . . .

- Some people think this is a story about. . . . But I think it is really a story about. . . .

- My ideas about . . . are complicated. In a way I think . . . , but on the other hand, I also think. . . .

You'll notice that from the start of the year until now, there has been a trend toward more writing about reading and less talking about reading. Think of yourself as an artist, and your teaching as your masterpiece. You have a palette from which you draw, and you'll use your wisdom to decide how much writing about reading and how much talking you want your children to do. Talking is more efficient, more supportive. Writing calls for an individual sort of accountability and engagement.

"So your writing might start like this:

> **When I first read this**, I thought it was a story about a girl who has to travel to America by herself. **But I have come to realize** that she isn't by herself, because all along the way, Rifka gets into relationships with other people. It is almost like she makes a substitute family.

"Decide which of these thought prompts you are going to try out, and think about how your writing will start. If you want help from a club mate, you have one minute to get help." The room buzzed. "Readers, eyes up here. When I say 'Go,' start to write. I'm going to do this too. We are all going to write fast and furious, not letting our pens stop, so we fill an entire page and go on to the next page. If you finish what you are saying using one of these prompts, you can take another and keep writing. You're only going to have three minutes, but I challenge you to try and fill the whole page, and more, in that time. Go."

The room was filled with the scratch of pens. After three minutes, I said, "Readers, it's time to stop. I want you to notice how much you all wrote. Hold your writing up so we can all see the sheer length of it. Wow! Readers, one reason I did this today was to show you that writing needn't take up half of reading time. In three minutes of writing, you can put tons of ideas onto the page. As you go forward, continue to be protective of your reading time, making sure you are reading at least forty or fifty pages a day, and remember that you can *also* write fast and furious to get lots of your thinking on paper, to help you change your ideas."

Becoming More Complex Because We Read

PART THREE

Strengthening Our Empathy for Quiet Characters

IN THIS SESSION,

you will teach your students that readers deepen our understanding by imagining the perspectives of even the minor, or absent, characters.

When I was seven, I couldn't imagine why my mother was so upset that I'd climbed to the top of the barn roof. It was thrilling. I could see all the way across the meadow; I could see the spines of the neighbors' cows! A few months later, I couldn't see how she could possibly have ended the wonderful game I'd invented: I'd tie a sheet to my jacket and hurl myself over the edge, the sheet flapping behind me like wings as I landed in a snowdrift. I still remember the sensation of flying and then landing, plunk, in a heap of wet snow. When I was thirteen, I couldn't fathom her decision not to allow me to drive in a car with my best friend who'd gotten her farm license in her parents' tractor. At sixteen, it was the height of injustice that I wasn't allowed to go on a cross-country road trip with friends. I can still feel my adolescent fury, remembering. Each of these instances seemed at the time unreasonable, even plain old mean. I imagined her plotting ways to remove all of the fun from my life.

Growing into adulthood, I didn't think much about those injustices but still held to some hint of the original feeling that I was unjustly roped in, curtailed. I mean, the things I would have learned, the friends I'd have made, had I only gotten to go on that road trip!

That sense changed the instant I had my own child. The moment I held my son in my arms, a switch was flipped. I was suddenly seeing the world not just through the eyes of a daughter, a sister, a wife—but through the eyes of a mother. A mother who would do anything to ensure her child's safety. Barn roof climbing? Absolutely not! Cape-wearing, okay, but *not* to leap off of the roofs of sheds! And tractor driving and road trips? Why bother asking? It was an extraordinary revelation. It felt like old neural pathways were suddenly forsaken to create new ways of thinking and seeing. Taking on another's perspective makes the world so much larger, so much different, and so much more complex.

I needn't have waited until I was a mother myself to be able to see my mother's perspective, though holding my own little baby in my arms certainly made it easier. The act of reading can be an invitation for readers to live vicariously. And the powerful thing is that through texts, we can not only experience events and places, we can also experience perspectives. Teaching reading involves helping our children imagine themselves into the minds of not just the main characters, characters whose inner lives are made accessible, but also into the shoes of other characters, even—or perhaps especially—those who aren't very likable.

GETTING READY

- You'll need to have finished reading Chapter 9 of *Number the Stars*; you'll revisit this chapter in the session.

- This minilesson calls for a read-aloud/think-aloud for which you might want to practice.

- Today you may want to add on to the chart "Making Our Way Through Historical Fiction."

- You may want to hand out copies of the thought prompts that spur people to change their thinking about texts. These can be found in today's share and on the *Resources for Teaching Reading* CD-ROM.

Jonathan Currie, a scholar of narratives, has pointed out that it's no surprise that readers generally identify with the main character in a story. After all, "we are more likely to sympathize with people when we have a lot of information about their inner lives, motivations, fears." Main characters are main characters because we're given narrative access to

> *Through texts, we can not only experience events and places, we can also experience perspectives.*

their points of view. Young readers sympathize with Annemarie and Ellen, rather than the young German soldiers, in part because they see through the girls' eyes. If the students had recently read *All Quiet on the Western Front*, for example, when they encountered the soldiers in *Number the Stars*, they might have recalled the voices of young Germans who had been drafted into a war they didn't want. One way that readers deepen their understanding of perspective is to consider whose perspective they have most access to as the story unfolds. In *Number the Stars*, for instance, the story is told in the third person, so many children will not be clear whose perspective shines through the book. It helps to teach them that because Annemarie is in every scene, and is the only character whose inner thinking is revealed to us, the book brings out her perspective.

Of course, if the first thing is to teach children to notice the perspective through which a story is told, the next thing is to help them to realize that one way to experience a story deeply and to grow important ideas as one reads is to deliberately consider the perspective of a character whose voice is relatively absent in the story. In *Number the Stars*, for instance, we are shown the night when the soldiers come to arrest the

Rosens from Annemarie's perspective. It is not hard to imagine Ellen's perspective. We see that she is paralyzed with fear. We know her as Annemarie's friend. Nor is it a huge stretch to imagine Annemarie's mother's perspective—the grief she must have for her own lost daughter, her fierce wish to protect this new one, and the hope that her own family will be preserved. It's more of a stretch, though, to imagine the perspectives of the German soldiers, because we have been given no access to their inner emotions at all, beyond a smile at a child or a chuckle. That smile and that chuckle are significant, because they hint at a complex humanity woven into the monstrous behavior of this scene.

And so, this session launches the third and final bend of this unit—a bend devoted to helping readers become more empathetic and able to understand complexity. This particular session supports a continuum of interpretation work around perspective that includes tracking who is telling the story and imagining the perspectives that are not explicit. This work matters tremendously—and not simply for the insight our young readers will gain into the stories they are reading. Our understanding of ourselves and others is constrained by the perspectives that are available to us. When we read, our natural sense of empathy is developed as we imagine unfamiliar perspectives, again and again and again. We want to teach our students to read with this intent, but also to carry perspectives they gain from books into their lives. The philosopher Maxine Greene warns that if students are not taught, in public school, to welcome strange and new perspectives, they will end up "seldom concerned with the common language that might link them to strangers and help them understand how it is with those others." That understanding of multiple perspectives, she continues, "fuses with a vision of spaces that are not closed in, that are open on all sides to the unexpected and the possible." It comes back, as ever, to the notion that we read to be greater than we are, to see the world differently, to cultivate a sympathetic imagination.

MINILESSON

Strengthening Our Empathy for Quiet Characters

CONNECTION

Tell students a story of being introduced to something by two different people, outlining how this gave you two different perspectives.

"Readers, the first time I walked into this school building, guess who led the way, guess who was my guide: A first grader! You see, I happened to meet my neighbor's little daughter by the front entrance, and she felt it was her duty to give me the grand tour. 'I'll show you around,' Susie said, leading me first to where the older kids' lockers were and the playground was. 'Under *this* tree is where my friends and I play,' she said. 'This end of the yard is where the younger kids go,' and then she pointed self-importantly to one swing, adding, 'This is the swing I fell from last week when I got a bloody knee.' Almost as an afterthought, she gestured vaguely toward the teachers' lounge and added, 'In *there*, though, is where *you*'ll probably go at recess.'

"Then, readers, I met the principal who gave me the official tour of the school."

"'Here's where you'll find me, and here are the mailboxes and the bulletins about whatever new programs are coming our way. We also post reminders beside the mailboxes,' the principal told me, beginning her tour. She started with an office and an area that Susie had bypassed altogether. The tour included a visit to the reading specialists' office, the book room, and to the inside of the teachers' lounge. She handed me class lists, introduced me to staff, showed me *her* side of the school.

"Readers, it was so interesting to see the same school in these two completely different ways. Susie and the principal had such different perspectives from which they viewed the school. I bet that if a tiny worm had shown me around this school, I would have been given access to a different perspective altogether." In my best little-worm-imitation voice, I droned, "Here's the stair to hide under to avoid getting trampled under kids' feet as they thunder to the gym. Under this cafeteria ledge, you'll find the best crumbs. Avoid open ground or the kindergarteners will see you. They're the most dangerous.

COACHING TIPS

When I spoke of Susie's tour, my voice reflected a first grader's carefree tone. I changed my voice to alter the mood into more officious seriousness when I began my account of seeing the same school now through the principal's eyes. Through this subtle tone change alone, I cued children to the contrast, the difference, between the two perspectives. A variation of this story might have been "Readers, the first time I traveled to the seashore . . . ,' followed by an account of how you saw the seashore first through your own tourist eyes and then through the eyes of a seasoned fisherman. Any anecdote that you choose for this connection must introduce alternative perspectives, ones that your children's imaginations can access.

"You see, readers, how it's the same school, from different perspectives? I bet right now, that *you* and *I* know totally different sides of this school. You and I would have given a newcomer totally different tours of the same school."

Ask students to consider how they'd approach a task, and then have them consider how someone unfamiliar and dramatically different from themselves might perform the same task.

"Right now, imagine that you have to give someone a tour of this school. Jot or think about a quick plan. Where will you take them first? What parts of the school do you think a new kid absolutely must know about?" After a minute's pause, I intervened, "Now, readers, think about or jot another tour. This time, try imagining how you'd give someone a tour of this same school if you were a bird and your nest happened to be in one of the school trees. What points of the school would you introduce a new-bie bird to?" After a few seconds of silence, I prompted softly, "Remember, you're a bird, now. Your view is aerial. You'll be looking *down* at stuff. Kind of the opposite of the worm who has to look *up* at stuff." [Figs. XIII-1a, XIII-1b, and XIII-1c]

Teachers, at this point, my story feels fairly sufficient in having done the work of a standard connection. I can slide into a teaching point about perspectives straight from here, but I don't. Instead, I stall the teaching point, first inviting students into a quick role-playing. My aim is to get children to imagine from the "inside" what they might do versus what an unfamiliar and unlikely character might.

You may decide that this example of a bird is too childish or out of character for your particular set of kids, in which case you might decide to ask them to consider the view of a new custodian or of a parent new to the district. You could, alternatively, ask children to pretend they were showing someone around their house and then to flip and imagine their mom was showing someone around the house.

Of course, it's an option to channel students to write rather than simply thinking. If you elect this option, you probably won't ask them to also role-play.

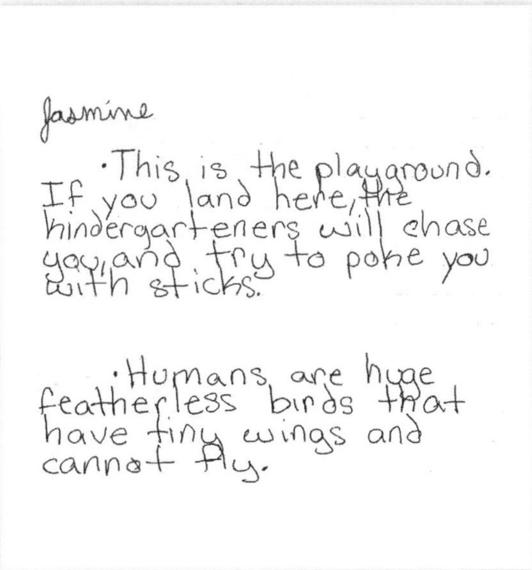

Jasmine

• This is the playground. If you land here, the kindergarteners will chase you and try to poke you with sticks.

• Humans are huge featherless birds that have tiny wings and cannot fly.

Figure XIII-1a
Jasmine assumes the perspective of a bird and gives a tour of the school.

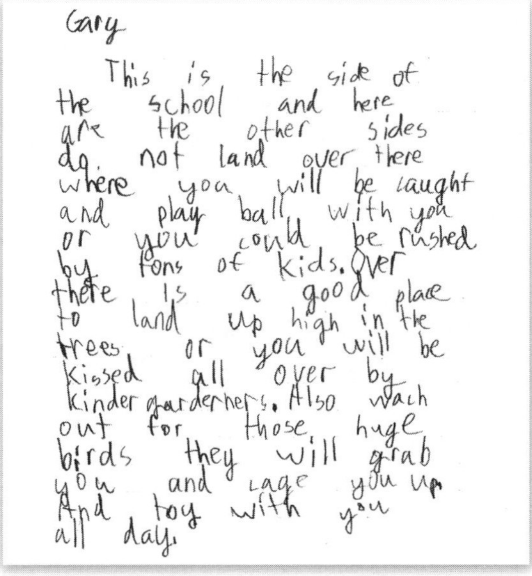

Gary

This is the side of the school and here are the other sides do not land over there where you will be caught and play ball with you or you could be rushed by tons of kids. Over there is a good place to land up high in the trees or you will be kissed all over by kinder garderners. Also wach out for those huge birds they will grab you and cage you up and toy with you all day.

Figure XIII-1b
Gary takes on the voice and perspective of a bird, rehearsing for the work involved in identifying with a minor character.

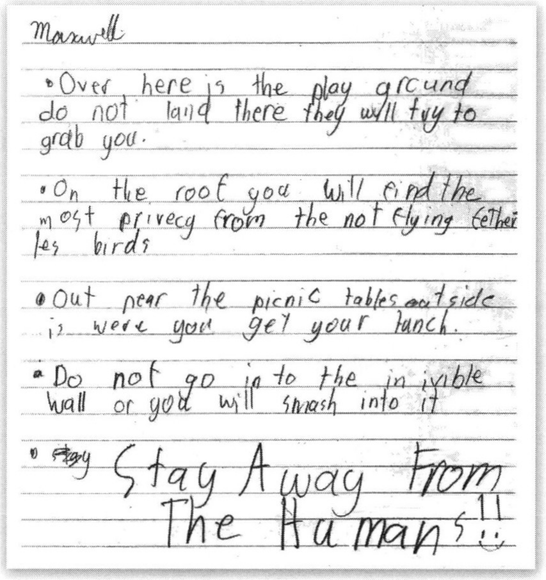

Maxwell

• Over here is the play ground do not land there they will try to grab you.

• On the roof you will find the most privecy from the not flying fether less birds

• Out near the picnic tables outside is were you get your lunch.

• Do not go in to the invible wall or you will smash into it

• Stay Away From The Humans!!

Figure XIII-1c
One more birds'-eye view of a school.

After about a minute, I said, "Partner 1, act out what you might be saying as *you* start taking a new kid on a tour of the school. Are you ready? Go!

After just a minute, I intervened and said over the hubbub, "Now Partner 2, act out what a bird might be saying as she gives another bird a tour of this school. Go!"

Review the notion that while it is natural to view the world through a familiar perspective, the deliberate adoption of unfamiliar perspectives will often allow insight into themes that we may have missed the first time.

"Can I have your eyes up here? Partners, I got the feeling that it was easier to role-play giving a tour as yourselves than it was to role-play giving a tour as a bird, right? Of course, it's easy being ourselves, because we *know* our own thoughts and emotions. Imagining a bird's thoughts and emotions isn't that natural, right?

"But readers, though it felt a little complicated to do so, I can *also* bet that now, since you've made that effort to step into the mind of a bird, you've thought about your school a bit differently than you've *ever* thought about it. I was listening in and heard Grace say that she imagined looking down at a rooftop instead of looking straight ahead at walls. Many of you, when you were pretending to be birds, talked about looking into the windows at the classrooms—so you were on the outside looking in. You developed a different perspective of your school building, didn't you?"

Recall the work children have been doing so far, bringing the talk to reading and interpretation of texts.

"These past few days, readers, we've been thinking about what our books might really, *really* be about. We've been pausing at parts of text that feel like they're written in bold, and we've asked ourselves, 'What's the point of this part of the story?' We've come up with tentative answers, with theories, and yesterday we talked about how one way to outgrow a theory and to get new ideas is to listen to the ideas of other readers, and to take those ideas on, wearing another person's ideas as if those ideas are our own theory, seeing the upcoming story through that lens."

Teachers, in an instance such as this, be aware that the activity could take a very long time, but it shouldn't. The point is really made clear from just the start of the activity. No one needs to hear the details of either tour!

Our kids by this point in the year have acquired some adeptness at picturing fictional worlds and the real world through the eyes of various characters—imagining how a penguin might feel toward its baby or how a Pakistani villager might feel about Greg Mortensen's help with opening up a school. Taking this natural reading work a step further, we've asked children to actually role-play an unusual or unlikely perspective.

The notion of perspective is fairly abstract. Children often don't really understand it until they've tried to imagine the world, or one scene, through someone else's view, trying to call to mind that person's (in this case, bird's!) history and experience.

Because we've just spent some time engaged in an activity that was not obviously connected to reading, it's important to funnel kids' attention back toward reading before making your teaching point. It will put the school tour perspective activity clearly in a reading perspective, and it will help your teaching point resonate. This also is a place to try to link today's teaching with the flow of the unit up until now.

Name your teaching point. Specifically, tell kids that one way to get a new idea for what a story is really about is to drop out of a familiar perspective and consider an alternative one—a perspective that we might not have otherwise considered.

"Readers, today I want to teach you that although it is easy to understand a story from the perspective of a main character (because the author lets us see his or her thoughts), it helps to also see a story through the perspective of other characters, characters whose feelings and voices might not have been brought out so clearly. If we try to think about and to see a story through the eyes of someone whose perspective is not shown, this—like trying to see the school through the eyes of a bird—gives us a new way of seeing, and more importantly, of thinking."

TEACHING

Remind children that taking on the perspectives of characters—people—different from ourselves allows us to see differently.

"Readers, you saw it was easy to think how *we, ourselves*, might give someone a tour of the school and much harder to imagine how a bird might do this. We *don't* have access to a bird's thoughts the way we have access to our own thoughts. In the same way, it is usually easy to understand the story from the perspective of a main character, to step into the shoes of the main character, and it is much harder to step into the shoes of other characters. Today though, I'm suggesting that trying to step into the shoes of those other characters helps us understand the bigger picture of what our stories might really, really be about."

Talk about the perspective through which the read-aloud book has been told.

"Let me show you what I mean. *Number the Stars* gives us access to one character's thoughts, to one character's perspective. Lots of characters are brought to life, but Lois Lowry tells the story through the point of view of one character. When reading any book, you can figure out whose perspective is especially shown if you ask, 'From whose eyes do I see all the other characters?' and 'Whose thoughts do I especially know?' If you're thinking, 'Annemarie,' readers, you're right. The book is written from Annemarie's perspective.

"If I want to develop a sense of what this story is really about, one way to do this is to try to *be* one of the *other* characters. To do this, I have to do a little bit of imagining, or

At this point, I might add a new bullet to the anchor chart for this unit, as this chart aims to capture the work that readers tend to do while reading historical fiction.

Figuring Out
PERSPECTIVE

• Whose eyes are seeing this story?

• Whose thoughts am I hearing?

• Whose voice is telling the story?

guessing, just like we had to do when we tried to see the school through the bird's eyes."

Set children up to listen as you read aloud a passage of the read-aloud, this time trying to experience this part of the story by bringing out the perspective of a minor character.

"Let me show you what I mean. Listen as I read an exchange between Annemarie and her Uncle Henrik. Annemarie, you'll remember, has just realized that she has been lied to, and so she goes to her uncle in the barn where he's milking the cow. We do not really know a lot about this uncle. All we really know is that he's unmarried and a fisherman. We don't really know *what* he thinks, *how* he thinks; Lois Lowry hasn't given us all that access to Henrik's mind. But I am going to use what I know about what's going on to try to imagine what he is probably thinking, like you all did with the bird." Picking up *Number the Stars*, I began reading from Chapter 9, fleshing out the inner thinking for Henrik every so often."

> [Annemarie] wandered to the barn where Uncle Henrik was milking Blossom. He was kneeling on the straw-covered floor beside the cow, his shoulder pressed against her heavy side. Annemarie leaned against the ancient splintery wood of the barn wall and listened to the sharp rattling sound of the streams of milk as they hit the sides of the bucket. Uncle Henrik glanced over at her and smiled without pausing in the rhythm of milking. He didn't say anything.

Looking up from the read-aloud, I started thinking aloud, as Henrik. "I'm busy with the cow, but really, I'm distracted with my own thoughts and worried, so I just smile, without saying anything. Maybe I'm a quiet kind of person, too."

> Through the barn windows, the pinkish light of sunset fell in irregular shapes upon the stacked hay. Flecks of dust and straw floated there, in the light.
>
> "Uncle Henrik," Annemarie said suddenly, her voice cold, "you are lying to me. You and Mama both."
>
> His strong hands continued, deftly pressing like a pulse against the cow. The steady streams of milk still came. He looked at her again, his deep blue eyes kind and questioning. "You are angry," he said.

Throughout this read-aloud/think-aloud, as I fill in the missing inner thinking for Henrik, I'm aiming to show children how this work helps us see another dimension to the story, how it brings us closer to the story's theme.

As you read this text, it will help you to imagine what you might say in a minute, when you pause to think aloud. Then you can contrast the way you'd be apt to think aloud with the way that I do this, and you may find there are intriguing and important differences. I am trying to draw on what I know from the story to co-create this character. I don't aim to stay in the actual moment, with the cow and the bucket of milk, so much as to show the way in which one draws on the text in order to consider the perspective of minor characters.

Looking up again, I thought out loud on Henrik's behalf, "My niece is angry and accusing but I stay calm, continue my work. I guess I've been *expecting* this. My niece is smart. I had a *feeling* she'd see through this Aunt Birte scheme. What am I going to say to her about this?"

"Yes. Mama has never lied to me before. Never. But I know there is no Great-aunt Birte. Never once, in all the stories I've heard, in all the old pictures I've seen, has there been a Great-aunt Birte."

Uncle Henrik sighed. Blossom looked back at him as if to say "Almost done," and, indeed, the stream of milk lessened and slowed.

Looking up I added, "My sigh means a lot. I'm saying to myself, 'She knows. Let me think. How do I deal with this? She's just a kid. I don't want her to have to know all this stuff. Knowing means shouldering responsibility.'"

He tugged at the cow gently but firmly, pulling down the last of the milk. The bucket was half full, frothy on the top. Finally he set it aside and washed the cow's udder with a clean damp cloth. Then he lifted the bucket to a shelf and covered it. He rubbed the cow's neck affectionately.

I added, "I'm taking my time. In fact, I guess I'm buying time, busying myself with the cow, all the while figuring out what to say to my niece, the angry, waiting Annemarie. I don't like lying to her, but I don't want to tell her how serious it is. I need to handle this situation carefully."

At last he turned to Annemarie as he wiped his own hands with the cloth.

"How brave are you, little Annemarie?" he asked suddenly.

I said, still as Henrik, "I took my time deciding, but I haven't asked this question with hesitation. My mind is made up. I *know* now what I'm going to tell Annemarie, if she can bear it."

She was startled. And dismayed. It was a question she did not want to be asked. When she asked it of herself, she didn't like her own answer.

"Not very," she confessed, looking at the floor of the barn.

Tall Uncle Henrik knelt before her so that his face was level with hers.

Notice that I draw on my sense of what this story is really about in order to bring out the perspective that is implicit but not explicit in this scene. Of course others could imagine Uncle Henrik thinking very different thoughts.

Teachers, though you're leaning on the read-aloud to do this teaching, the real work of forwarding the teaching point is actually being supported by your think-aloud—the small instances in which you look up from reading to articulate Henrik's inner voice. In demonstrating how to grant voice to a character where the author hadn't overtly provided it, you're filling in the gaps of the text, showing kids, very literally, how to infer.

"Readers, Annemarie made a direct statement to me. I'm about to be honest with her. So I stoop down to look in her eyes. What I'll say next is very, very important. I need her to take it very seriously."

"I think that is not true," Uncle Henrik said. "I think you are like your mama, and like your papa, and like me. Frightened, but determined, and if the time came to be brave, I am quite sure you would be very, very brave."

Looking up at students I spoke in Henrik's voice: "I believe she can handle the truth. I'm trying to give her more courage by showing her I believe in her."

Notice that I'm inferring. I'm doing the work that readers do. I could just as well have said, "Partner 1, you be Uncle Henrik. What are you thinking?" and in that way, I could have passed the baton to the children.

"But," he added, "it is much easier to be brave if you do not know every-thing. And so your mama does not know everything. Neither do I. We only know what we need to know. "Do you understand what I am say-ing?" he asked, looking into her eyes.

Halting the reading to be Henrik once again, I explained, "I can't tell her everything in too many words, but I've got to let her know that she must trust my judgment."

Be sure you read briskly. This minilesson is at risk of being very long.

Annemarie frowned. She wasn't sure. What did bravery mean? She had been very frightened the day—not long ago, though now it seemed far in the past—when the soldier had stopped her on the street and asked questions in his rough voice. And she had not known everything then. She had not known that the Germans were going to take away the Jews. And so, when the soldier asked, looking at Ellen that day, "What is your friend's name?" she had been able to answer him, even though she was frightened. If she had known everything, it would not have been so easy to be brave. She began to understand, just a little. "Yes," she said to Uncle Henrik, "I think I understand."

"You guessed correctly," he told her. "There is no Great-aunt Birte, and never has been. Your mama lied to you, and so did I. We did so," he explained, "to help you to be brave, because we love you. Will you for-give us for that?"

I spoke as Henrik: "There. I've told her the truth. I didn't want to, but once she showed the intelligence to guess something was up, I realized that she had grown up enough to face facts."

Annemarie nodded. She felt older, suddenly.

"And I am not going to tell you any more, not now, for the same reason. Do you understand?"

As Henrik, I say: "I'm relieved. I don't have to lie to my niece. Now I have her trust. And I can trust her."

Annemarie nodded again. Suddenly there was a noise outside. Uncle Henrik's shoulders stiffened. He rose quickly, went to the windows of the barn, stood in the shadows, and looked out.

"I'm tense, I've been this way for three years now, since the war. I hope that noise wasn't the Germans."

"It is the hearse," he said. "It is Great-aunt Birte, who never was." He smiled wryly. "So, my little friend, it is time for the night of mourning to begin. Are you ready?"

"There's no going back now. My little niece is now a grown-up. Now she's in on the war's secrets. It is the end of innocence, and so my smile is wry. This war . . . sigh."

Annemarie took her uncle's hand and he led her from the barn.

"I lead my niece, now knowing more than I wish she had to know, out to face whatever must be faced. I've changed her life by telling her, but I had no choice. It's this war that's taken my choices away." Ending on the note of Uncle Henrik's last thought, I shut the book slowly, signaling the end of the read-aloud."

Tell children that imagining this character's perspective has brought you closer to understanding what *Number the Stars* is really about.

"Readers, up until now, I had thought this story was about bravery and having the courage to help a friend through hard times. That's really because so far, I had been looking at this story through Annemarie's eyes. Now, however, since I've stepped into Uncle Henrik's head and become aware of his thoughts, I see issues that this story touches that I hadn't even paid attention to before. When I got into Henrik's head, I realized that as a grown-up, I have to *lie* to protect the kids in my family from knowing how dangerous life really has become.

Earlier I mentioned that one of the ways in which I teach is that I leak out my interpretations of the text in ways that set children up to do more skillful interpretations, when called to do so, than they could have done without this support.

Teachers, a think-aloud of this nature in which a character comes to life is guaranteed to be attention-riveting for children, but do remember that you'll want to lodge all this firmly into the larger work of this bend—that of developing children's interpretive skills. The upcoming portion of your lesson, therefore, will need extra emphasis. Remind yourself that getting into Henrik's head and considering his perspective was not merely a fun and interesting activity. It was a specific strategy that can be used to interpret the story more deeply.

"Readers, realizing that these are the lines along which Henrik is thinking makes me realize something that this book is really about. It's about bravery, yes, but also it's about tough choices—deciding to put even young kids in harm's way because there's no alternative."

Summarize what you just did for students to be able to replicate the process at other times, in other books.

"In all stories, it is natural to think and see the picture from the eyes of a main character because the author usually tells us what these are straight on. We don't need to wonder what Annemarie is thinking because her thoughts are all over the page anyway. But we don't always know what the other characters are thinking—we know what Kirsti or Mama or Peter or even the soldiers *do*, but the book doesn't tell us what they *think*. So we have to guess. And when we try to guess and imagine the thoughts of a character where these aren't explicitly stated, we see totally new angles of what this story might really, *really* be about."

ACTIVE INVOLVEMENT

Read another passage aloud, and this time, channel students to imagine the perspective of a character whose point of view isn't explicitly told.

"I'm going to skip a page, readers, to where the mock funeral for the fictional Great-aunt Birte is occurring. Again, Lois Lowry is telling us exactly what goes on in Annemarie's mind as Ellen comes to pay her respects—how she feels about lying to her friend and also how she realizes that it's for the best. What Lois Lowry *doesn't* tell us is any of what is going on in *Mama*'s head. I'm going to read aloud a paragraph, and as I do, pretend that you are Mama—like I just pretended I was Uncle Henrik—and jot whatever is going on in your head." As students got their pens and pads ready, I began reading."

Other people came as the night grew darker.

You'll remember that when teaching children to grow ideas about characters, we encouraged them to use lots of words, and again when encouraging children to grow interpretations, it helps to encourage them to say their ideas in different ways and use more than just a phrase or two.

Notice that stories, when they are well written, are about more than one big idea. One of the ways to enrich your understanding of a story is to grow another idea, and eventually to see relationships between ideas. This work receives a spotlight in the Common Core Standards.

Coach in ways that help students imagine the scene with enough detail that they can see through the eyes of a secondary character.

Aside, I quickly explained: "These are people who've come to pay their respects for the death of Great-aunt Birte."

> A man and a woman, both of them dressed in dark clothing, the woman carrying a sleeping baby, appeared at the door and Uncle Henrik gestured them inside. They nodded to mama and the girls. They went, following Uncle Henrik, to the living room and sat down quietly.

Aside, I added, "These people are here to pay their respects for the death of someone who doesn't exist. They're greeting Mama. Jot down what Mama might be thinking."

> "Friends of Great-aunt Birte," Mama said quietly in response to Annemarie's questioning look. Annemarie knew that Mama was lying again . . .

I paused briefly and deliberately at this point within the sentence, motioning for kids to jot. In a way this one sentence is significant to readers' understanding of Mama's changing awareness of Annemarie so I'm pausing, allowing children to note this. "Annemarie knew that Mama was lying again, and she could see that Mama understood that she knew." If you wish to do so, you could comment that this sentence is one of those that seem to be written in bold, and you could repeat it.

I noticed that both Lily and Max had written with a rapid urgency: *[Figs. XIII-2 and XIII-3]*

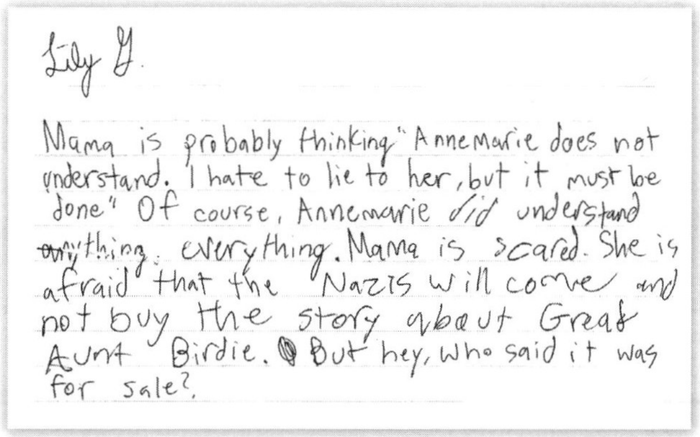

Lily G.

Mama is probably thinking "Annemarie does not understand. I hate to lie to her, but it must be done." Of course, Annemarie did understand ~~anything~~ everything. Mama is scared. She is afraid that the Nazis will come and not buy the story about Great Aunt Birdie. But hey, who said it was for sale?

Figure XIII-2

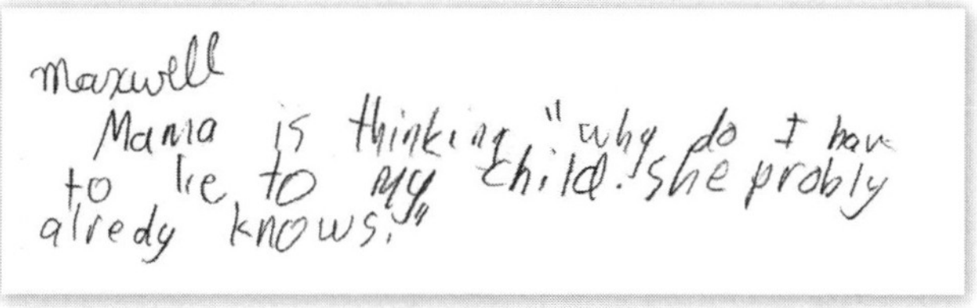

Maxwell

Mama is thinking "why do I have to lie to my child. She probly alredy knows."

Figure XIII-3

After a moment, I resumed reading.

> . . . and she could see that Mama understood that she knew.

While reading, I pronounced the last three words with deliberate slowness, implying that they are pregnant with significance, before I gestured for students to jot again.

> They looked at each other for a long time and said nothing. In that moment, with that look, they became equals.

Nudge readers to progress from imagining a perspective to interpreting the text.

"Readers, look over your jottings and see if you can come up with something that this part of the book might really, *really* be about. Share that thought with the person seated next to you."

As children shared, I crouched among the group, listening to conversations on my right and my left. Then I asked a few children to share their thoughts. Aly, with her usual insight, said, "I think this part is about Annemarie becoming a grown-up and taking on some of her mom's responsibility. Because her mother knows that this is no longer a little girl who doesn't know anything. Her mother sees her as an equal, as someone she can lean on."

Izzy added, "I think in this part that Mama is a little upset because her daughter is now part of this game and part of this war. But that she is happy too because there is one less person to lie to.

LINK

Reiterate that one way to grow a new idea about a book is to infer the thoughts and feelings of secondary characters and then to let this lead you to new ideas.

"I could walk through this school every day and not see what a worm sees, what a bird sees, what a first grader sees, or what you see. However, if I try to see this school through a worm's eyes, a bird's eyes, your eyes, I'll probably know this school a whole lot better than I do now. I'll see angles that I've been totally missing. To get what this school is really, really like, I'll have to consider it from multiple perspectives, right?

"Readers, it's exactly the same with our books. We could read through the eyes of the main character and only see so much. But if we try to look at the same scene through the eyes of characters whose thoughts the author hasn't made explicit, we see a lot more. As you read on, remember that in *addition* to pausing and reflecting on significant parts of the book, in addition to noting symbolic details, readers, you might consider perspectives other than those of the main character. If you do this, expect that your idea of what your book is really about will probably change."

Help Readers Make Themselves Different to Resee Important Passages

The Impressionist painter Monet is perhaps best known for a series of paintings of haystacks in a field. The hay is not stacked differently in one painting and another, nor are there animals grazing alongside the haystacks in one painting, a thresher at work in another. His goal was to show that time and color, season and daylight, affect the way we see what some may think of as a mundane subject—the haystack in a field. Each of his thirty haystack paintings captures a different glimpse of a haystack or two: One painting is a study of a clear summer afternoon, another of an overcast winter day, still another of early morning fog. Each canvas is saturated with the experience of that particular moment in time. The painter explored the effect of the light on each blade of hay, each patch of sky, each square of earth.

Seeing Texts in the Fresh Light of Further Reading and New Strategies

Just as Monet returns to the same site to see it in new light, so too readers return to parts of their books and find their own perspective has changed. If you watch what powerful readers do, you are likely to see that in an

---

> ### MID-WORKSHOP TEACHING POINT
>
> #### Readers Empathize Even with Characters We Dislike
>
> "Readers, let me interrupt you for a moment. I just learned something really important when I was talking with Gabe about the book his club read earlier, *Civil War on Sunday*. They returned to it today and were rereading it. When I asked Gabe about the characters, he talked a lot about how brave the Union soldiers were and how they were fighting what he called 'the bad guys,' meaning the Confederate soldiers. What was really interesting, though, is that Gabe has just come to the part in the book where Annie and Jack are working with a nurse named Clara Barton to pick up injured soldiers from the battlefield and bring them back to the hospital. Gabe, will you tell us what you noticed after rereading that part?"
>
> Gabe said, "Well, I didn't get it. Clara and Annie and Jack, they were on the Union side, right? But they didn't just pick up their own guys. They picked up the other guys, too. They picked up this Confederate soldier, and he wasn't even on their side; he was an enemy! And Jack realized the Confederate guy didn't really seem so evil after all when he saw him up close. It's like seeing him up close made him more like a regular person. And he felt sort of sorry for him."
>
> "What Gabe just said is such an important lesson—for our reading and also for our lives! He said that the Confederate soldier didn't seem so evil when Jack saw him up close. And that's the way it is with lots of our characters, and with people in the world, too. Sometimes before we get
>
> *continued on next page*

---

hour they may go back two or even three times to quickly reread or check something they've read earlier. It may be that they have an epiphany in a later chapter that sheds new light on earlier parts, and they quickly flip back to reread. Or something happens that makes them wonder if they missed something earlier. Or they feel the need to take in a passage more deeply, by rereading it. In most cases, they've learned something new and want that new insight to illuminate earlier parts, or even earlier books.

As Monet shows us, the same subject, when looked at in different lights, evokes very different responses from us. So, too, when readers use different strategies to think about and to view a text, it's not just the lens that changes. The text, too, seems new.

It is for this reason, among others, that students need to be able to have multiple strategies to use as they read, not just the strategy they've learned that day! We hope that as they learn a new strategy, they do not drop the thread of the old, but keep it close at hand to use when needed. Too often, students regard whatever we teach as a one-day assignment rather than a lifetime resource. They tend to use Monday's strategy on Monday to read, say, pages 130–150, and then they use Tuesday's strategy on Tuesday to read pages 150–180. What a loss! The work we teach, whether it is an invitation to make a timeline not only of the protagonists' experiences but also of history and to think between those timelines, or an invitation to reflect on the ways a reader's responses come from that reader's autobiography, or an invitation to think of the small objects that capture huge meanings, or an invitation to think about who has and does not have power in a text or, as in the case of today, an invitation to read with an ear to the voices and perspectives that are missing from a story—all this work is meant to be the work of a lifetime and to be work we do time and again, whenever we read and whenever the text and the moment call for this work.

You may find it helpful to, eventually, convert your teaching charts into reminder checklists for children to use.

Seeing Whole Texts, Rather than Small Sections, in a Fresh Light

Monet chose to paint a large scene to learn the most about light, knowing that examining just one bit of hay wouldn't tell him much about what he needed to know. Students, too, do well to consider the whole book, rather than a small section, as they use reading strategies. Today's work on considering the perspective of characters whose voices haven't yet been heard is work that can invite readers to reread, with new eyes, or it can help people read forward with new complexity.

I pulled my chair alongside the table where the Allies were quietly reading *The House of Sixty Fathers*. Some of them looked up as if to ask whether I wanted to talk with their whole club—as I sometimes do. I sig-naled to the readers to keep reading and took a moment to gather my wits.

I looked quickly at the readers' logs, checking on the pace at which they'd been reading. For a few members of the club, just keeping up with the club was challenge enough, but others would need independent books on the side, which I was glad to see they'd gotten. I could see from their folders of work that the members of the club had taken their first idea—"War makes you grow up fast"—and changed it to now be "When life is ruined by war, people find ways to survive." It looked as if this idea was soon going to be expanded to incorporate the idea that the ways to survive don't help just the body but also the heart to stay alive. They'd recorded a note about soldiers in Iraq adopting dogs, presumably paralleling this with Tien Pao adopting the pig. I also looked over the writing these club members had been doing prior to and during the day. The little scrawled responses that kids make to their reading are easy to overlook, to pass off as nothing much, but I have learned to pore over them. I was utterly charmed by Danny's sweet entries. "Danny, I see in your notebook that you are jotting about the story from the pig's perspective," I said to him, "You really have the voice of the pig!" [Fig. XIII-4]

I laughed inside at Danny's rather passionate role playing and

MID-WORKSHOP TEACHING POINT

continued from previous page

close to them and think hard about where they're coming from, we can make judgments about which characters (or people) are *good*, and which ones are *bad*. It is hard to do what Gabe, and what Jack, did and to allow ourselves to think about characters that we're all set to dislike—because they are on the "wrong" side of an argument, because they have a difficult personality, or for any number of other reasons. Yesterday we were saying that the point of a conversation is to be changed by what you learn. Today I want to say that we can also be changed by taking on the perspectives of characters we think we don't like, or shouldn't like. And the more we understand characters or people who are different from us, the harder it is to dislike them, and the deeper our understanding grows. Thanks, Gabe, for pointing that out to us. Everyone, try this out. If you find yourself really disliking a character, try to see things through that character's eyes. Even if you don't end up liking the character, you'll definitely end up understanding more!"

Readers Think and Talk About:
★ the setting—what kind of place is this?
★ the characters—their traits, desires, problems, relationships
★ new historical information
★ the sequence of events (what happens)
★ how characters begin to change
★ what the story seems to be about
★ what else it is about (more ideas)
★ important, **BOLD** passages
★ characters' perspectives

> Pig
>
> What is happening around me, why am being bad and nice, back and forth. Why am I always having to be hidden from the people around me. Pig would be more nonchalant is it was his choice. Pig would say "Why did I have to be so mearly treated so much of the time". Why was I Tien. Pao's big thing, why would he not just eat me".
>
> It must have shattered the pigs heart when it looked like everything was over I'm now. seeing that the way Pig was treated was like his baby sister was treated.

Figure XIII-4

took note of the way he began by saying the pig would be nonchalant—"it was his choice"—but then the pig's heart was shattered. What a change in that character! And what language Danny was using, capturing that change! (Looking at Danny's work, I thought again of my ongoing theory that some of the rhetoric which argues that boys need action-filled topics for writing, sci-fi books, macho topics, superheroes, comic books and so forth simply doesn't ring true for the boys my colleagues and I teach. Think of the boys in this series, or watch the boys on the DVD, and I think you'll agree they are every bit as engaged and every bit as ready for intimacy and empathy and deep human questions as are the girls. But I detour.) Looking again at Danny's work, I cherished the phrase, "I am now seeing. . . ." That's such a huge goal for readers: illumination.

So I talked with Danny and began the conversation not with research but with appreciation. He was happy to talk, excited about reading onward in the story with the pig's perspective as well as Tien Pao's in mind, and he and I read a little bit of the upcoming text sitting side by side, reading silently, me keeping pace with him, with Danny pausing at spots when his assumed perspectives enabled him to think something, to see more. I told him how important the one phrase had been in his writing, "I am now seeing. . . ." Then, before I left, I gave Danny a little personalized minilesson. I wanted to do more than pat him on the shoulder and say, "Good work."

I said to him, "Danny, I just thought of something that I learned once that really helped me, and your work is reminding me of it. Can I tell you about this lesson I learned?" Danny, of course, was happy to hear. "In a screenwriting class that I took, we watched a movie, *The Passenger*, and halfway through the movie, the professor paused the film and pointed out that the cameraman throughout the movie was shooting in really unusual ways—coming in from weird angles and so on. After my teacher pointed that out, she pressed play, and as I watched on, I was flabbergasted by the camera shots. The odd thing was I hadn't even noticed the camera work until my teacher said something. It's sort of like what you have been telling me about how all of a sudden you are seeing this story not only through Tien Pao's eye's but also through the pig's eyes. And here is the new point I want to make: When the class was over, I rented the movie so I could watch the first half with the eyes of knowing the camera work was unusual. And even though I'd seen that first half already, it felt brand-new. I caught my breath in new places and had different ideas about the story because I watched with a new perspective.

"Can you guess why I told you that story?" I asked, and Danny surmised that I was suggesting he could also look back on the first part of his book, looking at it through the new lens. I nodded, and we talked about how sometimes when reading, we take up a new strategy for just a time, and then we drop that strategy in the ditch, like we used to drop our ideas about books in the ditch. Becoming a more sophisticated reader means becoming someone who has more to bring to the text—more possible tools, more choices. And one of those choices is the choice to reread—even just three minutes of revisiting the first page of a novel can often be unbelievably powerful.

I thought of suggesting Danny consider also the perspective of the airman, but I don't really think much is gained by dutifully assuming the perspective of every single character in a story, or that it was realistic to think a ten-year-old could carry that many lines of thought while reading forward. So instead, I made one last point, "The other thing you might want to try, though, is to think about some of the other ways of making meaning that you've been learning about—strategies you learned about earlier—and see if they, also, can help you see more in this story." I pointed to our anchor chart that suggested ways to work with historical fiction.

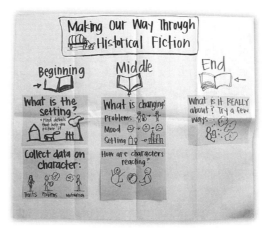

Readers Can Assume the Perspectives of Different Characters to See More in a Text

Ask readers to consider synthesizing different characters' perspectives to get a more complex interpretation of important parts of the text.

"Readers, think back to when you put pink Post-its—the ones carrying your idea about what your book was really about—onto the four corners of a board and talked together about coming up with a shared big-tent idea." (I'm referring to the teaching share for Session XI.) "I've been thinking of how that same board might be used in a slightly different way. Imagine that the Post-its on the four corners weren't your big ideas. Imagine they were, instead, the big ideas contributed by four characters with four different perspectives. For instance, if the big idea was related to a tour of the school and if a first grader, a teacher, the school principal, and a worm *all* sat around a board and contributed Post-its that went together into their big idea of a tour of the school, imagine what a complex big idea we'd have for a school tour!

"Sometimes while considering a scene in our book, it might help a club to sit around a board, not bringing our *reader selves* to the table but instead, bringing a single character whose perspective we may have decided to adopt. A club might stop at a part of our book that seems to be written in bold font and ask, 'What is really going on here?' or 'What might this part mean?' And different club members could take on the thoughts of a particular character."

Offer clubs a chance to try synthesizing multiple perspectives, from various characters, of an important part of the text. Coach into this work.

"Let's give this a go. Right now, let's have you and your club mates pick a part in one of your books that seems to be written in bold, and each of you take on one of the characters that has a role in that passage. (This means you'll have to find a part of your book in which three or four or five characters appear, although two of you could share a role.) Don't take more than a minute to decide on a passage or to decide who plays which character, or you'll eat up all your time doing that. But once you have that figured out, in a jiffy, do take a few minutes to really think yourself into whichever role you assume. You'll want to scan backward in the book for a minute to help yourself imagine what that character would be feeling and thinking, given the situation. Then, when you're ready, jot what you think that

COACHING TIPS

This teaching share is different than usual and you may decide to forgo it, instead letting clubs determine their own agendas. There are a lot of reasons to make such a decision. We included this option because it is different, and youngsters seemed to benefit from this new experience. We worried, though, that this felt more like a one-day activity than most of our share sessions.

character might say the story is really about. When you're all done, lay your Post-its side by side on the corners of your board, and begin talking to each other from within your character's perspective. In the end, your goal will be to see if you can come up with one shared answer to the question on your board: What is really going on in this passage? How does it fit with the whole book?"

I gave the children some time to do this and moved among them as they talked in their huddles, all still working in the meeting area.

The *Out of the Dust* club had chosen a passage in the chapter called "A Tent of Pain." The passage was told first person from the point of view of Billie Jo, the daughter whose pregnant mother has been burnt in a fire, caused by oil spilled close to the stove.

A Tent of Pain

Daddy
Has made a tent out of the sheet over Ma
so nothing will touch her skin,
what skin she has left.
I can't look at her,
I can't recognize her.
She smells like scorched meat.
Her body is groaning there,
it looks nothing like my ma.
It doesn't even have a face.
Daddy brings her water,
and drips it inside the slit of her mouth
by squeezing a cloth.
She can't open her eyes,
she cries out
when the baby moves inside her,
otherwise she moans,
day and night.
I wish the dust would plug my ears
so I couldn't hear her.

When I approached, the club members had already stuck their individual Post-its on a white board. *[Fig. XIII-5]*

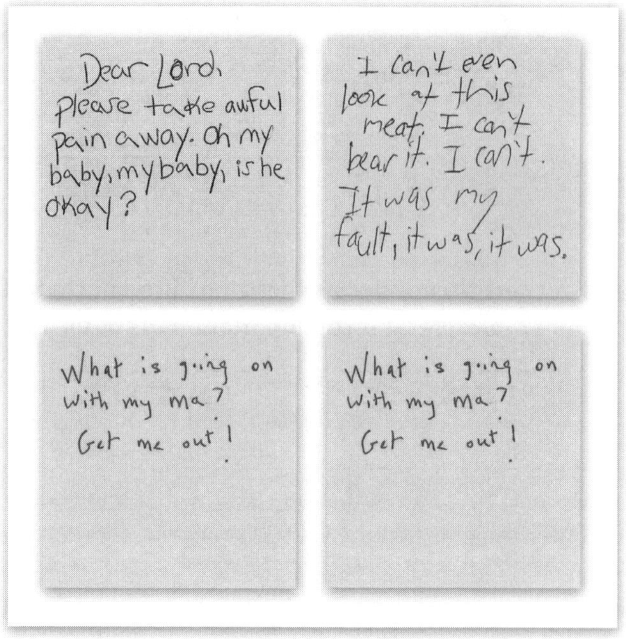

Figure XIII-5
A white board containing the ideas from four readers.

I listened as the group came to the decision that one big thing that was happening in this passage is that everyone is frightened about what will happen to the family. They referred to that claim—that everyone is frightened about what will happen to the family—as their "big text Post-it!"

Ask readers to show, for homework, that their thinking about their big ideas in their books has changed from a few days ago.

Time flew, and it was hard to stop the work that the club members were doing, but we needed to do so. "Readers, tonight, as part of your homework, go back to the big-tent idea your club had about your book a few days ago, and make some sort of a chart or a piece of writing that shows how your thinking is changing. You might show that you used to have one idea and now have several, or that you used to have a particular big idea and now it has changed. But one way or another, in addition to reading for forty minutes, think about how all this talking and thinking has taken you on a journey of thought. And don't forget the prompts I gave you the other day to support this sort of writing." I distributed little sheets of paper, containing those prompts.

I used to think ... but now I realize...

When I first read this, I thought... but now, rereading it I realize..

On the surface, this is a story of... But when you look deeper, it's really about

Some people think this is a story about... But I think it is really a story about ...

My ideas about... are complicated. In a way I think..., but on the other hand, I also think...

Imagining What's Possible and Reaching for It

IN THIS SESSION,
you will teach your students that as we build interpretations, readers draft and revise our ideas.

ézanne, when he first came to Paris, spent half of each day in the Louvre, practicing what the Old Masters before him had learned to do with ease. Rembrandt taught him to draw. Titian taught him to color. Goya taught him to put his soul in his paintings. Cézanne entered the Louvre Museum, and he entered a guild that spanned hundreds of years, a guild in which students were apprenticed not only to living teachers but to masters buried before they were born. That's because painting, like all the arts, is a craft. Only rarely does an artist come along like Picasso or Mozart who seems to come of age with the gifts of their forbearers in their fingertips. For most artists, there is a journey.

Writing is like this. "Writing is a craft before it is an art; writing may appear magic, but it is our responsibility to take our students backstage to watch the pigeons being tucked

GETTING READY

- In the connection part of the minilesson, you'll show an image of a Seurat painting from the Art Institute of Chicago. The image is available online at the museum's website (www.artic.edu) and on the *Resources for Teaching Reading* CD-ROM. To make the image available to your students, download and print a color image, show it on a computer screen or upload the image and project it on the smart board, make a color transparency, or get a postcard.

- In the teaching section, you'll reveal a chart that names qualities of good interpretations. You'll want to have the chart written ahead of time, because it's not one that you construct with your students; it's one that provides them with a checklist.

- You'll be helping students learn ways they can revise interpretations by helping them revise an anonymous classmate's interpretation of Eloise Greenfield's poem "Things." This will connect more to your students if, prior to the minilesson, you make sure that your children know this poem and that at least some of them have had a chance to write quick interpretations of it. It is available to print out from the CD-ROM.

- It would be helpful, though not essential, to have scrawled one interpretation onto chart paper. This might say: "'Things,' by Eloise Greenfield, is a poem about poetry, and it says that poetry lasts forever." Over the sequence of the teaching component, you will then revise this little interpretation.

- In the active involvement section of this minilesson, you'll ask children to reflect back on Chapter 10 from *Number the Stars*. It is essential that prior to this lesson, during your read-aloud, you have given students a chance to jot an interpretation of this excerpt (it can be just a Post-it) so that you can gather up some of their ideas and coalesce them into one representative draft that the class can work with.

- Be prepared to display a "Talking and Writing to Learn" chart during the share.

up the magician's sleeve," asserted Don Murray. Like Cézanne, young writers apprentice themselves not only to the teacher who stands in their classroom but also to published writers whom they'll never meet, but whose stories mesmerize them, whose poems delight, whose essays enthrall. And just as Cézanne painted hundreds of versions of his portraits before he was satisfied (or dissatisfied; he threw many out), apprentice writers expect to draft and revise their work.

> *Once they begin to read silently, young readers minds' often seem closed to us. They may be thinking thoughts of profound significance.*

The Poet Laureate Billy Collins describes pondering all morning before changing one single word in a poem, and then feeling, miraculously, that it is done. When we hear that Vermeer took three years to finish a single painting, working sometimes with a brush that had only a single horsehair to hold a droplet of paint too minuscule for the human eye to see, we wonder. But he knew. He knew that each revision mattered.

Reading is not so tangible. Once they begin to read silently, young readers minds' often seem closed to us. They may be thinking thoughts of profound significance. They may be calling up vibrant images as they read; their hearts may be sinking in terror and rising in joy. Who knows? (It's one reason we ask them to write. It's not just to deepen their engagement with books; it's also so that they create artifacts that show us what they're thinking as they read.) Yet reading, though it may feel invisible, is also a craft. Students can get better at it. They can learn the intricacies of its secrets. And as they learn these intricacies, like all artists, they'll draft and revise.

In this session, we offer students some guidelines for revising their readings, their interpretations, by telling them some qualities of good interpretations. We do this because unless you have on hand students' literary essays and mentor notebooks from prior years, you'll have no brilliant interpretations, at their level, to offer them. The great interpretive readers write at levels that are too academic for our students. Cézanne had had his sunlit afternoons in the Louvre, learning from paintings he used as mentors so that he could paint and throw away and paint again. The thing is, Cézanne was old enough to understand the Old Masters, if not to replicate them. We can't really offer our kids mentor interpretations from scholarly articles or from *The New Yorker* and *The New York Review of Books*.

So we offer a compromise. We, as adults, read these mentor texts: We listened to podcasts on NPR, collecting the words of people who care enormously about novels, those who put their interpretations into words. And then we gathered up some of the qualities these interpretations have in common. Just as most writers incorporate a few craft elements in stories (it would be unusual to have stories without settings or characters or where no one spoke), people who write and talk about books also have a few things that they do well. In this session, we share these with our kids.

MINILESSON

Imagining What's Possible and Reaching for It

CONNECTION

COACHING TIPS

Show your students a work of art, and tell the story of its creation, highlighting the fact that great work is the result of rough drafts and revision. Describe parallels with the writing process.

"Readers, pull extra close because I want to show you this amazing painting," I said, and then revealed Seurat's famous masterpiece, which hangs in the Art Institute of Chicago. "It's called *A Sunday Afternoon on La Grand Jatte*, and it shows a group of people in Paris.

"Do you see how it's all created out of little dots? The artist Seurat studied light and optical illusions. Then he started experimenting painting pictures out of little dots rather than big, sweeping brushstrokes, like artists had done before him. Gorgeous, right?

"To make this painting, Seurat worked for *two years*, drafting and revising, drafting and revising. Seurat hired a bunch of actors and models to pose for this scene. He has three dogs, eight boats, and over forty people dressed as soldiers, families, and fashionable ladies, and he has pets! So whenever he wanted to change something, he might get some of these actors back, set them up outside, and draft and revise again!

Teachers, in other places within this series I have encouraged you to make a list of all the many ways in which you can gather your students' attention at the start of a minilesson. You now have a new way to do this! You'll see that the students won't immediately know how this painting or the subsequent talk about the writing process connects to reading. This method of teaching is actually not all that different from the method we've used previously when a minilesson begins with a fairly long personal narrative. The kids listen, knowing that somehow this will end up being pertinent to reading. The same thing hopefully happens here. You don't have to use this particular painting, by the way. Most renowned paintings are the result of intense revision.

I let the children nudge and whisper for a moment as they processed this information. Then I called their attention back. "I know, it's amazing! The thing is, readers, that any kind of meaningful work takes drafting and revising. I've seen you, for example, write a story and take it through many drafts. You know something about the qualities of good stories, and so you have almost a checklist in mind as you revise. You consider whether your characters are compelling. You make sure there's tension in your story. You are aware that your setting can change in ways that are significant. You revise for these, and other story qualities, because you want your stories to fulfill their potential."

Figure XIV-1
Just as a sense of the qualities of good writing can guide writers, so, too, readers need a sense of the qualities of good reading.

Name your teaching point. Specifically, teach your students that readers take ideas through a process of drafting and revision, guided by a vision of the qualities of a good interpretation.

"Today I want to teach you that readers, also, take our ideas through a process of drafting and revision. And just as when we have an internalized sense for the qualities of good writing that guides us as we draft and revise in writing, we also need an internalized sense for the qualities of a good interpretation so we can draft and revise our ideas about the texts we are reading."

TEACHING

Tell students that readers are guided by an internalized checklist of qualities of good interpretations, and suggest one such checklist. Highlight that interpretations connect with the whole text, account for craft decisions in the text, and matter.

"As writers, you know some of the qualities of great stories, because you have read so many of them." I pointed toward the charts in our room from writing workshop.

"You carry that craft around with you, so that when you go to revise your writing, you have an internalized sense of what makes for compelling stories. *[Fig. XIV-1]* But I'm not sure you have that same sense of what makes for compelling interpretations. So, readers, let me tell you some of the qualities of a good interpretation." I revealed a chart I had prepared earlier:

There is a tremendous body of research that shows that students benefit from being given crystal clear ideas about what it is they should be aiming to do. Many years ago, Sadler showed that when teachers and students have a clear sense of what constitutes quality, this short-circuits the randomness and inefficiency of trial-and-error learning. Feedback, he found, helps students when it decreases the gap between what they are doing and a commonly held image of what constitutes good work. A problem is that "teachers' conceptions of quality are typically held largely in unarticulated form, inside their heads as tacit knowledge" (Sadler, 1989, p. 127).

Teachers, if you have time, you could first read aloud an effective literary essay or notebook entry and only afterward name what works in those texts through a list such as this one. The book "Breathing Life into Essays" from the Units of Study for Teaching Writing Grades 3–5 contains lots of wonderful literary essays, although that series will also have helped your students produce equally wonderful essays, so your files will be full, and the essays your own children have written will be more powerful than those written by others.

Good Interpretations . . .

- Connect with the entire arc of the text

- Account for craft decisions that the author made

- Matter beyond this one text and one day

"That means that experienced readers keep those qualities in mind. We have a kind of checklist, and we use this to guide us as we revise our ideas. And just as we know how to revise our writing, taking it through multiple drafts with mentor qualities in mind, so, too, we can take *our ideas about a text* through a process of drafting and revision, based on a sense we have of what makes for a good response to reading. We can even do that without writing our ideas at all—just by thinking or talking about a text one way and then another way."

Demonstrate the process of drafting and revising responses to reading. Introduce a short text and an interpretation of it that sums up the moral at the end.

"Earlier today, I asked a bunch of you to reread this familiar poem—you all know it— and to write a quick first draft interpretation of it. Let's read the poem again—let's read it chorally—and as we do, ask yourself, 'What would I say that this poem is really, really about?'

When I spoke about taking our ideas about a text through a process of rough drafts and revision, I gestured toward the work students had been doing as recently as their homework the night before, thinking about the big-tent ideas they had made, their overarching theories that synthesized the theories individuals had been developing as they read their books. I knew those ideas had already been revised and that many readers had developed a second idea alongside the first one. In most or all the clubs, the children's latest iterations of those ideas were the closest the club had to an interpretation that could now be assessed with the checklist in mind. [Fig. XIV-2]

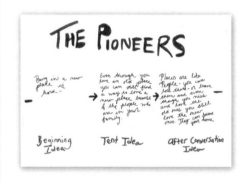

Figure XIV-2

Notice that even though the work has already been done by a few students and I do not need more students' texts to make my point, I engage the class for a second in generating their own quick interpretations. The secret power of a demonstration is that we do the work alongside of, one step ahead of, the learners. That way, they are not only watching with arms folded; they are invested.

"Earlier, when some of you had a chance to write your interpretations of this poem, I got a lot of interpretations that went like this," I said, holding up a page of student writing and reading, "'Things,' by Eloise Greenfield, is a poem about poetry, and it says that poetry lasts forever. Is that what a lot of you would probably say?"

I recommend producing a large-size version of this interpretation because you'll return to it more than once in the minilesson.

When I ask, "Is that what a lot of you would probably say?" I'm frankly looking for students to concur, and I convey this by the way I talk and by the way I nod my head as if to suggest that I'm just checking that my assumption is correct. The truth is, having done this with hundreds of kids and teachers, I know that most of us would produce a version of that interpretation. And I'm pleased that this is so because it means that today's teaching stands a chance of being dramatically helpful, because I'm going to suggest that a checklist of qualities of good interpretation can make a world of difference to readers with that sort of an interpretation of this text.

Examine an interpretation against the checklist of qualities, looking especially at whether the interpretation connects with the whole text.

"So, let's take this idea through some revision, using the qualities that are on our checklist. Let's start with 'Does it connect with the entire arc of the text?' So, let's look at the idea—'Poetry lasts forever'—and ask, 'Does "poetry lasts forever" pertain to the beginning and to the middle of 'Things'?'"

I paused to let the children look at the poem with this question as a lens. Then I continued, "I think we'd agree that the interpretation 'Poetry lasts forever' doesn't pertain to the whole text. The beginning and middle of the poem are about sand castles and candy that are gone now. That means that if I say that this poem is about the idea that poetry lasts, the idea doesn't hold true for the first two stanzas. How could I revise this interpretation so it relates also to the candy and the sandhouse from the first two stanzas, and the 'Ain't got it no more' chorus? All of that is a really big part of this text. Do you see that the interpretation—'Poetry lasts'—doesn't account for that part of the poem's message?"

You should feel as if this first item of the criteria of a good interpretation is familiar. Look back over the span of this unit, and there have probably been ten times when you have nudged readers to go from noticing a part that matters to thinking, "How does this connect with the whole text?" When you taught children to ground big ideas in tiny, concrete specifics, you angled them toward this as well. Those big ideas tended to pertain to large spans of the text, so again you helped readers work between detail and general, between part and whole.

So now you give children a checklist and suggest they double-check that their thinking fits these attributes. You've demonstrated, coached, scaffolded, and helped readers think about the relationship between a part of a text and the whole, and now you teach them to double-check that, yes, they've done this one item.

The children were with me, and in fact, many were developing solutions to this as I mulled over the problem, elongating my own work of solving it to give them time to beat me to it!

"Readers, do you see how the checklist for what makes a good interpretation helps me revise my first draft idea? Now I know that I need a different way to say what this poem is about, an idea that picks up the beginning, middle, as well as the end of the text. Let's see . . . Hmm, maybe I could say, '"Things," by Eloise Greenfield, is a poem about poetry, and it says that in a world where many things—sand castles, candy— don't last, poetry lasts forever.'" I adjusted the interpretation on chart paper so now it said this: [Fig. XIV-3]

REVISED IDEA: In a world where many things - candy, sand houses— don't last, poetry lasts forever.

Beginning → Candy
Middle → Sand houses
End → Poetry

Figure XIV-3

You should notice a progression to the teaching—and you should also notice that the same thing is taught repeatedly (after all, there are not all that many strategies that good readers do, really, and the hard part is to actually do them and do them with finesse). You should also notice that the same ol' things are taught in new ways.

If you want to involve the kids at this point, the best way to do it is probably to call for a turn and talk or a stop and jot. You'll be making every child give this a go. Then you can either call on one child, only with some foreknowledge, or you can proceed.

Name what you have taught in a way that is transferable to another text and another day.

"To say that poems last is an interesting claim, but to say that poems last *even while other things end* is much more meaningful. It shows why it's a big deal for this child to quietly compose something on her kitchen floor. Even when other things around her go away, she'll have those words—that poem—forever. Do you see how I did that? My bigger tip, readers, is that I want you to remember that a lot of your first draft interpretations will be about the ending of the book—the solution. But if you go back and name the problem, too, and bring the problem into the lesson you take from the text, that's a way to pick up the beginning and middle of the story.

"But of course my real point here is not that poetry lasts while other things end. My real point is that we, as readers, can carry an internalized sense of what makes for a powerful reading of a text, and we use that to help us see ways we can take our first, rough draft ideas and make those ideas even stronger."

You can practice thinking this way yourself. Pick any book you know well and come up with a theme that encompasses just the end—or solution—of the book. Then push yourself to revise that theme so that it also includes the beginning and middle—or the problem. For example, one theory about Sarah, Plain and Tall *is "This book teaches us that home is where the heart is." That relates to the solution of the story, the ending. A more encompassing theme could be, "Many of us go through life feeling homesick for places and ways of living that we have lost. It can help to remember that home is where the heart is."*

Teachers, take note that in an instance like this, you profit from the training that tells you to repeat the teaching point often. You and I both could easily have forgotten that the real point was that it helps to have an internalized checklist to guide our interpretations and could have repackaged this as a minilesson about interpretations needing to address the entire text. That, actually, is a subordinate point.

Big Ideas About <u>Number the Stars</u>

• Annemarie is becoming more brave

• People shield each other from danger by not telling the whole story

• Annemarie sees the world differently as a result of losing Ellen, and other parts of her childhood.

Return to the checklist and quickly repeat this process in reference to a second item—good interpretations account for craft decisions the author made.

I pointed to our checklist. "Let's look really quickly at one more of the items on our chart. We can read our new interpretation and think whether it accounts for the craft decisions Greenfield made in her poem." I read, "'Things,' by Eloise Greenfield, is a poem about poetry, and it says that in a world where many things—sand castles, candy—don't last, poetry lasts forever." I shook my head, and the kids did as well.

"If we want to revise our interpretation to bring in the author's craft decisions, what can we notice about what Eloise did to write this poem? Tell the person beside you."

After a minute, I reconvened the class and quickly summarized what I had heard them say. "You pointed out that Eloise wrote her poem in the language of an everyday person—using slang like 'Ain't got it no more' or the informal 'Still got it, still got it.' This, plus her reference to very ordinary pleasures like castles in the sand and candy at the local corner store, might suggest she is not just saying that poetry lasts—she is also saying that it is available to everyone. You don't need to get a PhD at Oxford University to write poetry. Sit on the kitchen floor, and you've got it."

I reiterated the newest draft of our interpretation. "'Things,' by Eloise Greenfield, is a poem about poetry, and it says that in a world where many pleasures—sand castles, candy—don't last, poetry lasts forever, and it is available to us all."

You're probably tempted to bypass the other two points on your list of the qualities of a good interpretation, as the minilesson has been long enough. I share that feeling, and so I'm zooming through this point.

Children may instead have noticed the repeating lines in the poem, suggesting the poem is about what we can and cannot hold onto. A sweet treat is a simple pleasure, but it's gone in a matter of minutes. A sandhouse will crumble. But a poem—words that can be passed from one person to another—that has holding power. "Still got it, still got it."

ACTIVE INVOLVEMENT

Recall some quick interpretive writing children did of a passage you'd read aloud earlier, and ask them to take one amalgamated interpretation you will have created and revise it, using the qualities of a good interpretation as lenses.

"Readers, let's try this work by revising the interpretations we made earlier today when I read aloud the section of *Number the Stars* where Peter reads the Psalm over Great-aunt Birte's casket, just after the German soldiers have left the house. I gathered up what you wrote and sort of synthesized them into one interpretation that resembles what a lot of you said." I turned the chart paper to reveal the big idea the class had created after discussing that passage of the text:

OUR IDEA

In *Number the Stars*, Annemarie finds her world scary, even with all the stars.

"Let's do what good readers do and think about whether that interpretation—we'll call it ours—shows the three qualities on our checklist." I referred back to the checklist.

Strong Interpretations

- True of beginning, middle, and end. They take in ALL of the text.

- True outside of this story or matter outside of the text.

- Consider why the author wrote it that way.

"I'll reread the excerpt, and as I do, you can work on revising this interpretation to make sure that it relates to the beginning, the middle, and the end of the book and that you account for the same author's craft decisions and that your interpretation matters. Write and listen at the same time. Try it."

This minilesson is getting long. You'll only be able to do the whole of it if you have learned how to nip at kids' heels to hurry them along. If your teaching tends to move slowly, tweak the above sections to make them encompass both the teaching and the active engagement (the craft part could be the active engagement, easily) and forego what lies ahead. Always be vigilant about your minilessons usurping time for reading.

Peter stood and drew the dark curtains across the windows. He relit the extinguishing candle. Then he reached for the old bible that had always been there, on the mantel. He opened it quickly and said, "I will read a psalm."

His eyes turned to the page he had opened at random, and he began to read in a strong voice.

> O praise the Lord.
> How good it is to sing psalms to our God!
> How pleasant to praise him!
> The Lord is rebuilding Jerusalem;
> He gathers in the scattered sons of Israel.
> It is he who heals the broken in spirit
> And binds up their wounds,
> He who numbers the stars one by one . . .

Mama sat down and listened. Gradually they each began to relax. Annemarie could see the old man across the room, moving his lips as Peter read; he knew the ancient psalm by heart.

Annemarie didn't. The words were unfamiliar to her, and she tried to listen. Tried to understand, tried to forget the war and the Nazis, tried not to cry, tried to be brave. The night breeze moved the dark curtains at the open windows. Outside, she knew, the sky was speckled with stars. How could anyone number them, one by one, as the psalm said? There were too many. The sky was too big.

Ellen had said that her mother was frightened of the ocean, that it was too cold and too big.

The sky was, too, thought Annemarie. The whole *world* was: too cold, too big. And too cruel.

Peter read on, in his firm voice, though it was clear he was tired. The long minutes passed. They seemed hours.

AnneMarie's realizing the world is a big scarey place. In the begining it didn't feel so scarey to help the others. like it would just be a sleepover. I think now AnneMarie is realizing how mean the world can be. so she's kind of growing up.

My new idea about this book is it goes with the story about the man who was walking on the beach and he threw a starfish back in... and another. The Johansens are saving people like 'starfish.

Finally, still reading, he moved quietly to the window. He closed the Bible and listened to the quiet night. Then he looked around the room. "Now," he said, "it is time."

As the readers continued to work, I voiced over. "You can show what you have written to each other and talk for a second. Think how to make our interpretation connect to the whole arc of the story (don't just write about this passage itself), and if you can, think about ways the author's craft decisions forward her meaning." I pointed to the chart as I ticked off these qualities.

Once I knew some children had started to radically revise the initial idea, I called on Fallon to share. She read her revision of the theory: [Fig. XIV-4]

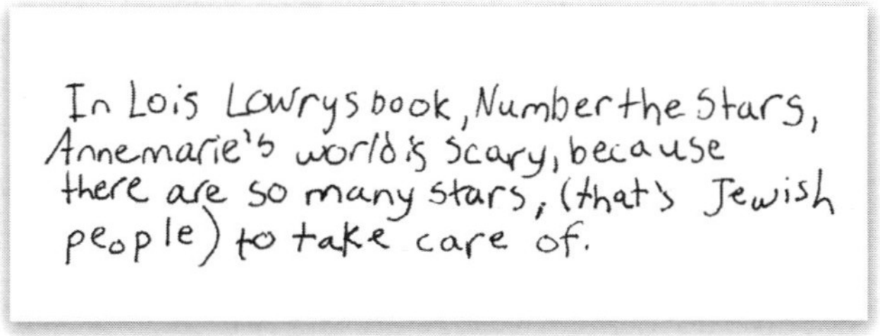

> In Lois Lowrys book, Number the Stars, Annemarie's world is scary, because there are so many stars, (that's Jewish people) to take care of.

Figure XIV-4

The children had lots of different ideas when they heard this passage. They were clearly somewhat mystified about the stars. Perhaps because the reference is to stars in the sky, they did not connect the reference to the star necklace, which is such a lasting image in the story. The latter quality, the craft of the story, will be the hardest for young children to analyze. If you are combining a reading unit with a historical fiction unit in writing, as I'd recommend, you can spend more time reading like a writer, and they'll be more alert to why authors do things in certain ways, to the effect of craft on the reader.

Teachers, you'll be surprised how perceptive and determined young readers will be as they push themselves to elaborate on their ideas with these lenses. They'll notice that Number the Stars is the whole book's title and start to ponder the significance of the phrase. They'll dig at symbolism and metaphor without needing the literary terms for these devices. One youngster we heard had a somewhat outlandish epiphany, that some of the Jews who escaped Denmark probably went to Israel, and that Lowry put these lines of the Psalm which refer to Jerusalem into this scene to suggest that journey. That's doubtful, but it's a good thing when young readers wonder at the motivations for craft decisions.

She paused, then exclaimed: "Oh, oh, and Annemarie actually held one star in her hand. She ripped that necklace off, and the star was printed on her hand!"

Aly put her thumb up and said, "That's the part I went back to—of the star in Annemarie's hand. But I totally changed our idea, to add in about God numbers the stars so he doesn't forget them and Annemarie not forgetting to take care of her friends." [Fig. XIV-5]

LINK

Point out that in this process of drafting and revision, their ideas ended up rising to the complexity of the story.

"Readers, as I listened to you revise your ideas based on your sense of the qualities of a good interpretation, what I noticed was that your ideas seemed to take in more of the story and become more complex. That's smart work. Before you head off to read, right now, hold the book you're reading today in your hands." I looked around the room, waiting for everyone to do that. "Now ask yourself, 'What's *this* whole story trying to teach me about life?' Or, you can say, 'What's this book *really* about?'

"Your club may have already come up with an answer, and that may still seem like the best answer, or you may have a different thought." I left a little pool of silence. "When you get to your reading spot, in addition to filling out your log, jot your answer to this question on the new pink Post-it that I've left there. Then as you read on, keep that Post-it out in front of you and remember that you'll probably be revising your idea of what your book is really, really about. I'll add on to our chart."

You can expect students' interpretations to meander a bit as they work to expand their initial ideas. They're not done with the book yet, either, so they're a little unsure where their idea might lead. One thing is clear: Their collective interpretation is richer than any idea they worked on alone.

You will probably notice that very few children talk about the craft decisions that Lois Lowry made and integrate that into their interpretive work. That's okay, but you'll want to imagine how you, yourself, would do this. For example, you could note that in the book, many of the chapter headings are phrased as questions. "Why Are You Running?" "Where Is Mrs. Hirsch?" "Who Is the Dark-Haired One?" "Is the Weather Good for Fishing?" You could wonder why Lowry uses this format. Perhaps it's because Annemarie, her unlikely hero, doesn't have even half the story when she sets out on her journey. She has questions, but there are no easy answers. And, as she comes to discover, sometimes to know less is to be able to act more.

God numbers the stars so he won't forget them. Annemarie won't forget her friends either. When the star of David pressed into her hand, it pressed something into her heart too.

And actually, the title doesn't say anything about god. So it could be all about Annemarie and her goodness.

Figure XIV-5

Making Our Way Through Historical Fiction

• Collect setting details. What kind of place is this? What does it feel like?

• Is trouble brewing? How is it changing? What feels important?

• Collect vital data about characters. Traits? Pressures on them? Problems they face? What drives them?

• What new understanding and historical information do you have?

• What is the sequence of events in the story, including jumps in time?

• Notice what's changing in the book. How are the characters' problems escalating? How has the setting or mood shifted?

• Think about how characters are reacting differently to big events and what we can learn from this.

• Pause at passages that seem written in bold and ask, "What is significant here?" and "How does it fit with what the whole store is really about?"

• Think about big ideas and the little details that hold those ideas.

• As you read on, carry your theory with you, but be open to new information that might change your theory. Expect to be surprised!

• Look back over the terrain of the text and ask, "What's this story really about?" We take into consideration the beginning, middle, and the end of the story.

As _readers_, we :
① sift through everything that's happened in our books
② see how everything is threading together
③ then ask ourselves, "What is this book _really_ about?"

· · · · · · · · · · · · · · · · · · · ·

As _writers_, we :
① think back across the terrain of our stories, remembering the moment
② ask ourselves, "What is this story really about?"
③ then explain in our notebook why that particular moment was so important to us and maybe the lesson we learned from it.

 ONFERRING AND SMALL-GROUP WORK

Coach Readers to Cultivate Powerful Responses to Books

In Session XII, we talked with children about people who enter a conversation with stiff backs and crossed arms, determined not to budge an inch from their starting opinions. We encouraged children to approach conversations with openness, instead of with stiff backs. The truth is that some of your students will approach *books* with an equally resistant posture, and this will be especially true for the texts that are a bit hard for them. They may read a couple of pages and think, "Yuck. This is way too flowery for me," or "Nothing's happening in this story. It is boring." Books such as *Out of the Dust* and *Freedom's Wings* are a far cry from the television dramas, movies, and action stories that children tend to choose.

The problem is that although a resistant reader can still plow through words, for a reader to really engage in reading, that reader needs to give herself over to the experience. Reading fiction involves caring enough about characters that those characters can affect us. So how do we help a child who hasn't yet connected with a char-

acter engage with the text? How do we help that child invest in the story of the book she is holding in her hands?

> ## MID-WORKSHOP TEACHING POINT
>
> ### Readers Talk with Passion About Books
>
> "Readers, I know you need more time to read—it isn't yet time to talk—but I wanted to be sure you read, keeping in mind that readers carry on book conversations in our own minds as we read.
>
> "I know you all have a pink Post-it on which you've captured an important idea you think your book conveys. As you read, keeping that idea in mind, remember, you can also be keeping the voices of your friends in mind. For example, maybe one of your book club members often listens to your ideas and challenges the particular words you've used, saying, 'I'm not sure that's the exactly right word.' Well, as you read on, let that friend's question be in your mind, and let it change your thinking. You might even pause in your reading to revise the words you've used on your pink Post-it.
>
> "Or maybe one of your friends is apt to say to you, 'But how does your idea go with the beginning?' You don't have to wait for your friend to say that to you. You can ask your friend's question to yourself as you read, and you can let that question lead you to go on a journey of thinking. We've talked before about going into conversations, expecting what others say to change us. Well...expect those conversations to change your thinking now, as you read, as you anticipate what your friends will say. So continue reading, with your pink Post-it in hand, and continue revising your thinking."

Helping Readers Connect with Books and Characters by Recommending Books Well

One of the challenges of teaching reading is to broker relationships between students and books, and especially books that children might not otherwise choose to read. If you want to break through students' resistance to books, it can help if you're willing to go out on a limb for a book. A humdrum recommendation ("This is a pretty good book, I think you'll like it.") won't make as much of an impact as a passionate one: "This is a haunting book. I find myself thinking about it all the time. It's become a part of my life, like a member of my family."

People who write reviews of books can serve as mentors, helping you discover ways to talk well about the things you love in books. The blurbs on the back covers of books can be resources, too. Listen to this description of *Sarah, Plain and Tall*: ". . . a tender story about the fragile beginnings of a family relationship on its way to permanence." Or this description of *Letters from Rifka*: "Told with unusual grace and simplicity, an unforgettable picture of immigrant courage, ingenuity, and perseverance." Especially in the case of books that are poetic or have an unusual structure, you may find that reading the early portion of the book aloud is the best way to draw readers to it.

When talking up the book, you'll probably want to help readers identify with the protagonist, because for most of us, it's that bond that draws us into a fiction story and keeps us reading it. Sometimes the reader will feel, at first blush, that the characters are nothing like her. You may want to help them see that the characters yearn for things that the readers, too, want. Billie Jo, the protagonist in *Out of the Dust*, wants, above all, to be close to her dad, to stop feeling wracked with guilt, to have a way to be happy again, and to come to terms with the loss of her mother. Children can identify with aspects of Billie Jo, and doing so will help them care about the book more.

Even your stiff-backed children are as full of emotion and desire for a meaningful story and life as anyone else. You may just need to drum up their passion at times! Your strugglers may find it especially easy to give up on a book. As tempting as it may be in such a case to focus on the mechanics of reading with these children, I find that often it can be more useful to rally that child's passion for the book.

I kept this in mind as I approached Tyrell, who I'd noticed had been less than enthusiastic about *Blast to the Past: Lincoln's Legacy*, a book he was reading on his own. I had thought it would be an engaging book so I was a bit surprised by Tyrell's lagging energy. I wondered if it was just ebbing energy after working hard in this unit for quite some time. Whatever the reason, his relationship with the book deserved some attention! Instead of focusing again on vocabulary or fluency (which I often did with this group), I decided to focus the conference on drumming up his enthusiasm.

Earlier in the unit, the club had been immersed in books (both picture books and the chapter book *Freedom's Wings*) that focused on the experi-

ence of slavery and escape to freedom, as well as a Northerner's view of slavery in the moving picture book *Nettie's Trip South*. Their most recent book, the Magic Tree House book *Civil War on Sunday* was a similar sort of historical time-travel adventure, so I knew that *Lincoln's Legacy* would have a familiar structure.

Sometimes drumming up enthusiasm can be accomplished simply through launching into an animated discussion. "What I *love* about books like this," I said, "is being able to sort of fall right into a piece of history. Fantasy books like this one and the *Magic Tree House* books are a bit different from straight-up historical fiction, but they really help me feel like I'm there. Maybe because the main characters are actually from our time, too, so it helps me imagine what it would be like to be suddenly transplanted in another time. It's really interesting to think about how certain buildings and things that we think of as having been around forever just hadn't been built yet! Abigail and Jacob have to navigate through a whole different world in this book. And it's also so scary to me to think about what our country might be like today had Lincoln *not* freed the slaves."

When I paused, Tyrell added, "I wonder if there would still be slavery. That would be terrible! Lots of kids in our class wouldn't be able to come to school!" After continuing the conversation for a bit, I was satisfied that the gleam had returned to Tyrell's eye and moved on to another student.

We can sometimes focus so much on the million things we know we need to teach that we forgot that simply sharing our love of reading does a lot to cultivate a reading community full of individuals who are passionate about books. Just as we make plans to teach other things, we can remind ourselves to consciously focus on this kind of teaching as well. Georgia Heard, in her book, *Writing from the Heart*, talks about assigning herself three things to love in a day. A teacher of reading might do well to assign herself the job of finding three things she loves about books each day.

We can teach a love of reading just as we teach anything else. The love of reading can be something we consciously take on and lead ourselves and our students toward, bit by tiny, lovely bit.

TEACHING SHARE

Readers See Messages in Texts, So the Mundane Becomes Meaningful

Ask readers to gather with their book clubs to talk about their ideas and allow those ideas to change and deepen.

"Readers, I know many of you have been revising your ideas about your book as you read, and that you may want to talk in your clubs about how your ideas are changing. Get together with your club now. You may talk again about that question—'What's this book really about?' Or you can talk about anything else that seems important to discuss. Remember to expect your thinking to change as you talk. Try using 'I'm learning' phrases such as these:

Talking and Writing to Learn

- I'm changing my mind . . .

- I'm starting to think . . .

- I'm realizing . . .

- So, if that's true, then . . .

- Can we try that idea on for a bit? If that's true, then how come . . .

- Could it be that . . . ?

COACHING TIPS

Be prepared to coach into children's thinking, perhaps pointing out examples of craft moves they might notice in their books or particularly significant details lodged early on in their books that support their interpretations. You may also want to encourage a club to think between two books they've read or between the book and events in the world.

As children talked, I listened to the American Dreamers, whose idea, after reading *Letters from Rifka*, had been, "As people move to new places, they hold on to things that remind them of their old home and the people they love." They were now reading *Maggie's Door* and wisely wanted to develop an idea that pertained to both books. I prodded them to look at each word and think, "Is this the exactly true word?" They revised their interpretation so that it wasn't just *people* who were moving and holding onto objects, it was *immigrants*. Unlike other people who move, immigrants were often forced to leave, and their journeys were full of struggle, which made the things they carried with them matter that much more. So their revised idea became: *[Fig. XIV-6]*

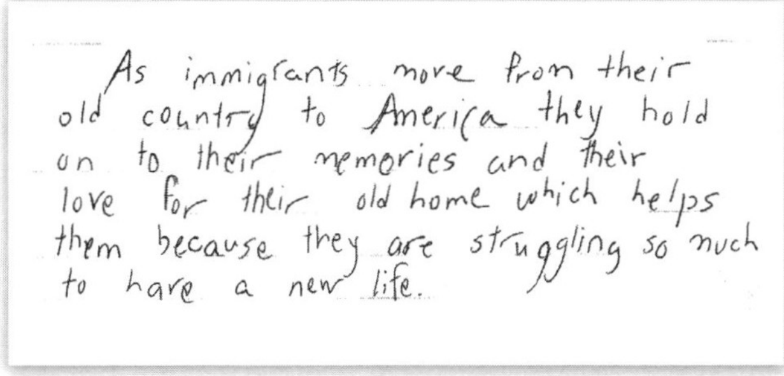

As immigrants move from their old country to America they hold on to their memories and their love for their old home which helps them because they are struggling so much to have a new life.

Figure XIV-6

As the children talked, I reminded them that there is power in going between big ideas and small details. They got going on a talk about the almost invisible objects the immigrants carried and soon were enthralled with the significance of grains of sand. When Nora emigrated from Ireland, she'd inadvertently carried sand from a sandy road in Ireland with her. *[Figs. XIV-7 and XIV-8]*

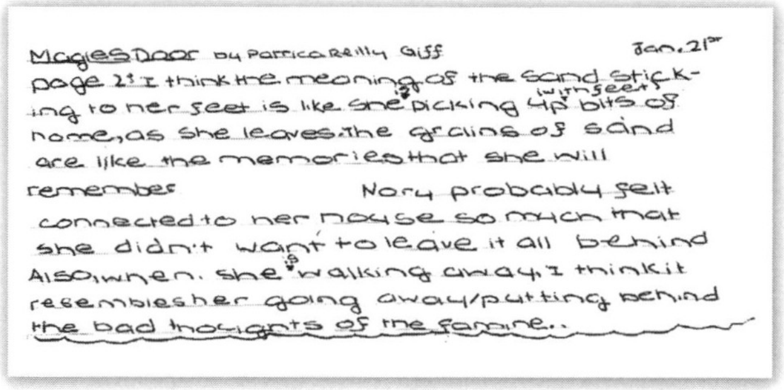

Maggies Door by Patricia Reilly Giff   Jan. 21st
page 21 I think the meaning of the sand sticking to her feet is like she picking up bits of home, as she leaves the grains of sand are like the memories that she will remember. Nora probably felt connected to her house so much that she didn't want to leave it all behind Also when she walking away I think it resembles her going away/putting behind the bad thoughts of the famine..

Figure XIV-7
Izzy's jottings about the grains of sand in *Maggie's Door*.

"The sand on Nora's bare feet" it seems to me as if the sand shidding to her is begging her to stay in Ireland.

Figure XIV-8
Note the way Grace's thinking stands on the shoulders of Izzy's thinking and vice versa.

Seeing Power in Its Many Forms

IN THIS SESSION,

you will teach your students that readers deepen our thinking by investigating power dynamics in our stories.

icture this: A group of youngsters gather around a teacher in a preschool classroom in Australia. She reads them *The Paper Bag Princess*. The picture book tells the tale of beautiful Princess Elizabeth, who has expensive princess clothes and lives in a castle. She is going to marry a prince named Ronald. Then a dragon comes and carries off Prince Ronald by his underpants, burns Elizabeth's castle to the ground, and incinerates her clothes with his fiery breath. Elizabeth puts on a paper bag and goes in pursuit of the dragon. Ronald pines in the dragon's cave until Elizabeth rescues him, at which point he harangues Elizabeth for being a mess.

The teacher finishes the story and prompts her children, "Talk to someone near you. I'm curious to hear what you think about the hero of this story?" As the children chatter, the teacher leans in. The smile on her face fades a bit. "What's that you're saying?" she asks the group.

"Oh, well, Ronald's the hero,' says a pig-tailed little girl.

"And he's a prince," adds another girl with braids down her back.

The teacher prompts, "But don't you think Elizabeth is sort of a hero here? She's the one who defeats the dragon."

"No," says one boy firmly. "She's the girl. She can't be the hero."

"Ronald's the hero," affirms another small boy. "He held onto his tennis racket when the dragon took him. That was really brave."

"Elizabeth should have gotten better clothes. Then Ronald would still love her," chimes in the girl with long braids. "Oh, and she should have been nicer to Ronald." All the children nod.

Are you picturing a teacher saying, "Yikes!" to herself? It was the Australian scholar Bronwyn Davies who first launched this action research project, which has since been duplicated in hundreds of classrooms, including dozens of schools that work with the Teachers College Reading and

---

GETTING READY

- You'll want to finish reading *Number the Stars* prior to this minilesson.

- You may want to have on hand some of the timelines and notes you've made about the book so that you can help children recall earlier scenes. You might, for example, have the excerpts on chart paper telling about when the soldiers stop the girls in the street or come to the house; pull those out, so that you, and the children, can recall parts of the story where the Germans are the ones with explicit power. Some are available on the *Resources for Teaching Reading* CD-ROM.

- Create a chart titled "Predictable Questions to Investigate Power" with two initial bullets, and be prepared to add to it throughout the minilesson.

Writing Project. The effort was part of a campaign to raise the self-esteem of girls. In schools across the nation, teachers began reading stories to impressionable youngsters in the hope that these stories would instill a sense of girl power. But the kids often didn't even see the girl power in those stories, resolutely refusing to let the female figure be the powerful one. When responding to story after story, many girls said things like, "Ronald's the powerful one. He's the prince." These interpretations showed that the power system the kids knew was so solid, so entrenched, that they

When we help readers read with the lens of power, it's as if we help them access whole new ideas and language.

just couldn't imagine how girls could have power, even when they saw a girl acting in powerful ways. Yikes. Bronwyn and fellow researchers rallied, with more books and more critical conversation: They began to explicitly talk about power with very young readers.

These kids were making a bad interpretation of *The Paper Bag Princess* because without even knowing what they were doing, they came to the topic of "Who has power?" with their arms folded, their backs stiff, their minds made up. They had prior expectations about power relations, and they weren't going to let this new voice in the conversation—*The Paper Bag Princess*—change their minds. This happens, too, with young readers of historical fiction. The Freedom Fighters at one point looked up from *Roll of Thunder, Hear My Cry*, shaking with rage. They had just gotten to the part

where Mama takes the children to visit Mr. Berry, who has been lit on fire by the white townsfolk. I assumed the children were raging against the people who had done this to him. But they were even angrier with Mr. Berry, for not saving himself, and with Cassie's family and the other black families, for "putting up with this." "They should *do* something!" cried the children, entirely frustrated and upset. It was not too different from the response I have seen sometimes to *Freedom Summer*. When an edict goes out that the local swimming pool will now be open to all people, all races, the town responds by filling the pool with tar. The African American protagonist, John Henry, watches his older brother, Will, work as part of the town's work crew, shoveling the steaming tar into the pool. Instead of being angry at the racism of this town, many young readers are angry at Will for doing work on the town's behalf. "Why didn't he refuse?!" they cry. Sometimes it seems that young readers become confounded by behaviors because they aren't seeing the way in which access to power is as real as access to a car, a house, a job. Helping children understand the role that power relations play in a story is a way of helping them to understand cause and effect, tension, motivation, and change.

What's really interesting about teaching children to look at their books with the lens of power is that it leads them to discoveries about the many kinds of power that exist in the world and about the role that resistance can play. When we help readers read with the lens of power, it's as if we help them access whole new ideas and language—and they come pouring out. "Maybe it's not just guns that give power," they'll come to say of *Number the Stars*. "Maybe friendship is more powerful than racism," they'll say as they finish *Freedom Summer*. "Maybe Anne Frank's words have more power than the people who killed her," a child will reflect. They start looking at everything with the lens of power: Who has it? How is it visible? How does it shift? How do people resist? Critical reading enables readers to have these epiphanies and insights.

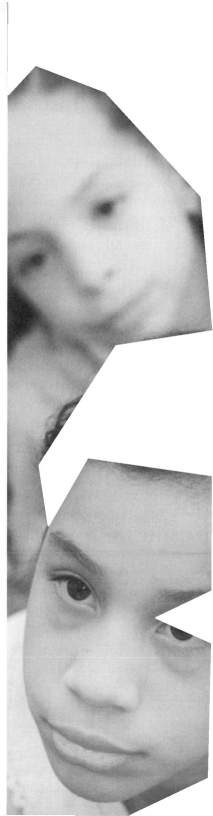

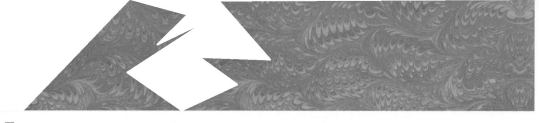

Seeing Power in Its Many Forms

CONNECTION

Tell students that endings of books give us an important vantage point and that it is especially important to note surprises, because they can often yield epiphanies.

"So we have finished reading *Number the Stars*. For readers like you and me, who have been thinking hard about the messages that books carry, the ending of a book is always a special time. When we reach the ending of a book, it is a bit like we've now climbed to the top of the mountain. When we get to the mountain top, we don't just race down. Instead, we use that vantage point to look back over the landscape of the whole story. We think especially about how things fit together—and about things that don't fit, too. We pay attention to bits that surprised us because those surprising bits are often sources of epiphanies, of new realizations.

"I'm pretty sure that as you think back on *Number the Stars*, there are things toward the end of the book that surprised you. Can you think what some of those surprises were—because remember, they're often worth pondering." I left a little pool of silence.

"There's a part that made my eyes fly wide open. Let me see if any of you noticed it as well. Do you remember when Annemarie asked what was so important about the handkerchief package that she'd rushed to the boat, and Uncle Henrik told her that scientists and doctors had worked together to figure out how to make a drug that would confuse the dogs, so they couldn't smell the people hiding in the boats? And *then* he told her that *all the fishing boats in Denmark* were getting those handkerchiefs. That one surprising part changed my sense of the whole story. Until now, I think my

This minilesson does not follow the usual pattern in which we first teach readers a strategy or a lens that they can use, show them how to use it, and then scaffold them as they give it a try. Instead, the minilesson starts with the harvest of such work—sharing some of the insights that critical reading can yield. You might decide to revise the minilesson so that you first forward your teaching point and then let kids join you in discovering the power of the collective resistance in this story, engaging them in that work alongside you.

In this book, Annemarie and her family are not lone agents of change but are part of a bigger movement. Kids can come to realizations such as this, and we help them all to grow important interpretive ideas by leaving a trail of bread crumbs.

pink Post-it, my big idea Post-it about this book, might have been something like 'Annemarie is brave, because even when she knows the risks, she makes choices to save her friend.' But I am starting to realize that this isn't just a story about one brave person. Listen with me to some of the passages and think with me about how these passages might get us thinking new things. You can just listen, or you can listen and jot."

> Many of the fishermen have built hidden places in their boats . . . down underneath. I have only to lift the boards in the right place, and there is room to hide a few people. Peter, and the others in the Resistance who work with him, bring them to me, and to the other fishermen as well. There are people who hide them and help them, along the way. . . .

> There are many soldiers . . . all along the coast. They are searching all the boats now. They know the Jews are escaping, but they are not sure how, and they rarely find them. The hiding places are carefully concealed, and often we pile dead fish on the deck as well. . . .

> . . . those damn dogs, they go right through dead fish to the human scent.

> "We were all very, very worried. We thought it meant the end of the escape to Sweden by boat.

> "It was Peter who took the problem to scientists and doctors. Some very fine minds have worked night and day, trying to find a solution. . . .

"Readers, what are you thinking? Turn and tell someone near you your thoughts about this rescue operation."

The children talked. "The Johansens weren't the only ones who had Rosens!" Izzy said.

Gabe nodded. He read her his jotting: [Fig. XV-1]

There were Rosens
everywhere. They were
in all the boats. Everyone
was hiding their own Rosens.

There were Uncle Henricks
everywhere too. All the
fishermen were doing it!

Figure XV-1

Here, we linger in some of the details that give a picture not just of the Johansens but of the powerful work of this little country in this dark time. Imagine a country without an army, a country that shared a border with the dominant force in Europe, resisting in this way. As I read, I used my voice to emphasize the pronouns and modifiers that manifest the incredible collective aspect of this rescue. What I know is that of Denmark's 8,000 Jews, fewer than 500 were lost to the enemy—fewer deaths than the 750 the Danish Resistance suffered. Unlike stories of refugees in Germany, which tend to be stories of individuals resisting in isolation, hiding what they do from their neighbors, the Danish story is one of an entire people uniting to protect their Jewish brothers and sisters. It's a story of the power of good people working together.

"I can picture it with all the dead fish on all the tops of the boats, and the people hiding below, and giant dogs sniffing everywhere. Those big fishermen must have looked funny with little fancy handkerchiefs—you know, waving them around," Fallon swung her arm around as if dangling a handkerchief in the face of some dogs.

"I sketched that!" Max showed her his sketch of black boots, dead fish, and a savage dog. [Fig. XV-2]

Stress that readers can come to realizations that nudge us to revise our ideas and go on journeys of thought; ask readers to consider how their ideas have changed.

Convening the class, I said, "I'd been thinking that this was the story of one brave family, but now I am thinking, 'Whoa! This is all of Denmark!' I'm definitely going on a journey of thought, one where I change my initial thinking.

"Readers, doesn't that just make you think about how forceful these people were, when they worked together? Resistance leaders like Peter organizing escape routes, fishermen building secret compartments in their boats, scientists creating drugs, ordinary families guiding their friends through the dark to the boats. It was a massive rescue operation. It was all of Denmark.

"Readers, when we started this book, I thought that it was the Germans who had power. They had the black boots and the rifles. They're the ones who made everyone afraid, who took people away, who came in the middle of the night. How many of you felt like I did?" The children nodded vigorously.

Figure XV-2
Max used a sketch instead of words to capture his idea!

When I was thinking about how the Danish seemed to be united in this rescue operation, it made me think of the many times in my life when I have read The Diary of Anne Frank. *Despite having reread it with practically every new edition (remember when the unexpurgated version was released, with her not-so-childish feelings for Peter?), I still tend to cling to my first understanding of the book. When I read it at ten, I pictured Anne in an attic in Germany because at the time, I thought the Holocaust was only in Germany. Later I found that in Holland, where she lived, almost all the Jews were deported and killed. The same in Norway. The same in the Netherlands. I tend to think of these countries as the same. But they weren't the same. The royalty of these other nations left, and the homes and property of Jews were not protected. What was it about Denmark, the home of Hans Christian Anderson, guarded by the little mermaid, that helped them accomplish something we would only hope for in fairy tales?*

"I used to think that it was the Germans who had all the power. But now, I'm starting to not be so sure. There might be other kinds of power. . . ."

The children nodded, "Yeah. All the people they had more power. It's the power of friendship."

Name your teaching point. Specifically, teach your children that it pays off for readers to investigate power, asking who has power, what form does it take, and how does power shift.

"Readers, today I want to teach you that looking at our books with the lens of power leads to all sorts of new thinking. When we investigate who has power, what form power takes (how you see it), and how power changes, that helps us find huge meanings in books."

Teachers, notice that I've just used a version of the thought prompt "I used to think . . . , but now I realize . . ." to convey that my thinking about this story is changing. These phrases have proved to be very helpful to kids, helping recapture their ideas at the beginning or middle of a story versus their ideas at the end. Remember in the previous minilesson, when I taught children that a good interpretation of "Things" can't simply reiterate the ending—that poetry lasts—but that it also needs to reflect the beginning and middle of that poem? Often when readers read the ending of a text where the problem gets solved, the moral lesson is a kind of tsunami that sweeps over all their earlier thinking. The thought prompts, "I used to think . . . , but now I realize . . ." help readers recall their earlier thoughts and see ideas that span the entire text.

What a beautiful way to name one of the themes in this book: "I used to think this was a story about Nazis, who terrorized a town in Denmark and the people in it, but I have come to realize that this is a story about a nation that didn't have guns, and didn't wear boots, but that found a source of power big enough to counter the power of Nazi violence. By working together to take care of their friends, the Danish people showed that good can be stronger than evil." Then again, one could capture the theme this way: "I used to think this was the story of a brave girl who had the courage to do what's right for her friend, but I have come to realize this is the story of a whole movement of people who did what's right for people they didn't even know, taking great risks on their behalf, and who showed, by doing this, that when we work together, good can win over evil."

TEACHING

Lead into describing power relationships with a simple analogy. Then share some of the questions critical readers ask, using them to prompt the class in rethinking the read-aloud through this lens.

"Readers, you can think about power in any relationship. I was watching a nature special the other day about wolves. Scientists think that the reason wolves have survived in the wild, even as their sources of food get scarcer, is that they are a pack animal. They hunt together, so they can bring down big animals like the moose. But they also survive because they are not always fighting each other over who has power—polar bears, for example, view every other polar bear, even their fathers, as enemies, but wolves live together. And wolves have settled the question of who eats first—there is an alpha mother and an alpha father in each pack, and they eat first, and they have the babies, too. The wolves have sorted out the question of who has power and what you can do with it, so this system helps them survive.

"Of course, you can't just figure out who has power by looking at who eats first! There are some questions readers ask to investigate power. At the start of the book, when you are getting to know a new place, it can help to ask, 'Who makes the rules? Who's in charge?'" I jotted on a chart those points.

Channel readers to join you in asking questions that reveal who has power in excerpts of the read-aloud text selected for this purpose.

"Join me, readers, in thinking about those two questions. I'll read some excerpts aloud, and let's think (I'll give you a tiny bit of time to talk or jot, if you want). So, let's see, the story starts with that scene where Ellen and Annemarie dash down the street, and then they bump into the soldiers. Oh, right, and the one soldier gives them orders." I opened the book then, and read aloud, in a harsh voice:

> "Go home, all of you. Go study your schoolbooks. And don't run. You look like hoodlums when you run."

"Let me read on," I said, and again read in a harsh voice:

> "Where did you get the dark-haired one?" He twisted the lock of Ellen's hair. "From a different father? From a milkman?"

You will see that during the teaching component of this session, I actually do hardly any demonstration. Instead, I simple provide guided practice to the kids. That is, I channel them to progress along through the sequence of work.

Predictable Questions to Investigate **Power!**

➤ Who has power in this place—Who's in charge?

➤ What are the obvious or explicit signs of power?

Then I said, "Share your thoughts." I watched Kobe show his club the quick sketch he'd made of two figures. The top showed a soldier yelling "Halt! Go home little children! No more running for you. We are the runners now." Just below was a second soldier banging on a door. He, too, was yelling, "Bring out your dark-haired children!" [Fig. XV-3]

Malik had jotted, "The soldier's power is to scare people. They seem like they will hurt children. They are bullies. Bullies with guns and mean faces and boots." [Fig. XV-4]

"Readers, when we looked at this text through the lens of power, asking, 'Who has power?' and 'What are the signs of power?' I think we all saw those soldiers as powerful—and it is a cruel power. But let me teach you one new thing. After a reader asks, 'Who has power?' the reader can then ask, 'What's the resistance?' because where there is power, there is resistance. People don't just give in. Let's try using that question as another lens, thinking about the forms of resistance in *Number the Stars*. Turn and talk."

When children first begin to analyze power, they will see it as a negative force—the force of tyrants and bullies or authority figures. Power to them is all about oppression or domination. In time, you will help them see that there are beautiful, generative powers as well. The lonely strength of those who sheltered Anne Frank. The fortitude of Gandhi defying the British Empire. Harriet Tubman, going back, again and again, to rescue slaves and bring them to safety. Soon, you begin to edge toward the idea that there is power that is good, power that is hope, power that brings grace.

Figure XV-3
Kobe captures signs of power

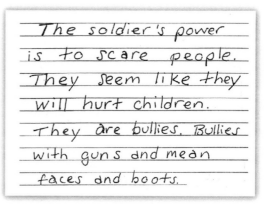

Figure XV-4
Malik's exploration of power

I called the children back. "What I heard you saying and saw you writing is that the Danish people resisted by working together; they didn't use guns for power. Instead, they used dead fish and handkerchiefs." I paused as if pondering. "So, are you saying even though the Germans have this obvious, cruel, armed power, the Danes have a sort of invisible power?"

Summarize the replicable process you've led the class through, doing so in ways that could be transferred to other texts and other days.

"Do you see that when readers want to think about our stories through the lens of power, it helps to look first at questions such as 'Who has power?' and 'What are the signs of that power?' But then it is also important to ask, 'What is the resistance? What is their power?' Doing this, we can realize that there are different kinds of power and that power is not necessarily a bad thing." I revealed the rest of a chart containing questions readers can ask ourselves when thinking about a story through the lens of power."

Active Involvement

Take your readers through the same series of steps, guiding them first with the questions critical readers ask.

"Readers, let's give you a chance to try this work in your books. First, you have on hand the book you're reading with your club. If you're just starting a new book, you might want to do this work in the book you recently finished reading. Let's just look at our chart. So, one of the questions critical readers ask is, 'Who has the obvious power in this place?' Think of your places: the deep South in 1933, the farm huddled into the dust, the prairie with its settlers. Do some jotting and give me a thumbs up when you've got an idea."

I looked over kids' shoulders. Aly had just jotted, "Mr. Wallace . . . Mr. Simms . . . Harlan Granger . . . all the white men." I voiced over as everyone worked, "Readers, Aly started by listing the characters that seemed powerful, and then she thought about what *group* they belonged to. Thinking about particular people as members of a group is one way to think about who has power, because sometimes it's not specific names so much as people in particular roles." [Fig. XV-5]

Children are used to seeing the more obvious signs of power: physical force, overt brutality—the power signals of a bully. It's harder to see moral power, because you see it best in its effects rather than in action. All along, in Number the Stars, *the Rosens and the Johansens seem powerless, but in the end, we learn that theirs is a power that is stronger than the power held by the Nazis.*

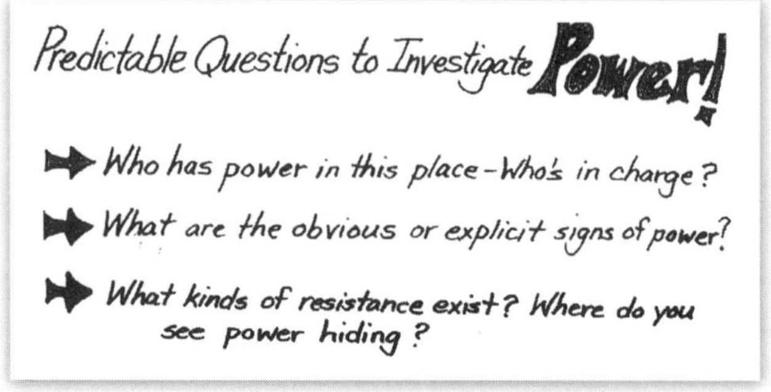

Predictable Questions to Investigate **Power!**

➡ *Who has power in this place – Who's in charge?*

➡ *What are the obvious or explicit signs of power?*

➡ *What kinds of resistance exist? Where do you see power hiding?*

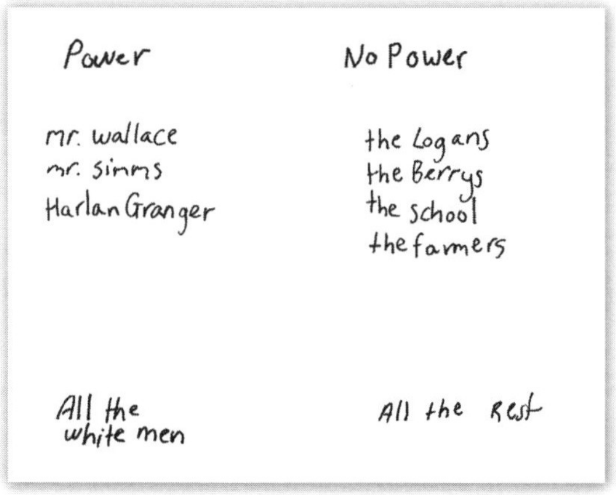

Power	No Power
Mr. Wallace	the Logans
Mr. Simms	the Berrys
Harlan Granger	the School
	the farmers
All the white men	All the Rest

Figure XV-5
Aly explores power in *Roll of Thunder, Hear My Cry* .

This is, in fact, an interesting question and one that you might choose to return to in your teaching. Often it's a person's membership in a group that gives or denies that person power. Youngsters don't often think about interactions as being not just between individuals but between groups of people. A starting place is to ask, "What groups do you belong to?" And of course, the answer is more extensive than we tend to realize at first. I belong to the group of elementary educators, to middle-aged women, to Congregationalists, to writers, to daughters, to mothers. . . .

I gave them another moment. "Readers, talk together, think back over the story, kind of retelling on your fingers the moments when this person, or this group, uses its power for good or for harm. In your mind or quickly on the page, make a timeline."

Sam and Josh, two members of the Freedom Fighters, started to work on a timeline of good power in *Roll of Thunder, Hear My Cry*. [Fig. XV-6]

Convening the class, I said, "Did you come to any ahas?"

Kobe's hand shot up, so I nodded for him to talk to us. "We just said, in *Skylark*, that we didn't really know who had power. Maybe Sarah, 'cause she was helping make the family happier. But a lot of people are unhappy now in the prairie because all this bad stuff is happening.

"And then," Malik jumped in, "I said everyone's leaving because they can't fight the drought on the prairie."

Kobe took the baton back. "And that got us to think that maybe the *prairie* has the power."

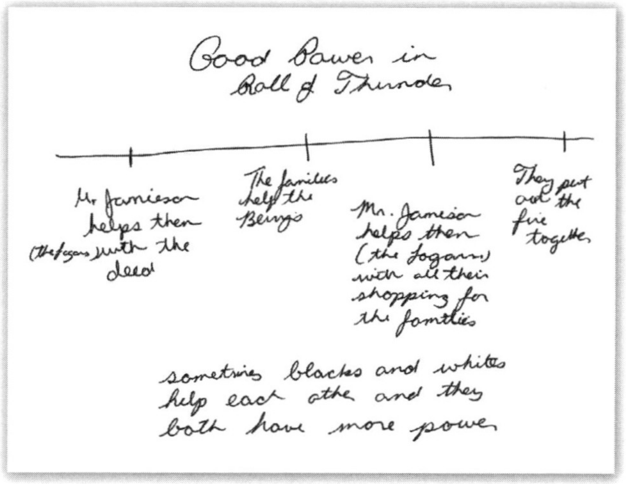

Figure XV-6
Sam and Josh's timeline on *Roll of Thunder, Hear My Cry*

LINK

Invite your readers to continue this work, thinking not only about power and resistance but also about perspective.

"Readers, it's time to read. Remember, it is always interesting to look at any novel through the lens of power. The lens of power and resistance to power often helps us understand more about why characters act the way they do. I know as you read today, you'll be asking, 'Where is there resistance? Are there resisters in my book, like the Danish, who are stronger because they all work together?' Notice, too, that one part of power is voice, and the person who tells the story will have more voice. You can read, though, like we learned the other day, trying to bring out the voices that would otherwise be silent. You have a lot to think about, and when you meet with your clubs next, which won't be until tomorrow, you'll have a lot to talk about, too."

Teachers, you can imagine how thrilled I was that these readers, who until now had mysteriously seemed to ignore the prairie, treating it as just a big farm in the novel, had articulated it as a powerful force. As students begin reading novels at levels R/S/T, the setting will, in fact, begin to play a much more significant role in their stories. It often operates on a symbolic level—usually as part of the problem that characters face. As their stories get even more complicated, the setting will be dynamic, changing across the story so that sometimes it is threatening and sometimes it is a refuge, as in Bridge to Terabithia.

If you are interested in teaching readers to be more critical, then there are a few units in Constructing Curriculum—*check the second half of it—that will help you do this. I also strongly recommend you draw on Randy Bomer and Katherine Bomer's book for teachers,* For a Better World: Reading and Writing for Social Action.

Help Readers See Hope in the Midst of Tragedy

You'll find, as your readers tackle novels at levels U/V and above, that there is a new quality to many of these stories that can be very hard for them to handle. That is the quality of tragedy. In prior stories, even complex narratives at the R/S/T level, such as *Fly Away Home, Bridge to Terabithia*, or **The Tiger Rising*, bad things might happen to good characters. The narrator's mother is dead in both *Fly Away Home* and in *The Tiger Rising*. Leslie dies in *Bridge to Terabithia*. So there is loss in these stories. But the characters die off-screen. The reader doesn't have to watch them die. But then the books change. In *The Lightning Thief*, Percy watches his mother get killed. The graphic realism of her death, like the graphic depiction of burning men alive in *Roll of Thunder, Hear My Cry*, marks a sharp change in the expectation that readers can deal with tragedy. Readers do need to learn how to deal with tragedy, or they'll turn away permanently from almost all canonical literature, from Toni Morrison's *Sula* to Steinbeck's *Of Mice and Men*. Tragedies happen in life, and what a gift it is if we can begin to help children cope with life, through learning to cope first with the tragedies in texts. In conferences, you can show your children that even though bad things happen in their stories, the stories themselves can still be meaningful and, even, uplifting.

It's important to teach readers who are reading books like these that terrible things can happen in a story, and parts, even that part, can still be beautiful. Part of maturing as a reader is being able to see beauty in literature that has tragedy in it. That's true for *Where the Red Fern Grows*. So many of us remember sobbing, and saying, through our tears, "Oh, I love this book. It is so heartbreaking. It is so beautiful." *The Yearling* puts readers through a similar emotional experience. There is great sadness, and beauty, too.

As you confer with your readers, therefore, take the time to help them talk about the parts of the story that they find frightening. Help them to find parts of the story that are, nevertheless, beautiful. Coach them to name their emotions as they read and to linger in the parts of the story where they feel the strongest. Often, figuring out what the story gets them to feel and think can help them handle their grief and channel it into ideas about social justice. And then, you can show them that readers who care are readers who are truly taking the story to heart, and that's what the

---

MID-WORKSHOP TEACHING POINT

Readers Know that Reading Means Eating the Nut and Throwing Out the Shell

"Readers, earlier today I suggested you think about people in your story not just as individuals but as members of a group, and then think about which groups of people have power in the world of your story. And some of you have been noticing mothers who seem quiet, or absent, in some of your books. And you're thinking, 'I don't agree with the way my book gives and takes away power.' You like the book, but there are things in it that you *don't like*.

"Here's the thing, readers. Remember, we talked earlier about how as the characters in your books grow up, they seem like they are becoming more aware. We saw that with *The House of Sixty Fathers* and *Autumn Street*, and we're seeing that with Annemarie in *Number the Stars*. Well, the other thing that happens as characters grow up is that people start to realize that most things aren't all good or all bad. That's true for people—even the people we adore aren't perfect—and it is true for books.

"Sometimes, even with books we adore, we're dissatisfied with a small part of the book. And that's okay. There is no perfect book, and as part of that, there is no book that will exactly match your view of the world. There is no book that will give every person an equal voice.

"For example, I love Disney movies. I like how strong Pocahontas is. I like how valiant Mulan is. I like how daring the Little Mermaid is. But the heroines of those books all look the same.

continued on next page

---

author wants! It's in the crucible of caring that we develop transformative ideas about justice and injustice.

Using a Strong Emotional Reaction to Develop a Big Idea

I drew my chair alongside Aly, who was reading *Let the Circle Be Unbroken* on her own. Her club, The Freedom Fighters, had recently finished the first book in Mildred Taylor's series, *Roll of Thunder, Hear My Cry*. I knew that Aly had been disturbed by a lot of what happened in the novel. She was bent over her notebook, forehead furrowed, deep in thought. I was curious to see what was swirling around in her head. "How are you liking *Let the Circle Be Unbroken*?" I asked.

"It's really good," she said, "But it's also hard to read. Not 'cause the book is hard, though."

"Oh? What's making it hard to read?"

"Well, it's hard reading about things not being fair back then. For example, I just wrote this." In her soft, melodic voice, she read, "I noticed that T.J. should get a fair trial because I have an eye for equality." *[Fig. XV-7]*

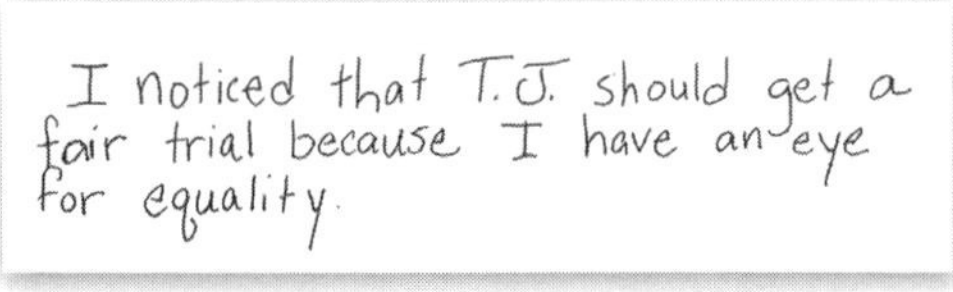

I noticed that T.J. should get a fair trial because I have an eye for equality.

Figure XV-7

MID-WORKSHOP TEACHING POINT

continued from previous page

They all have long hair and tiny waists and perfect faces, and they look like Barbie dolls. In that way, they're stereotypes. They reinforce the idea that for girls to be important, they have to be a movie star, Barbie doll kind of beautiful. I don't love that part of those movies.

"So the answer is this: Readers read books like we eat pistachio nuts. You eat the good parts and throw out the shells. You spit out the parts that are no good.

Some of you may have been swept away by *The Fountainhead*. It was only after college that I learned more about Ayn Rand's political views and then realized that this story only honors one—to me frightening—representation of the world. And many of us have people in our families whose belief systems are different from our own. We can disagree with those things while still loving the people!

"As you think about power in your book and you think about whose voice comes through loud and clear and whose voice is silenced, you might find yourself saying, 'This book makes it seem like men can't express their feelings, and I am sick of the world stereotyping boys in that way. I disagree with that.' Or you might say, 'This book makes little kids (like Kirsti) seem like they can't handle hard things, and I think that stereotypes little kids.' You can disagree with part of a book and still let the book sweep you away. Just remember—it's like eating nuts. You toss out the shells, that's all. That's what critical readers do."

"Yes, you've been reading with that lens—with an eye for equality, as you so eloquently put it—quite a bit this year. I know how important justice is to you."

"Yeah. I guess I just want to believe that people are good. And all these books I'm reading make me feel like they're not. It makes me so sad to see all this badness. Like, there's always one group of people who don't have any power. In my club's books, it's Black people, and in our read-aloud, it's Jewish people."

"That's true," I said. "Throughout history, it's often been the case that some people have powers and possibilities that others don't have." I paused to let her reflect on that, then said, "Would you be willing to try something that I sometimes do as a reader?" Aly nodded.

"When I have a particularly strong reaction to something in my reading, like when I have a weighty feeling like the one you just shared with me, I find it useful to lay out all of my thinking that might be related. I mine my notebook for any jottings that sort of fit with this one reaction—even remotely. Often what I find is that there's a really powerful idea hiding in my feelings. Would you mind taking a minute now to look through your notebook and Post-its and see if you can find jottings that in some way go together?"

Aly flipped through her notebook, using her fingers as markers, then looked through the Post-its she'd stuck into her copy of *Let the Circle Be Unbroken*. After a minute, she looked up. When I asked her what she'd discovered, she shared three jottings with me. The first was a bulleted list, followed by two related thoughts. *[Figs. XV-8, XV-9, and XV-10]*

"Are you noticing any patterns in them?" I asked, rereading them myself to see if I saw any.

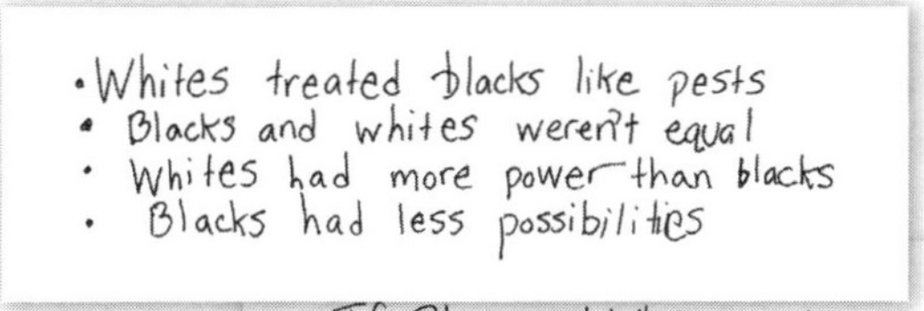

- Whites treated blacks like pests
- Blacks and whites weren't equal
- Whites had more power than blacks
- Blacks had less possibilities

Figure XV-8

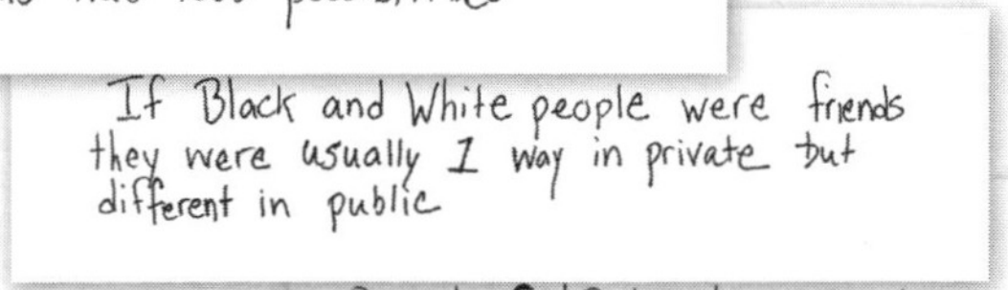

If Black and White people were friends they were usually 1 way in private but different in public

Figure XV-9

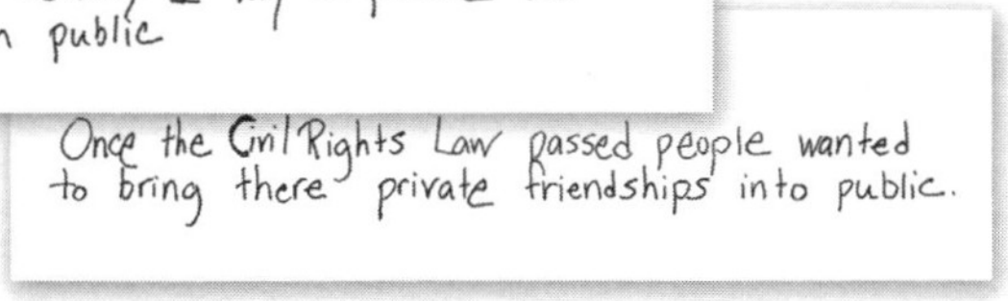

Once the Civil Rights Law passed people wanted to bring there private friendships into public.

Figure XV-10

"They're all about how Blacks and Whites weren't equal?" Aly asked, uncertain.

"Yes, there's that. What else do you notice? When I do what you're doing, I try to push myself to look really closely and keep thinking past my first idea," I said, rereading her notes as I talked to her.

"Well, it's kind of like I'm noticing how Black and White people are with each other. Like how White people treat Black people, especially."

"Do you think this is all White people, all Black people? Do you feel like you could paint the whole story with one big brush that says, 'This is how all the people are with each other'?"

Aly's expression lightened. "Well, Jeremy is good to the Logan kids. He walks in the rain; he comes to visit; he stands by them. I like those parts."

I agreed. "Yes, those are beautiful parts. Could you imagine those details were written here" (I jotted what she'd just said), "and just look across all these ideas you have, like we did when we looked across the ideas different kids brought to the table to come up with a big-tent idea? That day, we looked across different people's ideas, but we can also look across our own ideas and try to see if we can come up with an idea that is big enough to encompass all these thoughts. Hmm, what idea might we come to?"

Aly pointed to her entry about people acting differently in private and in public and to the one on which I'd recorded her idea about Jeremy. She said, "Well, Jeremy could have ignored the Logan kids. Or even made fun of them, like his sister did. But he tried to be their friend. It's his choice." Her face lit up. "And in *Number the Stars*, Annemarie's family could have not helped the Rosens. They could have even given them up to the Nazis. So it is like, people made choices."

"Aly, that's huge! Earlier when we talked, you told me that you notice unfair treatment of characters because you have an eye for equality. And now, it is like you are noticing where there is bad power, there is also resistance, places where people are making choices for the good, responding to injustice."

"Exactly!" Aly said. Her face lit up. "You know what else? This reminds me of my club's talk the other day about how some characters protest quietly."

"What are you thinking about that?"

"I'm thinking that Jeremy is another one who protests, only quietly. It's like he's saying, 'This isn't right. What does skin color have to do with a friendship?' So it's bad, but there is hope."

"Aly, at the start of the conversation you said that reading this book is hard because it is hard to see the pain in the world. Remember we talked about how characters grow up by becoming more aware and seeing more? Kids do, too. I think lots of kids your age start out like Kirsti and end up having to see that there's bad stuff in the world. You're looking that bad stuff in the eye, and it *is* hard to keep making choices for the good when you see all that depressing stuff."

"Yeah," Aly said. "But you wouldn't want to be like Kirsti and just think about pink cupcakes either."

"So what are you going to do next?" I asked.

"Read on?" Aly said. "I still have more in this book."

I nodded. "And as you read on, try to continue to remember that seeing more, even seeing the hard stuff, is part of growing up, right? But in the dark times, stars do come out."

TEACHING SHARE

Readers Pause to Think at the Ends of Our Books

Tell readers that at the ends of books, readers pause to think more deeply, drawing on all they know to think through the whole of the book.

"Many of you have been reaching the ends of books and moving to your new ones. Earlier, we learned that readers pause when we get to parts in a book that feel as if they've been written in bold, they are so important. I want to be sure you know that readers also pause when we reach the endings of books, and the endings of parts of books. We pause to look back over the trail we have traveled and to do some new thinking.

"Have any of you ever climbed a mountain—or climbed up the stairs in a building that is so tall it is almost like a mountain? Last weekend, I climbed St. Regis Mountain. The trail threaded through meadows and woods, up and up, and you couldn't really see where you were going or what was around you. Then there was light ahead, sunshine, and all of a sudden I was standing on a bald, rocky mountaintop, with sunshine and blue sky and the whole world stretched around me. It was like all of a sudden I could see clearly, with this new vision.

"Today, I want to tell you that when you reach the end of a climb—when you finally get there—you don't just turn around and race back down. Instead, you linger there for a bit, taking in the whole view, looking back over the trail you've traveled. You have a chance, at the summit, to really see.

"That's true if you are hiking, and it is also true if you are reading. If you are reading and you find yourself reaching an ending, it's like reaching the end of a mountain climb. You've gone through woods and you've emerged. Everything is illuminated. You know all there is to know about the story. So linger there for a bit, looking back over the trail you've followed, the story you've read. Now that you can see so much, it is almost impossible to *not* grow new ideas.

"Probably, some of the things you thought would happen didn't happen after all. Probably, some characters changed and learned lessons. That's always worth thinking about. And maybe you learned some lessons, too. You can use all the strategies you've learned, thought prompts, ideas from our charts—to think. So, readers, any time when you are reading, you can go on a journey of thought, starting with one idea and ending with another one. And you'll especially expect that to go on a journey of thought when you come to the ending of a section, or the final, very last page of your book."

COACHING TIPS

The content of this share will not be a new idea to your students. However, like most essential ideas, this one bears repeating. Make sure you don't talk as if this is just a little pinprick of an idea this is not worth much. Convey your reverence for the idea you are sharing. Lean in close and show with your own body language that what you are saying matters.

Sparking Nonfiction Against Fiction to Ignite Ideas

IN THIS SESSION,
you will teach your students that readers spark new ideas when we read relevant nonfiction alongside our fiction books.

nce children are immersed in a unit on historical fiction, their reading often spills out into the rest of the day. I remember the day Danny asked if he could look at *Rose Blanche* during snack. Danny knew a lot about World War II. He had a whole collection of books at home that he had gathered from the library, and he often contributed his expert knowledge to class discussion. Sam found this fascinating, so Sam scooted his chair close to Danny and looked over the book with him. Sam wanted to look at the picture of the kids behind the barbed wire, so he and Danny opened the book to that page.

They looked at the picture, each sucking juice from a juice box as they took it in. "Why are they wearing yellow stars?" Sam asked.

"They're Jewish," Danny said. "These were concentration camps. Mostly, everybody died. I read a book about it. They made them work, then they put them in gas chambers and ovens."

There was a long pause. Then, "I'm Jewish," Sam said.

"I'm Jewish, too," Danny said. Another long pause. Then, "It was a bad time for us. Things are probably not going to go so well for these kids."

GETTING READY

- Your children will be meeting with their clubs today, so be sure the work you do in the link and mid-workshop teaching channels them toward this.

- You'll need some texts for your kids. We've provided some fact sheets on the *Resources for Teaching Reading* CD-ROM, which you can shorten, alter, or appropriate for your own use. If you have the time to gather some articles, photographs, or books, make folders or baskets, as you did for nonfiction. You also could simply write a couple of texts with your colleagues. Put multiple copies into folders or envelopes, so students can mine these for bits of information they find fascinating. Invite students to add to the library as well.

- We have provided a picture of King Christian X, an Irish peasant girl, and some fact sheets on the CD-ROM that you will need for this session.

- During the minilesson, you'll use a fact sheet about the Holocaust from the CD-ROM, and, if you choose, you'll show some photos from the United States Holocaust Memorial Museum. The link for this collection is www.ushmm.org. Go to the "The Holocaust: A Learning Site for Students" section.

- At the end of the share, you'll begin a new chart on reading and talking across texts.

Listening to Danny, I was filled with thoughts about how nonfiction intersects with historical fiction, giving it a realism that is pretty sobering at times. Those of us who have studied Emmett Till, and that terrible summer at the nadir of the civil rights movement, are anxious about the two boys' fate in *Freedom Summer* in a completely different way. We know the risk they take is terrible. Our nonfiction knowledge gives an extra edge to the story.

As I gazed at Danny pointing out details to Sam, I thought how lucky kids are who are given the opportunity

> *One of the things we know about nonfiction reading and children is that kids who read nonfiction become teachers of it.*

to find out more about the topics they find fascinating or compelling. For it's not just that Danny had an intense curiosity. It's that he was lucky enough to have access to resources that let him satisfy this curiosity. And his classmates are lucky as well, because he is a natural instructor. One of the things we know about nonfiction reading and children—which we saw played out abundantly earlier in the nonfiction unit—is that kids who read nonfiction

become teachers of it. They are brimful of information, and they are eager to share it.

In this session, we invite children to dig around in nonfiction texts related to the historical era they're studying. Chances are, they'll find some material they find fascinating. Probably, they'll have some new insights about parts of their stories. The novels make them curious about history, and the history gives them new ideas about the novels. That kind of recursive process is authoring a reading life, and it's the same process that happens in so many walks of life. You get started on one thing; it sends you to another.

It's also true that just as two sticks being rubbed against each other light a flame, rubbing texts against each other sparks new thinking. This session will work with intertextuality, and it will help children author their own reading projects. Just as we—for a book club or for any subject we find fascinating—might gather articles, come upon podcasts, or pick up another novel to read along with the ones we've already read, so the children can learn to think of their reading life not as reading isolated texts but as pursuing their own passions and purposes. These final sessions of the unit especially foster self-initiation. They should help kids envision how readers come to think of some books as "going together." They should help them plan for work that lasts longer than their current book. This intertextual work may help children imagine reading projects for themselves, projects born of a broader vision, projects that include fiction and nonfiction, the real and the imagined, the possible and the dreams.

MINILESSON

Sparking Nonfiction Against Fiction to Ignite Ideas

CONNECTION

Describe stumbling across nonfiction related to your novels because you see the world through the lens of those novels, and also seeking out related nonfiction.

"Readers, you know how you put Post-its in your books, and you carry your books around, filled with all your notes? Well, readers, I don't put only Post-its into my books; I put newspaper articles, photographs, poems, and all sorts of related stuff. When I'm really into a novel, I kind of walk through the world, looking at everything through the lens of my book, and I'm always saying, 'That relates to the book I'm reading!' Then if I can, I file whatever I find into the pages of the book. Look, I'll show you a new picture that I just recently stuffed into my copy of *Number the Stars*."

I showed the students the picture. "I bet you know who this is. It's King Christian X of Denmark, riding his famous horse, Jubilee, through the streets of Copenhagen. I was in a bookstore the other day, and while I was waiting for a friend, I leafed through a book of famous photographs of this century. I almost missed this photograph, because I wasn't actively doing any research. But as soon as I turned to this page, something clicked! 'That's related to my book. That's King Christian and Jubilee!' I said to myself. Sure enough, the caption said that it was taken on King Christian's 70th birthday, on September 26, 1940. Later that night, I found the picture on Google Images so I could bring it to you, and printed it out, along with some information about the king and Jubilee, and I have that stuff filed into my book. I suppose I could move this stuff to a folder, but I kind of like having it all right there, touching the pages of my novel." I held up my copy of the novel, which had bits of paper and pictures stuffed inside the back cover.

"Readers, you can do this, too. You can gather information from outside any one of your books—facts, maps, pictures—and put bits of it together with your book. It's sort of as if you're making a text set, like we did when we were studying sharks and pen-

Teachers, your clubs may have started folders at the beginning of this unit. They may have timelines, maps, and other writing in these folders that club members have been creating, and they can add any nonfiction bits of information to these folders, making a collaborative text set. So, these reading projects may be literal or figurative, meaning they may exist as baskets, folders, or baggies, or merely as collections of texts that go together in a reader's mind. They may be collaborative text sets, created by all the members of a club working together, or they could be personal, with each child using a baggie to collect texts and snippets that talk back to the text. This is practice, showing kids how they can shape reading projects during vacations or the summer, when continued reading in fiction and nonfiction could really push them ahead as readers.

guins and so forth. It's like you're making a project out of your reading, gathering bits and pieces that relate to your books."

Name your teaching point. Specifically, tell children that readers look to nonfiction for information that sparks new thinking about our novels. We put bits of our nonfiction alongside parts of the story and see what ideas ignite when we rub these two things together.

"Readers, we often turn to nonfiction to spark new ideas about our novels. Just as two sticks light a fire when they're rubbed together, we can rub some bits of nonfiction up against parts of novels and see ideas ignite."

TEACHING

Show readers how the information they are learning from nonfiction sources can ignite their thinking.

"Let's just try, for a moment, seeing if this picture of King Christian X and Jubilee can spark new thinking. Let's see. . . ." I studied the picture for a moment. "I think the part of this picture that I find fascinating is how *cozy* it all feels! There's a girl on a bicycle, riding across the street just a few feet ahead of the king. The king seems to be laughing at her. And a little boy is reaching out to pat Jubilee. It's almost like they're a family.

"Hmm, so if I take this bit of information—that in 1940 the Danish were all cozy together, even the ordinary people with the king—what happens if I rub that up against *Number the Stars*?" I pondered a bit, as if mulling things over. "Well, it makes me think that maybe that's why the Danes took such good care of their Jewish brothers and sisters. Maybe they really did think of themselves as a family, and that's why they didn't hesitate to help each other. Families do that. They take care of each other."

I paused for a moment, as if noticing the copy of *Rose Blanche* that was on the shelf. "Hmm, I guess this makes me think, as well, that it's too bad they didn't feel their Jewish brothers and sisters were part of the family in Rose Blanche's town.

Denmark is, and was in 1940, a small country. There does seem to be something particularly intimate and interconnected about the people. King Christian's brother was king of Norway, and his sister was queen of the Netherlands. These two monarchs did not stay with their people under the German occupation. They fled into exile. King Christian X lived in his palace and kept riding Jubilee, without guards, among his people. You, of course, might find some other bit of nonfiction information fascinating that you'll rub together with the novel. Any bit is sure to spark some new thinking.

Name what you have done in a way that is transferable to another text, another day.

"Readers, do you see how I took a bit of information that I learned, in this case from a journalist's photograph, and I just tried it out alongside my novels, to see if it sparked any new thinking? Readers of historical fiction often do what I've done."

ACTIVE INVOLVEMENT

Give your students a chance to practice rubbing a bit of nonfiction information up against the read-aloud text by giving them a fact sheet pertaining to the topic of your read-aloud and inviting them to talk between the fact sheet and the novel.

"Let's give you a chance to spark something. Let's keep going with *Number the Stars* for a moment, as practice. Here are some facts to try rubbing alongside what you already know."

I handed out a fact sheet about the Holocaust that I had printed from the CD-ROM.

"Readers, take a moment to read these facts or look at these photographs. When something sparks an interest, think about these facts through the lens of *Number the Stars*. See if you can blow some wind over your spark and ignite some new thinking. If you have ideas about other books as well, of course, blow wind over those sparks. When you've got a little flame of an idea, turn and talk with someone near you."

They did so. I listened for a few moments and then gathered them back.

Convene your class and ask particular individuals to bring their conversations to the larger group.

"Readers, you rubbed two texts together, like people rub two sticks against each other, and I think sparks of thought have been generated. Can we share some? Let's hear some ideas."

Colleagues, I'm expecting that you are noticing, as I am, that this new idea comes late in the day, when the series is coming to an end. It has tremendous possibility and could easily have launched a whole new bend in the road of this unit. I regret that I don't have time to write three more sessions, to tap the power of this work and allow kids to really become magnets around the topics that are central to the reading they've done. But really, in a way, that's as it should be. This book should be stirring your imagination, helping you think of minilessons you can author and work you and your kids can do together that extends beyond these books. So go at it! Take this session as the beginning, and extend it.

- Approximately 456 Danish Jews who were captured during the war were sent to Theresienstadt, an internment camp. An internment camp was a camp where prisoners either worked in terrible conditions, or were sent on to other concentration camps. Prisoners from all over Europe were sent to Theresienstadt. These prisoners were supposed to be well taken care of, but of the 15,000 children who ended up in Theresienstadt, only approximately 90% survived.

- Pictures of children during the Holocaust from the United States Holocaust Memorial Museum (ushmm.org):

Two brothers in the Kovno ghetto in Lithuania, one month before their deportation to the Majdanek camp.

Soon after the liberation, survivors from "Children's Block 66," a special barracks for children at the Buchenwald camp.

Although you will want to teach readers to look across historical fiction to learn information and ideas, those texts may not always be precisely true. In Exodus, *for instance, there's a story about how when the Germans wanted the Danish people to wear the yellow star, King Christian insisted that all Danes would wear it. It turns out that story is a legend. So you want to be careful about quoting historical fiction as if it were nonfiction. It's not. But often the gist of the history is true. I looked up more about King Christian, and it turns out the Germans never brought yellow stars to Denmark. But the king had suggested that maybe everyone could wear them if needed. What matters is that* Exodus *gives me a little more information about how the Danes thought about their Jewish brothers and sisters, information that fits with what I've already learned in* Number the Stars.

Kobe gave a thumbs up to signal he wanted to share his idea. "I think it's amazing that the king would say he was going to raise the flag—even if the Germans shot him! The king really seems stubborn and brave, just like the Johansens!"

Brianna's expression was troubled as she put her thumb in the air. "I noticed how few children survived in the camps. Ellen would have been doomed if those soldiers had gotten her."

I nodded. "That bit of information makes that whole scene in *Number the Stars* seem much scarier, doesn't it?" I said.

"I felt the same," added Rosa. "Only I was looking at those photos, of the kids who died. Like that picture of Anne Frank. It makes me think about the kids who didn't have people like Annemarie to save them."

"Right," said Danny. "Even like Rose Blanche. She died all alone. Sort of like these kids. It was a bad time to be a kid."

I interrupted the children. "I can see that reading a bit of nonfiction, like bringing the lenses of perspective and of power to our books, has stirred up all sorts of new thinking. Some of you, I can tell, are more drawn to statistics, and some to stories, and some to pictures. You'll find, readers, that when you turn to nonfiction, just as when we paused in the bold parts of our novels, different bits of information will kindle something in different people. That's what makes collecting stuff a kind of personal reading project, because each one of you will pull together bits of information that particularly spark something for you.

LINK

Send students off to collect some nonfiction information which they can rub against their novels.

"Readers, I know you'll be dying to do this work with information about the era in which your club has been reading. I'm going to hand out some nonfiction material related to your era to each club. Try rubbing bits of this information up against your stories to see if this can spark some new thinking. And, readers, I hope you'll begin to think about the reading you've been doing as not just a series of books, but a whole reading project. You'll probably find that you can rub the books you have already read against each other, as well as the nonfiction material against those books, and remember, your whole goal is to learn, to change your mind. You should be saying things like, 'I used to think . . . , but now I am realizing. . . .'"

Teachers, one or two of your students are certain to turn, in their thinking, to other books. It's inevitable; they're so brimful of stories by this time in the year. You can choose whether to follow this up by talking more extensively about the notion of reading across books, trying the same bit of information against more than one novel.

Teachers, it's close to the end of this unit of study, so this session is constrained. Instead of launching kids into wide research, I distribute fact sheets that may contain just a fact or two, a photograph or two. I especially want readers to spend their time at the intersection of fiction texts and nonfiction texts, and I want them to review their historical fiction texts, gleaning from them all the information that's embedded in them. Because time is limited, I don't want to inundate kids with bins of related nonfiction, or I know they'll spend their time reading widely rather than thinking across texts. You may, however, add another few days or a week, even, to the unit, allowing time for more extensive research.

Teach Readers Strategies for Interpreting Pictures and Images

There are myriad images available for the historical eras that your students are immersed in, from the haunting images of concentration camp inmates in the archives of the United States Holocaust Memorial Museum (www.ushmm.org) to the panoramic Hudson River paintings in the online collection of the Metropolitan Museum (www.metmuseum.org) to the depictions of families working in sweatshop conditions in the Lower East Side Tenement Museum (www.tenement.org). It's no longer hard to build a library that is image-rich as well as text-rich. Once you do start adding in images to the text sets your children tackle, you'll want to teach your students a few essential strategies to work with these images.

One of the first things you may want to teach your children is the difference between paintings and drawings, which are an artist's interpretation of a scene, and photographs, which capture a single moment in time. Paintings and drawings are more like historical fiction. There may be some historical license. Photographs are more like journalism. They tend to be accurate. (This is not to say that photography has not come to be highly interpretive and artistic. It's merely that most of the photos that your students will encounter in this study are snapshots, military records, and journalism.)

> ## MID-WORKSHOP TEACHING POINT
>
> ### Readers Mine Historical Fiction for Information that Sparks New Ideas
>
> "Readers, so far, you're looking to *nonfiction material* for bits of historical information that might spark new thinking for you, and you all are finding information that is definitely changing your thinking. The Allies, for instance, have been reading that almost all the Jews in the Netherlands, where Anne Frank was hiding, were murdered or deported—70% of the Dutch Jews died. And 74,000 Jews from France were deported and killed. This club is realizing that it wasn't only the Germans who were dangerous—in many places, the locals, the collaborators, were also dangerous.
>
> "But this is what I want to teach you. It's not just nonfiction texts that can tell you information about the world at the time in which your books are set. Your fiction books, too, can teach you true stuff. What is required is for you to look across a cluster of historical fiction books, asking, 'What true things do these books teach me about those times?' And I think you'll find that you can learn information and ideas from fiction just as well as from nonfiction.
>
> "The Allies could have learned just by thinking hard about *The Butterfly*, that neighbors in countries other than Denmark often didn't protect the Jews. Remember how Monique and
>
> *continued on next page*

Once your students make sense of what they are holding, sorting out whether it is a reproduction of a painting, a family snapshot, and so forth, teach them to practice close observation. Just as when we reread a poem, we can revisit an image to see more. Images merit prolonged attention and support journeys of thought. At first, we tend to see the most explicit and largest forms. You'll want to teach your children that it is valuable to describe what they see, and then give words to what they notice about the mood, the atmosphere of settings, the expressions and posture of people, and the details of clothes and objects. You'll prompt them to incorporate the information from the caption into their observations. Then you can show them how to lay images alongside their novels, bringing their response to one to interact with their response to the other.

Teaching Children to Closely Observe and Interpret Pictures and Images: Conferring with the Immigration Group

The Immigration group was huddled around some pictures depicting the Irish Famine era. Between them, an atlas lay open to a page that revealed the vastness of the Atlantic Ocean that separated Ireland from New York.

They were deep in discussion when I approached, so I seated myself unobtrusively on the periphery to observe their thinking.

Grace held the wood-engraved image of an Irish peasant girl huddled outside the cottage from which her family had been evicted. (See CD-ROM.) "This wood engraving was printed in a London newspaper in 1886," she announced, peering closely at the caption under the image.

"That's like, um, thirty years since the Famine. Strange. . . ." Grace seemed to pause for words. "This girl. . . . She could be . . . she could be Nory." Grace was referring to a main character in *Maggie's Door*.

Nodding in agreement, Emma steered the conversation in another direction. "Listen to this man's description of what went on inside the coffin ships." Emma proceeded to read aloud an excerpt from Stephen de Veere's description of what he encountered on an Irish immigrants' ship in 1847.

> Hundreds of poor people, men, women and children of all ages huddled together without light, without air, wallowing in filth and breathing a fetid atmosphere, sick in body, dispirited in heart; the fevered patients lying beside the sound, by their agonised ravings disturbing those around. The food is generally ill-selected and seldom sufficiently cooked in consequences of the insufficiency and bad construction of the cooking places. The supply of water, hardly enough for cooking and drinking, does not allow for washing.

Izzy was wide-eyed. "That's a lot like what Sean and Nora had to go through, too."

Emma nodded, "They called them coffin ships," she added. After making this brief connection to *Maggie's Door*, the club's talk veered toward a

---

MID-WORKSHOP TEACHING POINT

continued from previous page

Sevrine have to hide from their French neighbors? And in *The Lily Cupboard*, another book the Allies have been reading, every time *anyone* comes to the farm, Miriam has to get in the cupboard. So the historical fiction books that you all are reading are teaching you true stuff about those times, aren't they?

"Each of your historical fiction novels can teach you about the times. To learn as much as you can, pay attention to patterns, to things that come up in more than one book. Both *Roll of Thunder, Hear My Cry*, and *The Gold Cadillac*, for instance, have incidents of black men driving expensive cars through white neighborhoods. The Freedom Fighters have been noticing that pattern, and they said, today, 'One thing we're learning is that it was dangerous for black families to drive fancy cars into white communities.'

"See how I said, '*One thing we're learning is.* . . .' I've never lived on the prairie, but I know what it looks like from *Skylark*. I've never made butter, but I know how to do it from *Sarah, Plain and Tall*. I've never had to hide in a cupboard because my neighbors might turn me in to Nazis, but I know, now, in which countries that would have been pretty likely and in which countries it would not have been. I know because I read for information, as well as ideas."

---

discussion of how long one might last without food and water and to references to a teenage girl who'd just that day been pulled from the rubble left by the earthquake in Haiti. She'd survived there for more than a week. After listening for a minute longer, I decided to intervene and bring the conversation back to the discarded image of the wood engraving and to the connections to the historical fiction they'd read.

"Readers, can I interrupt for a minute?" I asked, and then I took some time to admire the diverse sources that they'd integrated into their conversation. I reminded them that just a month earlier in our non-fiction reading unit, I'd had to nudge them to look between the charts, photographs, captions, and text that were all on a single page of their nonfiction texts. Now they were reading *Maggie's Door* and bringing in what they learned from NBC, and an atlas, and the words written 150 years ago to describe ships such as the one on which their protagonist traveled. "You're taking my suggestion to think about a text as being layered with other texts really far, and that's terrific," I said.

I continued, "My suggestion to you, though, is that you probably need to slow down and spend a bit more time talking and thinking of the information. So, for example, Grace, when you said that the girl in the image could be Nora, that's meant as the beginning of a conversation, not the end of it. You just said that—and it was an important idea—and then you raced on! When artists create an illustration, they're trying to tell a story. The artist might be trying to show how spooky or deserted a place is or how hot it is. The artist could show us smiling people to make us feel happy or crying people to make us feel sad. In fact, you and I could almost 'read' an image and ask that question, 'What's this image really about?'

But to do that, we need to pay attention to the tiny details in the image, to study how the parts of it go together, to develop theories about the back story or about what might happen *next*." I stated the teaching point more explicitly. "What I'm saying is that we can take a lot of what we know about reading *texts* and apply those strategies to reading *images*. We can look at a picture and think, 'What's the story here?'"

Teachers, you might be wondering, what happened to the rule of teaching one thing at a time? It is true that throughout the series, I've modeled sticking with teaching *one* strategy at a time. It may look like I just rattled off close to *six* different things to do while "reading" an image. If you noticed that the list of things I just recounted seems exhaustive, note that I haven't, in fact, introduced a single *new* strategy. I'm now reiterating a list of previous teaching points that were initially applicable to reading books. And I'm suggesting that readers apply those same strategies to the reading of not just texts, but also images.

Returning to the children, I said to them, "Let's try with this image. You've already studied the caption and connected this image to Nory from *Maggie's Door*. How might you read this illustration like gold?" The children looked at the image for a bit.

Then the talk began. "Why isn't she sitting on a chair? Why on this table?"

"Maybe she wants to get away from the cold ground."

"She doesn't have shoes."

"These three bundles are probably all she owns. It is sad, really."

"This girl, like Nory, might have made it to Brooklyn. She might have started out Irish and ended up Irish-American."

"It makes me think, that immigrants like this girl—or like Sean and Nory—didn't really have a lot of choices. She could have been thrown out of her house, and she probably had no food, no job, no money. They were desperate."

I noted with some satisfaction that studying an image in greater detail had enabled the group to add nuance to their understanding of *Maggie's Door*. I made a thumbs up and left as the club continued their new line of conversation without me.

TEACHING SHARE

Readers Seek Information About Parts of Our Stories We Find Fascinating

Share the story of a child who has begun to learn, on his own, about the topic of his book. Suggest that others might do the same work in their reading lives.

COACHING TIPS

"Readers, I'd like to point out something that happened today during Danny's club meeting. Danny's club noticed that he was sharing bits of information that didn't come from the nonfiction they were reading. It turns out that on his own time, Danny has become an expert on World War II. He knows details about concentration camps; he knows about the strategy of resistance fighters; he knows about all sorts of stuff that his club mined today. Danny didn't find all this out by sitting around. He traded books with friends, he went to the library, and he even visited the Holocaust Museum with his family. He lives his life alert to the subjects he finds fascinating. As a nonfiction reader, Danny has a lot of agency. He is in charge of his reading life."

"So, readers, as you go off today and even after this unit is over, I want to remind you that historical fiction gets us stirred up about a whole lot of new stuff—things we hadn't even heard of before we started reading. And as we get stirred up, we think of our reading life as an ongoing project—one that extends beyond the walls of this classroom. A novel about immigration won't say, 'At this point in your reading, you could go, *"Oh. My. Gosh.* I didn't know this about how hard it was to get into this country through Ellis Island and how badly people wanted to come. I have to know more. I must know more.'"

"I guess what I'm saying, readers, is that today, you read bits of information. But it doesn't have to be just bits. You'll want to keep learning. Work with other club members, with family members, and on your own. Get yourself to libraries, museums, and the Internet. Take charge. Read more on a topic, and as you do so, let the new information spark new thinking."

Finding Themes Through Different Texts

hink of a baby, holding her bare toes and belly-laughing when your face reappears in a game of Peekaboo. She'd thought you were gone for good, but lo and behold—you're back! To the baby, it's astonishing that your face reappears. She has yet to learn that objects persist even when they're out of sight.

The road from literal to abstract thinking is long. Research is clear that reading can speed up this journey. What is a book, after all, but an invitation to step into a world that is an abstraction. Not long ago, children were babies, playing Peekaboo, astonished that the out-of-sight face didn't cease to exist, but instead remained and returned. Now these young readers seat themselves beneath a barn door as a spider spins a web to save a pig's life, or they climb aboard a yellow school bus, anxiously watching a thin boy with a rash on his legs getting beaten up.

It's an accomplishment that a youngster can work with language to create the abstraction of a story. Then, to top this off, readers are taught that within books, there is more there than meets the eye. The spider didn't just save the pig. She got something in return—something we can't literally see and is never even explicitly named, but we can feel and sense. It is no small achievement for readers to come to realize that the stories they read are about ideas. Conversations can now center not only on the spiders and bus rides and ravaged coyotes but also on the abstract themes that underlie the stories in children's books—on ideas pertaining to war, friendship, homesickness, and loss. As readers talk across texts, they talk across experiences of loss or of friendship. They reach for words to distinguish one experience of loss from another. They consider consequences of one loss and another. They elaborate not just about objects and events and people but also about concepts—about identity, freedom, personal choice, sacrifice, home, and journeys. They sit and watch not only a spider, at work at her web, but sojourners, coming to America in different times, dif-

GETTING READY

- You'll be working with a big idea generated by one of your book clubs, ideally involving a story that is familiar to your students and an idea that is likely to ring true in other stories.

- Be ready to discuss the "Making Our Way Through Historical Fiction" chart during the link.

- Although your children will be talking with their club mates in the meeting, as usual, they'll also be turning to talk with members of a different club. If you think your students need some help negotiating this process, then you may want to practice this before the minilesson begins so the transition is smooth.

- You've finished *Number the Stars*. We strongly recommend you also read *Freedom Summer*, a text that is beloved in most of the classrooms we know well and is central to the minilesson about allusion that comes in the next session.

ferent ways, and for different reasons, and freedom fighters across different eras and different worlds. All of this helps readers progress on the continuum from literal to abstract thinking.

In a reading and writing community, children become at home in the world of ideas. Whereas we've encouraged children to give themselves over to the story and to allow themselves to be swept off their feet by a story, now we've reached out a hand to halt them for just a bit, asking them to look at the terrain that they've traveled in their reading, to note the common patterns, to see similarities and differences. At first glance, kids have noted the obvious—that all

> *As readers talk across texts,*
> *they talk across experiences*
> *of loss or of friendship.*

books about the Holocaust mention Nazi soldiers and the shutting down of Jewish shops, for example, or that all books about civil rights refer to Martin Luther King's "I Have a Dream" speech. In this minilesson we'll challenge readers to note deeper patterns, moving them beyond noting *historical* connections across books to noting *thematic* connections. And so once again, talk now turns from literal to abstract.

Although this unit aims to support interpretation, when interpreting literature, readers do not wash our hands of the grit of the story. Ideas matter, but the ideas come carrying the sand from the roads that Nory walked along in Ireland. Abstract ideas alone won't make anyone sob great, heaving sobs. And so the unit began by inviting readers to step into the character's skin, to live within another world. It is when *we, the readers*, shiver as a Nazi hound sniffs at the basket

we're carrying or when *we* watch a beloved shopkeeper being stomped by a shiny black boot that we can begin to realize, "That could be me," and we think, "What would I have done?" It is from the gut-wrenching agony of living in the other world that we recognize that this story is a call to courage.

The children are good at this by now. As they live and breathe inside of stories, they are becoming adept at constructing ideas. They're ready to realize that an idea that is true in one book may also hold true in another and that an idea that was embedded in another person's life is also relevant to today. Universal themes are not actually universal; that is, every theme won't be in every book. But a theme is an idea that is true in many places, in the stories we read and the lives we live.

As children begin to recognize themes, they're also ready to conceptualize the notion of text sets. So far, we've organized text sets for them. Sure, they've added in, finding a book here or there that they pursue in independent reading or bring to their club. But in general, we made the basket of books for World War II and for westward expansion, and we've constructed those text sets according to a historical era. Today's session invites children to organize books by theme rather than by era.

Who knows? They might put *Roll of Thunder, Hear My Cry, Number the Stars,* and *Witness* together, around a theme of girls learning about violence and learning to be brave. They might put *Skylark* and *Out of the Dust* with other stories that show man struggling with the destructive power of nature.

Just as the nonfiction session beckoned you to extend the unit, this session, too, can't help but stir you with a sense of "What if . . . ?" What if there's more time, and children can read across books organized by theme? But text sets can be a metaphor. Readers don't really have to put books in baskets to enjoy finding ways in which books go together. And in the end, the most important connections will be between the stories in books and those in real life.

MINILESSON

Finding Themes Through Different Texts

CONNECTION

Explain that as readers get opportunities to talk about books, we are able to layer our thinking about events with thinking about ideas.

"Readers, this whole year long, we've had grand conversations about books, and one of the things that has happened over and over is that those conversations have helped us to think in ways that are more layered. We think about people and places and events in a story, about things like 'Rob's mom is dead.' But we also think about ideas like 'Sometimes when people are really sad, we hold our feelings inside us, like a bulging suitcase.' Do you see that this involves layers of thinking? On the one hand, we think and talk about events like 'Annemarie ripped the star necklace off Ellen and then Annemarie held that necklace herself,' and on the other hand, we add another layer, and that is a layer of ideas. 'Annemarie was willing to take that risk because she knows friend take care of each other.'"

Name your teaching point. Specifically, teach your children that readers who think deeply about stories come to realize that some ideas are true in more than one story.

"And so this is what I want to teach you today. It is important when we read to think about people, places, events—and also about ideas. When you have thought about an idea in one story, sometimes that thinking helps you find ideas in another story."

COACHING TIPS

You definitely do not want to suggest that thinking about ideas is superior to thinking about people and plot. In good literature, the plot is never something one discards, leaving just some elevated, abstract idea! All of us read great stories for what happens and the people to whom things happen. And all of us gather with others to talk about stories, and much of our talk is about the evolving plotline. We spend most of our time envisioning, predicting, and empathizing. So just because this lesson shines a spotlight on the fact that readers also think about ideas and themes, you definitely do not want to create some feeling that one way of thinking is higher than another. What is higher, or more sophisticated, is thinking that is layered, not thinking that is abstract.

David Rock, author of Quiet Leadership, *spoke to all the staff developers at the Teachers College Reading and Writing Project. He let us know that brain research has shown that when people solve a problem, when we come to an aha of our own, the brain releases endorphins that produce a little rush. Kids need to have their own epiphanies. So the session doesn't front-load the fact that a good theme pertains to tons of books and to our lives as well. Instead, the minilesson tries to bring kids along so they get the rush of discovering. "Hey, the idea I had about this book, it goes with that book, too! and wait—it applies to my life as well!" That aha produces a true rush, so the teaching point hints at this without spelling it out.*

TEACHING AND ACTIVE INVOLVEMENT

Ask each club to agree upon a big idea that their book represents, working to say that idea in just a sentence or two. Do some quiet engineering so children word their ideas in ways that will pertain across books.

"Readers, I know you've been doing lots of idea work with your clubs, really grappling with what your stories seem to really, really be about. I expect you've got a bunch of ideas going about each of your books—a bunch of those pink Post-its. I need you and your club to take a quick second to do that same work we have done repeatedly, when you brought your pink Post-its together and came up with one big idea for your book. Turn and talk with your club, and consolidate all the ideas you've got going into one idea, for now, that you all care about. Think of it as one snowball. I know you have more than one, but for now, just make one idea."

The members of each club pulled together and consolidated one idea, out of all the ideas they had been developing over the last few days. Listening, I could tell they were getting somewhat long-winded about their ideas, which wasn't going to work well into my plans for the minilesson, so I intervened. "Remember, think of this idea as a snowball. So if your idea has got all these pieces hanging onto it, try to pack it into a smaller container, into a smaller snowball. Try to be able to say the idea your book is giving you in a sentence or two. I'll show you why in a moment.

"I'm going to ask the Dust Bowl Club to start off by saying the interpretation that they've developed as they read *Out of the Dust*. They're going to sort of lob their idea over our heads, into the air. Now here is the thing. It *could be* that their idea fits into one of your books as well. If it does, then stretch your hands up into the sky and pull that idea down to your book." Here I paused, demonstrating how I look up to see this "idea" just over my head, and then reach up and firmly pull it toward my chest. "And then, if the idea fits your club's book, your club (and only that club) will have a minute to say how the idea fits your book.

"Everyone, remember, if the Dust Bowl idea applies to your book in some way, reach up and pull this idea down and then begin talking about it with your club." I got into ready position, hands stretched wide and flexed in anticipation, as if I might just be catching a snowball. When the students also looked ready, I nodded to the Dust Bowl Club. (While they had been talking before this part of the minilesson, I'd made sure that they had a clear interpretation and were ready to share it with the class.)"

Teachers, as children agree upon ideas, you will want to listen for a club or two who have an idea that you know will turn out to apply to many other books as well as their own. You'll then use that idea in the minilesson. Most themes actually are broadly applicable, so this will not be difficult, but you may need to help clubs word their ideas in more concise and abstract ways. Instead of saying, "This is a story about Annemarie learning she could be brave when she had to be," you'll want to help clubs word their ideas more like this: "People can be braver than they realize when the situation requires it." You may literally reword ideas, because explaining how to do this would be cumbersome and you won't have much time. Substituting the word people *for the specific name of a character will help. You may not have time to teach kids to do this themselves right now, but eventually give them that pointer.*

Bear in mind, teachers, that I already know that almost any idea will pertain to almost every book. But remember, I want the kids to have the rush that comes from discovery. I'm fully expecting that there will be lots of hands reaching into the air, and a giddy rush from seeing that "Yes, yes, that idea goes with our book!" And then, from across the room, "Ours, too. It goes with ours, too." But I want to let the class come to this discovery together, and to let the kids feel as if they are teaching me. You may find this is too coy, in which case, of course, alter the teaching to fit your own style. But if you're just nervous that it won't work," trust that we've tried this often and it's incurably exciting.

Sarah made her hands look as if she held a snowball, or bird, and gestured as if to send it flying, and said, "We're thinking that our book is about how people need to find your home, the place where you belong.

"Okay, freeze everyone," I called. "Now think, could that idea be huge in one or more than one of your books as well? If it fits any one of your books, grab the idea and swoop it to the center of your club's conversation. Ready? Okay, Sarah, throw the idea out again and this time, if it fits your book, grab it and begin talking it over in your club." Sarah repeated the idea.

Suddenly, across the meeting area, hands reached up, as one child and another scooped the idea that the *Out of the Dust* group had lobbed into the air and convened a conversation around it.

When the idea had first been thrown out, the Pioneers looked at each other in amazement. They were delighted. This wasn't their idea, but it sure fit their books! After they reached up and scooped it down, they started talking a mile a minute. "It's just like Sarah!" Lily exclaimed! "Sarah was trying to feel the prairie was her home. And the kids were trying to help her feel like she belonged with their family."

"Yeah," Kobe added. "Like in the last one, before *Caleb's Story*, um. . . .

"*Skylark*," Brianna reminded him.

"Yeah, *Skylark*," Kobe continued, "Caleb writes her name in the dirt. He wants her to know it's her home. The prairie is her home. And he was all worried she wouldn't stay. But then, at the end, Sarah writes *her* name in the dirt. Like she's saying it is her home now."

Meanwhile, of course, the American Dreamers had also grabbed at the idea. "It goes with *Letters from Rifka* and *Maggie's Door*," they said. "Sean and Nora are on *their* way to a new home, and so is Rifka. They're all working so hard to get to new places." Izzy paused, thinking it over.

"Well, it's like they *want* to belong to a new place," Emma said, trying to build on Izzy's idea, "but they don't really belong anywhere yet, because they're on this giant trip, or journey. But they really want to belong, or be home, in America."

"Everyone, please look up here. I'm amazed, aren't you? This is an interpretation that the Dust Bowl Club developed specifically for their book *Out of the Dust*. But we lucked out and it went with almost every one of your books!

John Gardner has said that all stories are really a variation of "man's journey toward home." I had already heard this quote from Gardner and had chosen the Dust Bowl theme specifically because I knew it would resonate for many of the clubs. I'd also helped the club word it in this consolidated way so that the idea would be especially universal. There's often a bit of behind the scenes preparation for discovery teaching!

Almost any book yields themes that are broadly applicable. Freedom Summer, for instance, is about, among other things, children learning that adults can be cruel to each other. So is Number the Stars. Both books are also about how individuals can stand up for what is right and protect each other's interests. And they are both also about love being a stronger power than hate.

Don't let too much time lapse before moving to a second theme.

I'm acting as if it was just sheer luck that made the first theme universally applicable, although I know that is not so.

"Let's try another idea. Kadija, when we all look like we are ready to catch another idea, will you lob one of the big ideas of the Allies just over your head? If the idea seems to fit someone's book, that club can grab it!" I got myself in position to "catch" another big idea. Kadija threw out the idea, "When times are hard, people find ways to survive and to keep up their strength." Again, club members scooped up that idea and found, with giddy excitement, that it applied to their books.

"This is amazing," I said. "Let's try some of the ideas from earlier in the year—like, let me lob an idea from *The Tiger Rising*: Sometimes, when people experience loss, they can't talk about it. They almost wall that pain up. Does that pertain to any of your books?"

Again, the room was filled with a buzz—most notably, talk that Annemarie's family hadn't been able to speak of Lise since her death. And the club reading *Out of the Dust* agreed that Billie Jo's dad couldn't talk to her about *her* mom's death either.

Implicit in this is the idea that one book holds many themes. That's true. Great literature is full of themes. It is also true that no one theme is present in every book, so a theme that is lobbed into the air will not pertain to every book. "Universally true" is a generalization, meaning that it holds true in many places.

Talk to the class, suggesting this is no coincidence. The ideas apply across books because these are ideas from real life.

"Readers, what do we make of this? We could say it's a huge coincidence. But I do not think that is the truth of it. And I don't think the authors copied each other's ideas. I think the truth is that when we really uncover the deep things that a story is really about, we'll find our big idea isn't confined to just that one book. And the reason for this is that the authors just scooped their idea—as you did—only they scooped it out of *real life*. When you find a big idea—one that is repeated in lots of books by lots of different authors across lots of time periods—here's the big thing: You'll find it repeated in real life. When an idea applies across lots of books and applies also to real life, some people call it a *universal* idea or a *theme*. This means an idea that could be true almost any place in the universe!"

There are instances like this throughout the series where you may decide to open a topic up for class discussion rather than telling children your idea. You'll make the decision in each particular instance.

LINK

Encourage your readers to use themes as a lens to look across books, and to be open to conversations with other clubs.

"So, readers, the truth is that our ideas and interpretations overlap in ways that fit into many books—and into other texts like poems, songs, and even movies. Once you open your mind to the possibility that the idea you form as you read one text doesn't just fit into that one text, that it fits into many other texts as well, this also means that when you want to grow ideas about a text, you can be on the lookout for ideas that

Teachers, it is helpful for you to realize that when most of us read and find themes within a book, some of what really goes on is that we already know a lot of themes that exist in the world and that are commonly found in books So to some extent, we are attaching those themes that already exist to this particular text. Sharing this information means letting kids in on the tricks of the trade.

already exist in the world that you can attach to your book. And this means that when you read whatever book you are reading right now, you won't just be filing nonfiction articles in between the pages. Here's a cool thing: You'll be filing other books between your pages. You'll read along and say, "Ah, here they are, silent in the face of a terrible loss, like in the *The Tiger Rising*, and *Baby*, too.

"As you read today, will you be thinking about themes—about the universal ideas that seem to be true across some of your books, and by that I mean books you've read across this whole year? You may spend a good deal of your time getting out books you read earlier and looking across them and across the books your club has read, too, and asking, 'Have I read a couple books that are really about the same idea? How do the messages in these books compare, one with another?' In your club meetings, you'll have a lot to talk about.

"This seems like an important thing to add to our chart as something readers do at the end of a historical fiction book."

Making Our Way Through Historical Fiction

- *Collect setting details. What kind of place is this? What does it feel like?*
- *Is trouble brewing? How is it changing? What feels important?*
- *Collect vital data about characters. Traits? Pressures on them? Problems they face? What drives them?*
- *What new understanding and historical information do you have?*
- *What is the sequence of events in the story, including jumps in time?*
- *Notice what's changing in the book. How are the characters' problems escalating? Has the setting or the mood shifted?*
- *Think about how characters are reacting differently to big events and what we can learn from this.*
- *Pause at passages that seem written in bold and ask, "What is significant here?" and "How does it fit with what the whole story is really about?"*
- *Think about big ideas and the little details that hold those ideas.*
- *As you read on, carry your theory with you, but be open to new information that might change your theory. Expect to be surprised!*
- *Look back over the terrain of the text, and ask, "What's this story really about?" We take into consideration the beginning, middle, and end of the story.*
- *See one book as an invitation to do further reading, letting the new information you're learning spark new thinking.*
- *Think between this book and others you have read earlier, asking, "How are these similar? How are they different?"*
- *Notice universal themes and ideas across books. Ask, "Does the big idea in this book fit with another book I know well? With the world at large?"*

CONFERRING AND SMALL-GROUP WORK

Support Readers in Moving from Literal to Abstract Thinking

Today your readers may move directly into clubs or they may read silently for a while. Either way, the mid-workshop teaching point interjects into that work and does not launch clubs.

MID-WORKSHOP TEACHING POINT

Readers Look for Ideas Shared across Books to See More

"Readers, can I stop you for a minute?" I waited until all eyes were on me. "You know how we just talked about finding themes that are common across several books? A few minutes ago, Kobe came up to me and pointed out that farming is mentioned a lot in two of the books he's reading. He was wondering if maybe farming might be an idea that applies to both books.

"Listening to Kobe's question made me realize one thing I want to caution all of you about. Finding any ol' similarity between two books doesn't necessarily mean that the two books share a common theme. For example, I could say 'There's a kitten in *this* book.' (I held up Lowry's *Number the Stars*.) And I might say, 'Hey, there's a kitten in *this* book, too!' (With my other hand, I held up Polacco's *The Butterfly*.) Readers, the fact that both books mention a kitten may or may not mean anything. There's a pig in *Charlotte's Web* and pigs in *Animal Farm*, but the pigs in both books are as different as can be. We can hardly say, for example, that the tiger in *The Tiger Rising* makes that book similar in theme to *The Lion King*. The question we'd need to ask ourselves is, in Kobe's case, 'Does farming in this book

stand for the same thing as farming in this *other* book?'

"To figure out whether a literal similarity between books also suggests a thematic similarity, we'd have to first ask ourselves, 'Does the physical thing that is similar in the two books have something to do with a big idea that is similar across the two books?' Here (I held up Polacco's *The Butterfly*), Pinouff, the kitten that Monique gave to Sevrine, was a small, cuddly thing, a source of comfort to a little girl during a hard time. (I then held up *Number the Stars*.) What about Kirsti's kitten? Did this kitten do the same for Kirsti that it did for Sevrine? Did it provide her with comfort during a hard time? Hmm, you could say it did. She had no one really to play with, no pink cupcakes in her world. Kirsti must have found some relief in this new kitten she found. It's possible that the literal similarity represents an abstract idea that is similar across the books, and that would be worth developing. So return to your readers, your thinking, your connecting."

Conferring and Small-Group Work

There are some typical profiles of readers in our classes. Common among these are readers who love to have big ideas, but they don't love to back them up with real details from the text. Often these thinkers slip into cliché. "It's like all that glitters isn't gold," they'll say. Or "A bird in the hand is worth two in the bush." At the other end of the spectrum are the kids who

have Post-its on every page, and their notes are full of details. They observe everything but construct little from these observations. Interestingly, in both cases, it is helpful to teach into the relationship between details and big ideas. In this conference, you'll see some moves you can make to help very literal readers begin to make more meaning around details that they notice are repeated in more than one book.

Teaching Readers to Move from Noticing Details to Discerning Their Significance

As I approached the Allies, I saw that they had *Number the Stars* and *The Butterfly* spread open side by side. When I asked them what they were working on, Kadija informed me that my discussion of the kittens in the two books had gotten them thinking about other similarities between the books. Earlier on, our class had discovered that these two books were alike; we'd noticed they both show two girls, one Jewish, one Christian, who become friends during the war, and that in each story the Christian girl's family hides the Jewish girl, but we hadn't pushed beyond these fairly obvious comparisons. Knowing that the books were rife with symbolism and likenesses, I was pleased to see this effort and aware of the possibilities.

The club had made a T-chart with *Number the Stars* on the left and *The Butterfly* on the right. I peered at it and saw this: [Fig. XVII-1]

Number the Stars	The Butterfly
- Annemarie took Ellen's Star of David necklace	Sevrine gave her Star of David necklace to Monique
- The girls notice the soldiers tall boots	Monique calls the soldiers Tall Boots
- They took Mrs. Hirsh who owned a button shop	They took Monseur Marks who owned a sweet shop

Figure XVII-1

Of course, the club could have gone on with this chart, noting other literal similarities—that there was a local resistance movement against Nazi occupation in both books, that Jewish families were protected by Christian neighbors in both, that soldiers in each book displayed needless cruelty through small actions. I wanted to nudge the club away from adding endlessly to this chart of *literal* similarities, however, and to see how far they were in their ability to note *thematic* similarities between the two books.

"Great work! What a sensible graphic organizer you've got going. Filling out a T-chart is such an efficient way of comparing details in books. I have a question, though. Are you aiming to find things that are *literally* similar (like they each have a kitten in them) or things that are *thematically* similar (like in both books, people find ways to get comfort in hard times)?"

My question met with a minute of silence as the club members thought about this. My suspicion was that this group hadn't really pondered this distinction before launching into their discussion. "Theme," Brandon finally piped up, noting his club members' hesitation. I knew I had to research further. Brandon's confident assertion might be nothing more than a vague awareness that this must be the answer I'd been wanting. After all, I'd been harping on themes lately. "Show me what you mean," I prodded. I listened as Brandon, aided by Danny and Kadija, walked me through a surface-level list of similarities between the two books as outlined on their chart.

"May I teach you one thing to help you take your next step?" I asked, after hearing what they'd done so far. Waiting for the club to nod assent, I said, "You've walked me through the similarities between the books. Now, against each of these, you might write out what each similarity really stands for. Look at the first one." I pointed to where the club had written out their first entry.

"You might ask yourselves, 'What did this necklace mean to each Jewish girl? What did it mean for her non-Jewish friend? Why did the necklace change hands?' Discuss these a while to see what ideas—or themes—you might uncover that could be true in both books."

I took notes as the club pondered and debated the significance of the Star of David necklace among themselves. Eventually, Brandon said, "In both books, the non-Jewish friend took a really big risk. And in both, she knew she was protecting something that meant a lot to her friend. Like, it was like she was protecting her friend's religion." Intervening before the club conversation spiraled away from this comment, I asked, "Do you all agree with what Brandon just said? Brandon could you repeat your comment?" As he did, Kadija nodded vigorously. She definitely agreed. Looking at the rest of the club, I elicited their agreement.

"Let me name what you just did. You didn't just note the common things that *happened* in each story. (I pointed at the T-chart.) You took something that happened in each of these books and you discussed what this might *mean*. And you realized that in each book, it means much the same thing. Let's jot this deeper meaning that was common to the two books." Drawing an arrow leading out of the first entry, I neatly printed Brandon's words as he repeated them for my benefit.

"So, you started out with an on-the-surface, or literal, similarity. (I pointed at the chart.) And from this, you developed a *thematic* similarity. (I gestured to where we'd written out Brandon's words. *[Fig. XVII-2]*) You did this by looking at what *happens* (I pointed to the chart again,) and talking about what this happening might actually *mean*. (I again pointed to Brandon's sentence.) That is a great way to dig out the thematic connections between our books, a great way to see how two books might really be saying the same thing even though the characters and setting and details of what happens might be totally different."

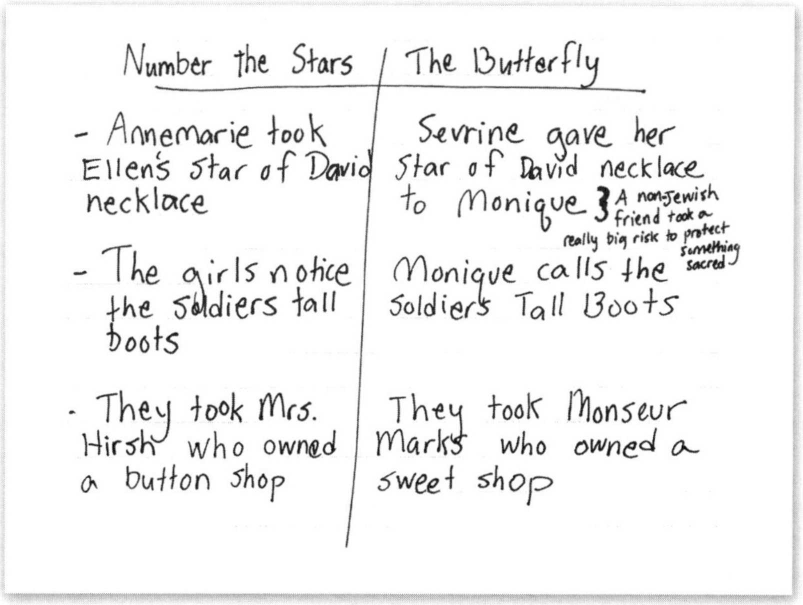

Number the Stars	The Butterfly
- Annemarie took Ellen's star of David necklace	Sevrine gave her star of David necklace to Monique ⟩ A nonjewish friend took a really big risk to protect something sacred
- The girls notice the soldiers tall boots	Monique calls the soldiers tall boots
- They took Mrs. Hirsh who owned a button shop	They took Monseur Marks who owned a sweet shop

Figure XVII-2

Readers Combine and Recombine Books, Learning About Themes

Orchestrate a share in which one club member creates a museum out of the club's books, and others cycle through, hearing about those books.

"Readers, pretty soon our unit is going to be over, and you'll need to figure out whether you are going to continue to read historical fiction, and if so, what you'll be interested in. So I've been thinking that you might want to learn about some of the eras that others have been reading, and some of the books they've read. So for our share today, let's have one person from each club stay in your club's meeting place with all your club books out in front of you. Everyone else will go from one meeting place to another, and in each place, you'll hear a bit about the era and the books. You won't have long to do this, so just get the highlights."

Suggest children consider ways to create text sets of books that go together by theme.

Children swarmed the room, looking altogether as if this was a speed-dating event! After a bit, I intervened. "Readers, I just had a thought. It might be that when you go on into your life, you could decide to put books together into baskets of books that go together by theme, not by historical era. Would you mind getting with some kids from clubs other than your own, and in the next five minutes, see if you and these other readers can come up with a basket of books that go together. Like, one basket could be 'man's search for home,' and another basket could be 'War makes kids grow up fast.' This will be up to you. Get started, and I'll distribute baskets so we can do this for real, and you can make labels for the themes that bring books together."

Both Brianna and Sam jotted their thoughts about books with shared themes. *[Figs. XVII-3 and XVII-4]*

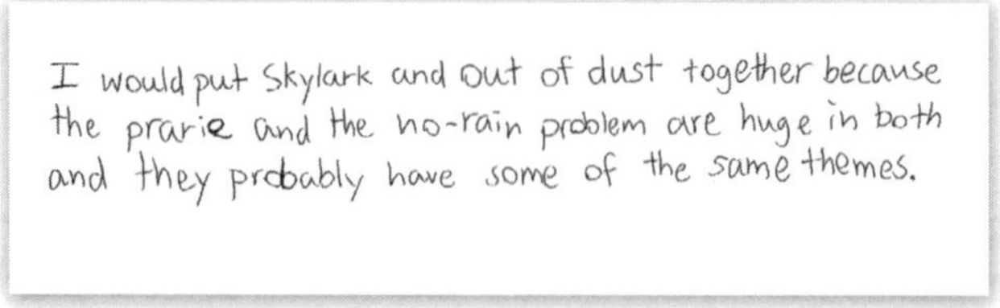

> I would put Skylark and Out of dust together because the prarie and the no-rain problem are huge in both and they probably have some of the same themes.

Figure XVII-3
Brianna creates a theme-based text set.

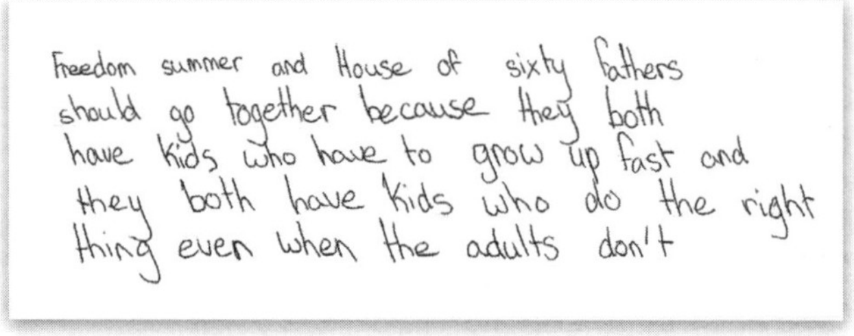

> Freedom summer and House of sixty fathers should go together because they both have kids who have to grow up fast and they both have kids who do the right thing even when the adults don't

Figure XVII-4
Sam puts two books together, starting a thematic text set.

"Readers, it is time to stop. I'm glad we have new baskets, new text sets. But readers, I also want to be sure you know that text sets don't have to be real baskets of books that sit in a classroom. They can be collections of books that in our mind we see as beginning to go together. They don't have to be just books, either. They can include nonfiction articles and movies. In your mind and in your conversations, you can think of texts as going together, and just as we've gathered nonfiction facts and stuffed them into our books, we can think of all these books as sort of being pieced together."

Conveying Complex Ideas Artfully

he end of this unit is fast approaching. I hope this is not the end of your units of study. I hope you've progressed quickly enough through them that summer is not right around the bend for you. I hope there is time in your year still for you and your children to turn toward units in *Constructing Curriculum*. You'll find those units are scaffolded more lightly that the ones we've experienced together. Those units will require you and your colleagues to fill in more of the gaps—and that's as it should be. I've tried to scaffold your teaching, and I hope that the result, like a good pair of training wheels, has let you feel the wind in your hair and the sun on your back. But everyone knows that a scaffold is only a scaffold if it is gradually removed, allowing work to continue without the same amount of support. And so I hope you find a unit in the *Constructing Curriculum* book that feels just right for you and for your kids. For older students, perhaps it will be the fantasy unit next; for younger, perhaps mystery or humor. Either way, as you and your colleagues progress from here to a unit that you develop together, I'm pretty sure that you'll think back on the units of study that we've now

taught together, and you'll use our shared vocabulary to think about the new work that you'll be doing.

Perhaps you'll say to each other, "We need one of those 'Making Our Way Through Historical Fiction' charts." Perhaps you'll say, "We'll probably want to start with our own *Exodus*." Maybe you'll ask, "What text will be our *Number the Stars*?" You'll be talking in code with each other, and this will be powerful because the terms you use will come loaded with rich memories and associations, with tones and textures of life within previous units. It's totally different to say, "We need to find our *Number the Stars*" than to say, "We need to find a touchstone text for this unit" because when you say the first, you are saying, "We need the felt sense we experienced with *Number the Stars*. We need the tone, the tenor, the tears, the turning points of that book." When you think about supporting your children as they read fantasy, with so many characters each with weird and wonderful names and with their own distinctive traits, you'll probably say to each other, "Remember how the unit on historical fiction suggested kids could make two parallel timelines—one of the unfolding historical events and one

GETTING READY

- Before this session, you'll want to have read aloud and had class discussions about *Freedom Summer*, the historical fiction picture book that has been one of the touchstone texts in our classrooms for years. If your children don't know this book, you'll want to alter the teaching section of the minilesson so you allude to books that they do know.

- Be prepared to display the "Making Our Way Through Historical Fiction" chart during the link.

of the protagonist's progression of experiences? Maybe we need our own version of those timelines." And soon you'll invent a graphic organizer—maps, character trees, something—that you and your colleagues will refer to as "our timeline."

As you embark on this new work together, drawing on all the prior experiences we've shared together, you'll be thinking in allusion, and that's the subject of today's minilesson. My colleagues and I have had some trouble writing this prelude. It's the very last page of the book that is being writ-

> *A scaffold is only a scaffold if it is gradually removed, allowing work to continue without the same amount of support.*

ten. "Why *did* we decide to teach allusions, so close to the culmination of all the units?" Mary and I asked each other. "Was this just one last little tip we could shoehorn into the unit before it was torn from our hands and raced to the printing press?" I've mulled over that question, waiting for this prelude to surface within me, holding our publisher, Heinemann, at bay for one last day, taking one last chance to think, "Why *did* we teach this, anyhow?"

I have my answer. We're teaching allusion because really, this is a metaphor for how all of us live and learn. I'm hoping that the books that children have read aren't just "been there, done that" experiences but that they become part of each child. How I've loved Katherine Paterson's beautiful description of writing and of reading (1981).

Writing is something like a seed that grows in the dark, or a grain of sand that keeps rubbing against your vitals until you find you are building a coating around it. The growth of a book takes time. I talk, I look, I listen, I hate, I fear, I love, I weep, and somehow all of my life gets wrapped around the grain. The process is the same when we read. You take that grain of sand and keep rubbing it against your vitals until you find you are building a coating around it. The reading of a book takes time . . . I read, I talk, I look, I listen, I hate, I love, I weep and somehow all of my life gets wrapped around the grain of sand. (p. 26)

Maybe Katherine is describing not just how a person writes and reads but how each one of us lives. Perhaps we human beings grow deeper, with each experience laminating itself onto us, becoming part of what we carry as we go forward in life.

Surely, it is true that all of us see upcoming books and new books through the lens of those that we have already read. Watch the videotapes of book clubs in action on the fourth section of the DVD, and you'll hear the children alluding to old books as if they are friends. In one of the videos on the DVD, some children are talking about *Bud, Not Buddy*, thinking about how Bud is distrustful of people and emotionally closed. If you watch this DVD, you may find yourself gasping at the leaps of insight these children take. They discuss symbolism and make allusions with the familiarity and ease of much older readers. As they discuss Bud's "physical and mental" suitcase, they note that the suitcase represents Bud himself—everything he keeps to himself—and, too, acts as a reminder of the journey he has survived. After a few minutes of discussion, one boy in the club practically jumps out of his chair as he alludes to Rob's suitcase in *The Tiger Rising*. "Remember how Rob kept all the things to himself?" he says, and we can see the light

bulb in his head as he alludes to the earlier text and realizes that the suitcases in both books perhaps are representative of something similar.

When I've shown those videos to teachers across the country and to participants at our summer institutes, I know they are thinking, "Who *are* those kids?" They ask, "What grade is this?" but I know they are partly asking, "Is this a private school? Is this a gifted class?" I understand the question. I'm floored, too, by the kids' leaps of insight. I don't bother to explain that, no, this is a New York City classroom, that it isn't a special class or special kids, because of course, in a way, the kids *are* gifted—gifted with a teacher who wears her love of reading on her shoulder, who teaches with power and passion.

Your kids will also astonish you. Time and again, you'll sit alongside their conversation, and you'll gasp at their insights. You'll get goose bumps over their analogies, their literary language, and their passion and power. You'll want to call the video people in to your classroom. "You won't believe this," you'll say, and the rest of us—we'll watch your kids, and we'll ask, "Who are these kids?"

Powerful teaching leaves a lasting legacy. Kids are different because of your teaching. They approach tomorrow's books, seeing them through the lens of yesterday's books. More, they approach tomorrow's reading, carrying with them the lens of all yesterday's lessons, yesterday's discoveries, yesterday's stories. Those charts in your classroom—by now, hopefully your children will have picked through them, discarding the parts that no longer matter and taking the parts that do matter into their being. Let yourself be speechless with awe at what children can do when they've been gifted with the miracle of powerful teaching.

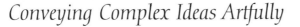

Conveying Complex Ideas Artfully

CONNECTION

Provide examples of literary allusions that your children will easily recognize, setting children up to notice what you're doing.

"Readers, we've been realizing that the boundaries between one story and another aren't as firm as they might seem. And you know, the truth is that often while I'm reading, something in my book will remind me of something from another book that I've read. Sometimes this is a theme, like we talked about yesterday, but sometimes it's a kitten, or a sunset. Sometimes it's an object or an emotion or a specific episode that gives me this huge rush that comes from the gates opening and another story rushing in. Reading *Number the Stars* with you was no different. There were points in Annemarie's story that made me think about *other* stories I know. Let me read from my jottings. Listen and see if you can tell which other stories I'm talking about."

I opened my copy of *Number the Stars* and unpeeled a Post-it from within its pages to read aloud. On it, I'd written this idea: "For three years since her death, Mama and Papa hadn't said Lise's name. However, after the night when they narrowly escaped from the Germans finding out Ellen's identity, Mama and Papa's *suitcase opened*—they mentioned Lise for the first time."

I looked up meaningfully at the mention of a suitcase. "Readers, give me a thumbs up if you know the other text I've connected to here."

"Readers, I know you figured this out in a second, right? Lise's parents reminded me of Rob in *The Tiger Rising*, who kept his pain locked up in a suitcase and couldn't speak his mom's name after her death. Both books show that it isn't easy to talk about someone whose death was premature and unexpected.

COACHING TIPS

I merely want students to recognize the text to which I'm alluding. That is enough at this stage. I'm not looking for a longer or deeper intertextual discussion just yet. But I've deliberately made a connection that will, I hope, feel like the gates have opened for them, and the other text has rushed in.

"Listen to my next jotting and see if you can figure out the text I'm alluding to now."

Picking out a second Post-it from within my book, I read aloud, "Annemarie's Mrs. Hirsch was Monique's Monsieur Marks—what kind of world was it where selling buttons or candies amounted to a crime?"

Again, after allowing students no more than ten seconds—enough time for them to recognize that I'm comparing the arrests of Jewish shopkeepers in *Number the Stars* and Polacco's *The Butterfly*—I intervened. "Readers, I heard you guess that one, too—you're right, Mrs. Hirsch reminded me of Monsieur Marks in *The Butterfly*, shopkeepers arrested just for being Jewish.

"See if you can pick out the allusion in yet another jotting I made." Lifting another Post-it out of my copy of *Number the Stars*, I read aloud, "With the kind of hands that crushed butterflies, the Nazi soldier tore Lise's baby photo in half and dropped its pieces to the floor." Looking up I added, "Hands that crushed butterflies. Turn and tell your partner what text you think I might be alluding to."

I waited for about five seconds this time, enough for kids to make the mental connection that a Nazi soldier in *The Butterfly* had crushed a butterfly to death—showing the same needless cruelty that the soldier in *Number the Stars* revealed when he tore Lise's baby photo and ground the pieces under his heel.

"Oh my gosh, Readers, you are amazing at picking out the allusions I've made in my Post-its! An allusion is a reference that creates a link to a well-known story. When we make this kind of reference, we call to mind the feelings and thoughts associated with part of a story we all know. Sometimes an allusion can just be a few words, and everyone will know what is meant. If one of you was trying to do something elaborate to fool me, I might comment, 'Are you trying to pull off Great-aunt Birte's funeral?' and you'd know what I'm talking about. If I knew someone to be a bully, I might just say, 'There goes a Threemonger,' or if I saw someone I didn't trust, I might just whisper to you, 'He's a Beauchamp all right,' and you'd get what I mean. That's because in this reading community, we know the same stories."

Teachers, note the casual way in which I've slipped the word alluding into my talk. It isn't that we expect students to know what the word means yet. They probably don't. But since we have them successfully engaged in the actual task of identifying allusions, we can use the precise word to name their process. Later in this minilesson we'll bolster this with a more direct explanation of what an allusion is.

Of course, these examples work only where listeners know the allusions well enough to recognize an offhand reference to these texts. In this case, both allusions (Polacco's The Butterfly *and DiCamillo's* The Tiger Rising*) have served as communal mentor texts. Students haven't just read these books; they've engaged in deep conversations about them and can therefore easily guess the source just by hearing the word* suitcase *or* butterfly.

Help your students know that people who share a common background allude to their shared background knowledge all the time

"Readers, our talk, even outside of reading, is full of allusions. In normal conversation we refer to famous people, historical events, or movie details to explain ourselves better. When the horrible bombs went off in the London train stations, newscasters said, 'It's another September 11,' and we all closed our eyes, dreading another incident of sudden violence and chaos. In the school hallway just this morning, I heard some boys say of a friend, 'He's a real LeBron type,' meaning that he's such a great basketball player; LeBron James went straight to the pros at eighteen, skipping all the college teams, he was that good.

"You'll be wondering why I'm talking about allusions all of a sudden. Readers, listen closely. For this whole year, we've been living a reading life to the hilt, doing the sorts of things that real readers do—participating in book clubs, having conversations about our books in which we talk not only about what happens in our story but also about what those happenings might mean. We're exploring the big ideas in our books.

"Sometimes, though, our ideas about our book are so big that it is hard to find the precise words to explain them. Why does the imprint of the Star of David in Annemarie's palm make us feel like catching our breath? What should we make of this kitten that Kirsti has befriended? How does helping the Rosens affect and change the *Johansens*? And what does the big starry sky at night have to do with all this? Sometimes, these big questions from the text have no easy, packaged answer. Sometimes, the text might just evoke a feeling or a mood that we can hardly put in words. And that is totally okay! We don't need to find the one word that will capture a mood or feeling that a text evokes."

Name your teaching point. Specifically, teach your children that when readers have ideas that are too big to easily explain, readers often communicate by making allusions to texts that are well known in their community.

"Today I want to teach you that if your head is so full of ideas, your chest feels like it wells with all this *huge* stuff you have to say, and yet you find yourself sort of sputtering and hemming, you need to know that people who read and who care about books often have things to say for which no ordinary words will do. And the good news is that we can use the same techniques that authors use to say things that are too big for words. One of the things we can do is we can reference a beautiful detail, significant theme, or lasting image—anything really—from a story we all know, and by doing

I expect that in most of our families, talk is full of allusions. One of my family's jokes revolves around my brother Hugh being in such a hurry that he drove off from the gas station while the nozzle was still in his car, spewing gasoline everywhere. So it's common for me to say to him, "I've been so busy. You know, I keep doing things like driving away with the gas nozzle in the car." We have a good laugh at the inside joke. Your children will make allusions with each other, and so if you want them to understand and use literary allusions, you may want to overhear their shared language and say it back to them.

When you're alert to the art of allusion, you'll begin to notice it in speeches, articles, books, songs—everywhere. Within these units, each time that we talk of "scaffolds," we allude to Bruner's scaffolding theory. Each time we mention the zone of proximal development, we allude to Vygotsky's research, and when we talk of readers "responding" to the text, we allude to Rosenblatt's work. Within a community of literacy teachers, these allusions are shared, accepted, and common to the extent that they scarcely merit explanation.

so, we conjure up that whole story, and people who know it say, 'Ah yes, yes. I know what you mean.' That's called making an allusion, and literate people do this all the time."

TEACHING

Retell the story of a time when a student tried again and again to communicate something to you and then resorted to an allusion that all of a sudden made his meaning clear.

"Readers, yesterday after we were talking about themes in our books, Isaac came up to me. He was struggling, the way we all do when we have huge ideas, to find words for his idea, which was something about the book *Freedom Summer* showing that real friendship is not easy. I saw that he had jotted on a Post-it. *[Fig. XVIII-1]*

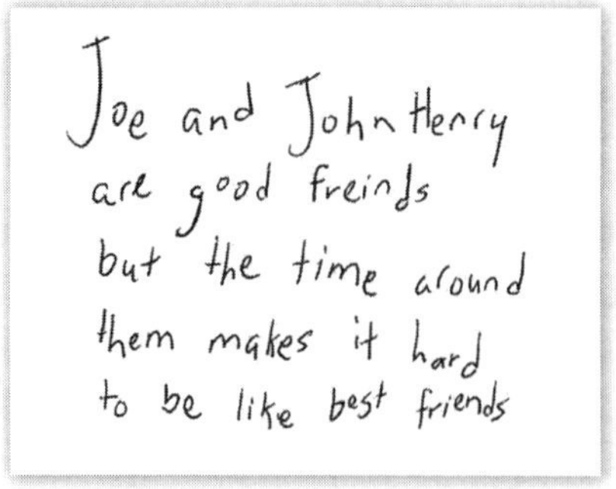

"Here's how our conversation went," I said.

"I asked him, 'Are you trying to say that being best friends is not easy?' Then I pushed, 'Explain to me what you mean, *real* friendship is difficult?'

"Isaac said, 'No, not like that.'

"'Is it that friendship isn't simple?' I asked.

"'Yes and no!' Isaac said. I could tell he was getting frustrated with me.

"'Is it that friendship is complicated?' I asked.

"Readers, by this time, Isaac had sort of stopped answering, and he was looking away from me, kind of like he was giving up on me ever understanding."

"Readers, as you can guess, we were both getting a little frustrated. Then Isaac paused, and thought, and said, '*Real* friendship isn't easy. Like the Johansens' friendship with Ellen's family.' I got it, then.

"Readers, give me a thumbs up if you, too, recognize the allusion Isaac made. Then turn and tell your neighbor what comes to mind when Isaac alludes to the Johansens' friendship with Ellen's family when he wants to say that real friendship isn't easy."

The children turned and began talking. I listened in and overheard Izzy say to Emma, "It's like the kind of friendship where your families are different kinds of families."

In this next part, I recall a conversation I had with a student. Because I'll be showing how we struggled to communicate a big idea, I'm sure, first, to tell the student that I would love to share his process with the class. You could also have the student role-play with you. You'll know your kids, and you'll know if you have a moment to rehearse beforehand.

Figure XVIII-1

I used my voice and hands to mimic our conversation, giving a sense of heightened frustration. I had cleared with Isaac ahead of time that I would be exaggerating the content of our conversation slightly, so that students could see the problem. Isaac was "in" on the lesson and was quietly smiling to the side.

Meanwhile Sarah was telling Jack, "I think that every friendship has a test to see if it is really a *real* friendship."

Step back from the story to explain how the allusion communicated more than ordinary words could convey, using this as a way to talk about allusion.

"Readers, I hear you talking about how *real* friendship can challenge us—that it isn't always easy to fulfill the role of a friend. When I heard Isaac's allusion, I was flooded with images from *Number the Stars*—Annemarie's palm bearing an imprint of the Star of David, Mr. Johansen stepping up to a Nazi soldier, bravely handing him Lise's baby photograph, Annemarie running and tripping to deliver a handkerchief to Uncle Henrik, lying to the soldiers with their ferocious dogs. I was reminded of the *length*s that the Johansens had to go to to protect their friends. And Isaac's allusion made me realize that the same sort of thing is true of *Freedom Summer*, in which a white boy rushes into an ice cream store with a beating heart, lying to the shopkeeper because he can't think of eating that ice cream without his friend. And I understood that real friendship isn't always easy.

"But there's more. In a way, *Number the Stars* and *Freedom Summer* have more than just this in common. That's why Isaac's allusion was so brilliant. In both worlds, it was risky being friends with a person of a certain race or religion, and both books sort of say that *real friendship* doesn't look at the risk factor.

"Isaac's allusion called to mind all these associations between the two books. I knew exactly what he meant. Real friendship isn't always easy. Do you see how, when Isaac made this allusion to the Johansens and the Rosens, he called to mind for us a whole host of emotions and understandings? All of a sudden we understood the kind of friendship he was talking about. His idea, which had been too big for words, was suddenly communicated, through the power of his allusion. They're magical, really, allusions."

Teachers, note that I'm taking greater mileage out of Isaac's allusion than merely using it to teach how powerful thoughts might be effectively communicated. I'm also reinforcing the point of the previous minilesson—that the theme of one book will be echoed in another. Allusions, in this case, might well be a tool for kids to recognize patterns across stories.

ACTIVE INVOLVEMENT

Tell children about a school in which every teacher and child reads books in common, and show how those books give the entire school a shared language, one that can be used on the playground and in the hallways to communicate.

"Readers, I want to tell you about something that's happening in lots of schools across this city. Lots of schools have something called 'Book of the Month,' and this means that on the first day of every month, every teacher in the school reads the same book aloud to every student in the school—it's usually a picture book—and every classroom in the whole school has a grand conversation about the book so that everyone takes it into his heart, her heart. And you know what else? The special teachers—the art and music teachers—they read it, too. And the principal, the paraprofessionals, the people who watch over kids at recess, and the custodians. The reason that people all read this book is that it gives the whole school common texts that allow people to communicate about things for which there are no easy words.

"So if the whole school read *Hansel and Gretel*, then anyone in the school can track down a class that's gone off to the library without letting people know where they went by saying, "Why didn't you leave a trail of breadcrumbs so I could find you?" Or if the whole school read *Ira Sleeps Over* (you know that story about Ira worrying his friend would laugh if he brought his blanket to a sleepover but then found out his friend slept with a teddy bear named Tah Tah?), any teacher in that school can say, 'We gotta be able to trust each other in this class, remembering that everyone of us has our own version of a teddy bear named Tah Tah.'"

Suggest that the class read-alouds provide a common reference that can be drawn upon in allusions, and ask children to share allusions they could make to those texts.

"You know, we haven't really been thinking about the way the books we've read this year can give us, in this class, a shared language, but they can. And right now, I'd love it if you and the person beside you would talk and think about times when you could allude to our shared books to say something to each other. You might want to celebrate someone's determination—like Rosa's determination to get that God's eye (the weaving with Popsicle sticks) right. Remember how she worked on it over and over and would not give up? Was she acting like a character we all know? Or you might want to talk about some of the things that happen on the playground or in the cafeteria that aren't right. Let's think for a minute, before we say anything, of a way you

Carmen Fariña, who'd been a principal and then a superintendent in the New York City Schools and then became Deputy Chancellor, has written about this in a book called A School Leader's Guide to Excellence: Collaborating Our Way to Better Schools. *As a principal, she initiated something called "Book of the Month" as a way to turn her school into a kinder, gentler place. At the start of the month, she gave each of the grown-ups in her school a beautifully wrapped picture book, with a letter in which Carmen explained why she'd chosen this book for the community. Afterward, I'd hear teachers saying to kids, "You just showed the courage of Ruby Bridges, the way you did that," and, "I feel like you could be* In Charge of Celebrations *(referencing Byrd Baylor's book) and help us find a way to honor that." In a classroom community, of course, the read-aloud books from across the year provide a resource that can be drawn upon for making allusions, and the truth is that this is far more than a figure of speech. This is also a way to be sure that stories inform us as we live our daily lives.*

could allude to a book that we all know to say something for which there are no easy words."

I let the room go silent, and sitting in front of the class, did my own thinking about this, knowing that in some magical way I could mentor kids just by sitting there, thinking. Then I said, "Turn and talk."

Kobe said to Malik, "Oh! I know. We could say that trying to win a race on the playground is like being Searchlight."

"Yeah!" Malik said, "Or if we let the first grader win or something, we could be like Stone Fox."

LINK

Send children off to read, reminding them to think in allusions when they have ideas for which no ordinary words will do. Remind them also to draw on all they have learned as they finish up their books.

"Readers, as you go off to read today, when you have ideas about your books for which there are no easy words, see if you can think in allusions and if this helps you to say the feelings that are welled up in your chest. You can make allusions to movies, to historical events, to songs, to experiences, but you'll find that allusions to literature are especially powerful, because the stories are so powerful.

"And readers, remember that you are the author of your reading life. You'll be doing a lot of other work as well. If you want to look at the chart about what readers of historical fiction tend to do, it might remind you of some of the work you can be doing. Off you go."

Making Our Way Through Historical Fiction

- Collect setting details. What kind of place is this? What does it feel like?

- Is trouble brewing? How is it changing? What feels important?

- Collect vital data about characters. Traits? Pressures on them? Problems they face? What drives them?

- What new understanding and historical information do you have?

- What is the sequence of events in the story, including jumps in time?

- Notice what's changing in the book. How are the characters' problems escalating? Has the setting or the mood shifted?

- Think about how characters are reacting differently to big events and what we can learn from this.

- Pause at passages that seem written in bold and ask, "What is significant here?" and "How does it fit with what the whole story is really about?"

- Think about big ideas and the little details that hold those ideas.

- As you read on, carry your theory with you, but be open to new information that might change your theory. Expect to be surprised!

- Look back over the terrain of the text, and ask, "What's this story really about?" We take into consideration the beginning, middle, and end of the story.

- See one book as an invitation to do further reading, letting the new information you're learning spark new thinking.

Support Readers in Intertextual Work

Today, the mid-workshop teaching point will come after thirty minutes of reading and will launch clubs, marking the transition between independent reading and book club work.

MID-WORKSHOP TEACHING POINT

Readers, in Reviewing Books, Include Their Passionate Responses to Them

"Readers, many of you are finishing your books and wrapping up the unit. I have one tip I want to give you for when you finish a book and get yourself ready to talk and write about it. This is my tip: As you get ready to talk with people about books you've read, you want to prepare not only to share your thinking about what the book is really, really about, but to also share your reaction to the book. And if you look at mentor texts of interpretations, such as the book reviews written in *The New York Times* or essays published in famous magazines like the *New Yorker*, you'll find that great responses to literature almost always talk about why the reader loves the book. It is pretty rare for a writer to take the time and effort to write about a book they detest. Most of the time, people who write for newspapers and magazines only *want* to inform their readers about books they think are important.

"This means, readers, that you'll hear sentences such as, 'The truly beautiful thing about this story is . . .' or 'The reason I love this book is . . .' or 'The most unforgettable moment in this story is . . .' or 'Something incredible that happens is. . . .' Do you hear how intense, how fervent, those sentences are? The reader wants others to *love* the book, to find it deeply significant. I've jotted some of those sentence starters here on a chart, because I think they might help you ramp up some of the ways you are thinking about your books.

"Don't forget this, readers, because as you read and as you think back over books you've finished reading in preparation for sharing them, you can be collecting things to love. A good interpretation is one that shows the reader cares and wants others to care, too! It can be emotional. It can be excited. It can use literary language. It invites others to see new things, to find new parts of the novel to love. So back to work, reading in ways that allow you to fall in love with this book—and to convey that love to other readers."

Conferring and Small-Group Work

The Civil War Club had finished *Riding Freedom* and seemed to be deep in conversation when I approached. *Riding Freedom* was a bit of a departure from the Civil War, though the story takes place during the same time period. I decided to add this book to their club's reading because not only did I have four copies, but it is an unusual, engaging story (about a girl who lives her life as a boy so that she might become a stagecoach driver, something a woman was not allowed to do at that time) that illustrates some of the same themes that come up in the other books the kids in that club were reading. It was also a bit more of a challenging read, and I thought it would be a great way to finish out the unit.

The kids knew by this time to keep on talking when I approached, which they did, with barely a glance in my direction as I pulled up a chair. They seemed to be arguing. I listened carefully. I was listening to see, of course, if their arguing tone was really arguing, or if it was productive, impassioned discussion—or some combination thereof!

"Charlotte is just as brave as Annemarie!" Rosa was insisting. "She had different problems, but she was so brave! She did everything by herself. That makes her braver I think."

"Well, Annemarie could have gotten killed for what she did, running down to her uncle in the boat. She had to stand up to soldiers and everything. Charlotte was brave, but mostly she just hid," said Gabe. "She didn't show her real self. I think Annemarie was braver, even though Charlotte did stuff by herself."

"No, no, no," Tyrell was interrupting. "No, I think Charlotte was braver. She had to totally change her whole self around and be a boy! For her whole life! Until she *died*!"

The discussion was certainly impassioned, which I appreciated with an inward smile at the students' earnestness. I knew that they could probably use that passion, however, to discuss something that went a bit deeper than which character was braver, a topic that seemed destined to soon begin going in unproductive circles. The readers were definitely poised to make some interesting connections between the two books they were discussing. I wondered if they had started making comparisons because of the minilesson's work with allusions. They weren't at this point making allusions with their comparisons. They were simply examining the two main characters. I hoped with some nudging that they might be able to find an allusion in one of the texts that could deepen their thinking.

I broke in as Max and Gabe started to protest Tyrell's point. "Boys, hold up. Wow, it is so great to hear the energy in your voices as you talk about these characters! It's also wonderful that you're looking between the two books that way. I can see why you might compare Charlotte and Annemarie. They're both really strong, brave girls."

"Except Charlotte was braver," interrupted Tyrell with a grin.

I continued right along, "*But* it doesn't seem like your conversation about which of them is braver is helping you discover anything new about the books or the characters. It seems like you've each already decided who you think is the braver one, and you're just holding your position. It's great that you're using parts from the book to back up your thinking, though. You know, I don't think you would have done that so naturally early on in the year! Here's what I'm wondering, though. I wonder if, instead of thinking about how these characters are different—who is braver and all of that—I wonder if you might think together about what is similar about them. I think you all agree that they're both brave. But what other qualities do they share? Sometimes thinking about that can help us pick out some important themes that are happening in both books. They are definitely both brave."

"I was thinking that lots of the characters in our books are brave. Rob is, too. He's brave about letting the tiger out, and letting his feelings out, too," said Gabe.

I was glad to see that Gabe was pulling in *The Tiger Rising* as well, and that he had clearly taken in and remembered the larger messages we'd discussed as a class.

"They're brave about different stuff though. Rob is brave about something just in his own life. Annemarie and Charlotte have to be brave about something in the world that's not fair to everyone," said Rosa.

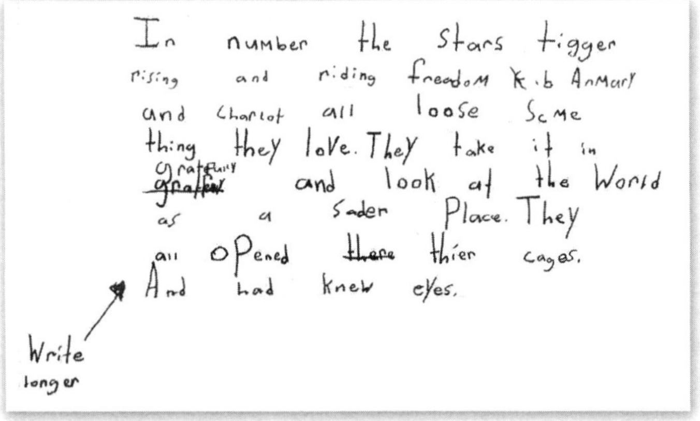

Figure XVIII-2

"That's a really interesting point, Rosa. Jot that down for later, but right now let's keep thinking about what they may have in common. Rob too."

"Well, they all did lose something, right? They all did lose something they love?" added Tyrell thoughtfully.

"Wow. They did, didn't they. You know, I think this might be a great time to all stop and jot. Think about what you've heard your club-mates saying and what you're thinking about the things these three characters have in common. You might even try to find a way to make an allusion that describes their commonalities. It's fine if you don't, but give it a shot. I'll be back in a couple of minutes. Go ahead and share your jottings with each other when you've finished."

I gave the club a few minutes to write, hoping that one of them might be led to make an allusion, but glad at any rate that the level of their conversation had been deepened. Looking for commonalities between the characters was already a first step toward finding a resonant image or idea that would describe their thinking.

When I came back to the club, Tyrell was reading: [Fig. XVIII-2]

After listening to Tyrell read, I took a deep breath. Wow, I said to myself. And, "Wow," I said to the club. "What an important allusion you just made, Tyrell. We all know exactly what you mean when you say they all "opened their cages." It means so much more than the words you said. It means everything we know about how hard it was for Rob to open the tiger's cage, and to open up the cage around his own emotions and let himself really feel. And when we think about all of that as it relates to Annemarie and Charlotte—both opening their "cages" and breaking free—it's so much more meaningful. I am so glad you kept pushing yourselves today and got out of the "who was braver" rut. Remember, you can push yourselves and each other to do that even when I'm not around."

A Conference that Teaches a Reader to Wrestle with Multiple Perspectives and Plotlines

I pulled up alongside Emma, one of the members of the American Dreamers Club. She was reading *Brooklyn Bridge* by Karen Hesse, on her own, having fallen in love with Hesse's writing when her club read *Letters from Rifka*. (Her club, meanwhile, was reading *Water Street*, by Patricia Reilly Giff, the sequel to *Maggie's Door*.) Like Emma, I am enthralled with Karen Hesse, who conveys her messages not only through the content but also through the craft of her books and who uses a larger range of literary devices than do many authors of children's books. I had gotten hold of a copy of *Brooklyn Bridge* to read alongside Emma. I hadn't read it yet, but was curious to see how it was structured and how Emma was handling the craftsmanship of a Hesse book on her own.

"Emma, I see you are reading Karen Hesse's new book! I know she has become a favorite author of yours. I've always loved her work too: *Just Juice, Letters from Rifka, Out of the Dust*. I got myself a copy of this one to read, too. How is it going for you? What's happening so far?"

"It's really, really good," she gushed. "It's about this boy named Joe Michtom and how his family started this teddy bear company in Brooklyn and so they have a lot of money now, but it's hard for Joe because he doesn't see his parents as much anymore. There are a lot of other people in the story too, lots of Joe's relatives, and those characters are pretty interesting, too."

"What are they like?" I asked.

Although I hadn't yet started the book, I'd looked at it enough to know that a lot of the family members wove in and out of the text. I'm aware that as children progress toward higher bands of text difficulty, they're often required to juggle lots of characters and lots of perspectives, and I wondered how Emma was doing at keeping track of all the characters and their different story lines. I noticed she had created a character map on a Post-it to help her remember the different relationships. I decided to probe a bit to understand if she was making sense of all the many characters.

"Well, he has these funny, kind of interesting, um, what's that word for someone who is kind of strange and different but not really in a bad way?" Emma interrupted herself to ask.

"Unique? Eccentric?" I offered.

"Yeah, eccentric!" She nodded, pleased to be using a sophisticated word to describe the characters in her book. "He has these three eccentric aunts, and there are a lot of other relatives and friends who live in the neighborhood. Most of them are immigrants. Actually, did you know that Joe's family came from Russia just like Rifka's?!"

"Oh wow. That's so interesting!" I said and, glancing through her book, noticed Post-its suggesting she was bringing *Letters from Rifka* to bear on this new immigration book. Two Post-its highlighted her thinking. *[Figs. XVIII-3 and XVIII-4]*

"Emma," I said. "This is so unbelievably cool. Do you remember how Rifka used that Pushkin novel as sort of the frame for her letters about immigrating to America? It is almost like *you* are using *Letters from Rifka* as sort of the frame for your work with *Brooklyn Bridge*! You could practically do as Rifka did and put little passages from one book at the front of every chapter in the next book! It is very grown up and literary to do what you are doing—to sort of have one book out on the corner of your desk as you read another book, and to often go, 'These are sort of the same

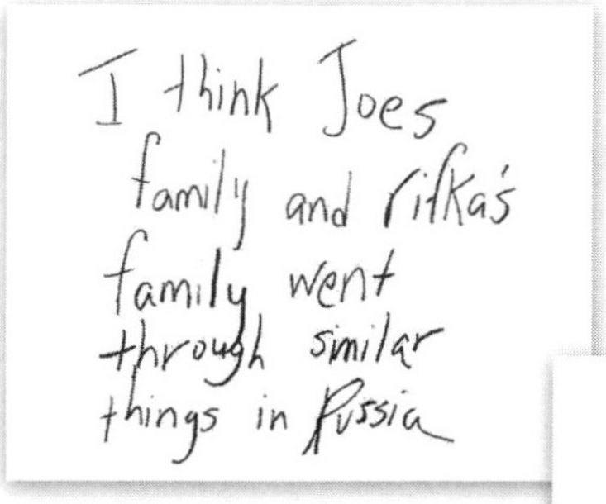

Figure XVIII-3

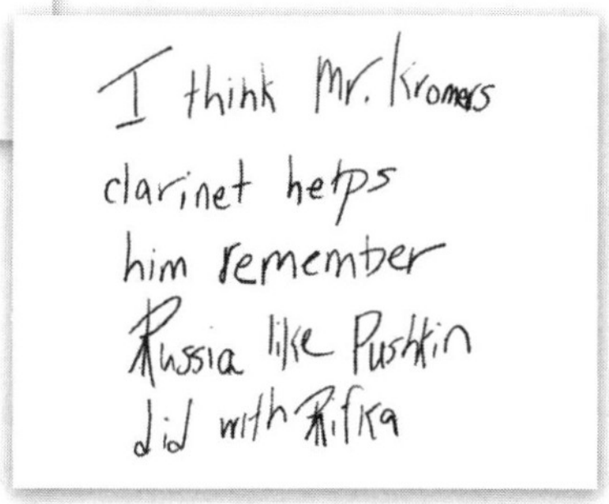

Figure XVIII-4

because. . . .' It is something I would love to have you teach the other kids, because the whole room could be doing what you are doing, and it would be *so cool.*"

I wondered if Emma would seize on my mentioning of that possibility, and she didn't. I figured that she seemed to be already integrating the two books in a natural fashion, and that was the important thing. I needed to learn more to help her. Recalling the journalists' rule of thumb—that the more you know the more you can learn—I figured I would rely on what I knew from the few pages I'd read so far of the book. Straight away what had struck me was that Hesse shifted from one perspective to another and varied the font to reflect those alternating perspectives. At one place, Emma had written about the italicized passages, "I love these stories—they are kind of spooky." I inquired about that.

"Well," she began. "They're almost like ghost stories or something. They're about kids who live under the Brooklyn Bridge and who don't really have anywhere to go. They're all on their own. They're all orphans, or just have no one to take care of them. In this one," Emma pointed to a story titled *Max and Karl*, "these two boys come to America and then one of their moms dies and the other kind of goes crazy, so they end up being on their own and living under the bridge."

As Emma told me about this story embedded into the text of the book, I wondered immediately about the connection between the story being told by the main character, Joe, and these other "spooky, ghost-like stories." The way she was talking about these sections as being like ghost stories made me think that she was probably not looking for connections between them and the main plotline. I decided to explore this further.

"Emma, do you remember those questions that we've been asking about passages in books that seem especially important—questions like how does this part fit into the whole of the book, and why do you think the author wrote in this particular way, and what is this part really about?" She nodded. "I want to teach you that really, those questions can be asked whenever you want to think deeply about any part of the text. I know when we talk about those italic chapters, they aren't written in bold (they are written in italics!), but you could try asking those deep-thinking questions about them and see if that helps you grow some really important ideas."

Emma looked over the list of questions and then said to herself, "Okay, so why do I think Karen Hesse included these italic stories in the book? How do they fit with the whole story that Joe is telling, about him and the others?"

She leafed through the book. "Hmm, I'm not that sure. They live under the Brooklyn Bridge, and Joe lives in Brooklyn, so?" She shook her head, and said, "I don't know."

I could tell that it hadn't occurred to Emma to read and think between the two story lines, nor had she paused to think about the significance of these shorter stories and the way in which they fit within the larger arc of the book. Since higher-level texts sometimes require a reader to tuck information they are collecting about a character or a story into their mind, hold onto it while they read on, and expect to learn more or find connections as they read further into the story, I knew I had something to teach Emma that would deepen her ability to read not only this book but also other more complicated books down the line.

"Emma, I can tell this book is really intriguing you, especially after reading *Letters from Rifka*, and it's so cool that you are using your knowledge of the immigrant experience to add to your understanding of this book. So now, I'm going to give you an important tip that will make read-

ing this book even better for you than it already is. In sophisticated books like this, the author doesn't just do weird things, like write short sections in italics or jump between one character's point of view and another's because that'd be cool for kids to read—though it is!" Emma grinned and nodded quietly.

I continued, "When authors do weird things, those are times to ask yourself questions that get you thinking deeper. And you need to ask those questions, already knowing that for sure, the author is doing this on purpose, to convey some deeper, larger meaning. It is your job to figure it out." I showed Emma the italic passages in *Skylark*, pointing out that this was true also for this book, and suggesting that if Emma could figure out her book, she could perhaps give that reading club some pointers, too.

"Now, I don't know this book," I continued, "but I'll bet there is a way these stories in italics intersect with Joe's story and add to the whole meaning she is trying to convey, otherwise Karen Hesse wouldn't have put them in. And, it's your job to read with your mind open to clues about how the stories go together or fit. It's almost like you're reading a mystery, and I *know* you love mysteries."

"That sounds kind of cool. Like I have to find clues for how they fit!" Emma said, getting excited.

"Exactly! You might not necessarily find all of your clues right away, either. Remember how Peter popped up in the beginning of *Number the Stars* and then he didn't show up again for a while? You saw that he comes back to play an important part in the story. So that little subplot about Peter wasn't in the start of the book for no reason, but readers don't realize how that part will fit into the whole until they read on. As you read *Brooklyn Bridge*, you can be on the lookout for the way Joe's story (I held out one arm) and the stories about the kids under the bridge (I held out the other arm) fit together or intersect, too (I crossed my arms), even though we might not know yet what it means.

"And remember, this book isn't the only one where the author does some weird stuff and you, the reader, are supposed to ask those questions. Nor is this the only book that contains different subplots, substories where the reader is supposed to think, 'How will these fit together?' Lots of more complicated books ask you to keep track of more than one story line at once."

Readers Can Make Texts More Moving with Their Responses

Share an example of a student's response to a text that makes the text itself more moving. Suggest that responses can do that with texts.

"Kwami has been reading *Out of the Dust* with his club. He's been fascinated by how Billie Jo, the main character and the book's narrator, damaged her hands. Listen to Kwami's writing about Billie Jo. Listen to what he has said, and get ready to talk about what you notice in his writing." I nodded to Kwami, who held his notebook open and read: *[Figs. XVIII-5a, XVIII-5b, and XVIII-5c]*

> Billie Jo brushes past Pa hiding her deformed hands from his staring, the staring that is halfway between fury and self-pity. #Hands with cuts, with open flesh. The pain in the hands symbolizes the pain over ma's death, the pain of dust chewing up their bone dry wheat. Maybe they'd be happier with a little money, maybe they'd be happier with some wheat, maybe they'd be happier out of the dust.

Figure XVIII-5a

Figure XVIII-5b

Figure XVIII-5c

"A few minutes ago, Kwami tugged on my sleeve full of excitement. He had been thinking about his piece of writing and today's teaching on allusion, and he had found what he believed was an allusion. He said to me, 'Billie Jo's hands are like Rob's legs.' I could see that he was onto something and waited while he gathered his thoughts. Then he said, all in a rush, 'It's like, with Billie Jo, her damaged hands remind her that her mother's dead, that maybe it was her fault. Even though they hurt her, the biggest hurt is the sadness she feels about her mom being dead, and that it was her fault. And, well, in *The Tiger Rising*, Rob's rash is like this reminder that he is sad 'cause of his mother, so in both of them, it's like their bodies are kind of like, crying.'

"Readers, by comparing Rob's rash and Billie Jo's deformed hand, and then suggesting that both the hands and the rash are reminders of these characters' internal hard times, Kwami made a beautiful connection, and I think it is pretty convincing to think that Rob and Billie Jo's physical ailments represent deeper hurts. It's not that Rob's rash and Billie Jo's burn aren't real, but it's almost as if the authors of those two characters use them to show deeper hurts for which there are no words. And now Kwami has given voice to those hurts.

"I was moved by the insight and empathy Kwami showed in this response. I wanted to share it with you because I suspect you will be moved and inspired by it, too. Keep Kwami's response with you as you read on, responding yourselves."

Every once in a while a child writes something so masterfully crafted that you want to whoop with joy. You also want to learn what from your teaching allowed him to do so many things in one piece of writing so seamlessly, so richly, to such success. When you find a piece like this one, rejoice. And share it with the children in your class. You won't just be making that one child famous; you'll also be conveying to the other children, "All of this you, too, can do as you read and write." Of course, the truth is that writing like this, which could be used to demonstrate so many teaching points, is rare. You may want to save it for your celebration.

Making a Mark on History

IN THIS SESSION,

you will teach children that paying attention to the choices that characters make gives us a fuller picture of history—and of human nature.

When I was young, my parents gave me books about Albert Schweitzer, the great missionary doctor who built and staffed a hospital in Lambaréné, Africa. Winner of the Nobel Peace Prize, he captured my heart when I was very young because he cared for thousands of people in need of a doctor and because he cared also for animals of all sorts—including a pelican and a motherless monkey. I aspired to be like him.

He wasn't my only hero. I wanted to be Kitty, that brave nurse in *Exodus*; I wanted to be Peter Marshall, a preacher; I yearned to be the mother in *Cheaper by the Dozen* who adopted a slew of kids from all over the world; I wanted to be Jo in *Little Men*, who created a school that doubled as a haven for homeless boys. I grew up surrounded by heroes and full of aspirations to find ways to make my life matter.

I recently gave my sons my own version of the books that were so important to me when I was young. For Christmas, I gave both Miles and Evan a copy of Tracy Kidder's *Mountains Beyond Mountains*, the inspirational story of Paul Farmer, a Harvard-trained doctor who has dedicated his life to a hospital complex he's created and led in Haiti. Before they even began reading the book, I took them to my favorite page, a dog-eared section in which Paul Farmer describes pulling out all the stops to save one emaciated sick boy, spending well over $30,000 to fly him to Massachusetts General Hospital for surgery that nevertheless came too late and didn't save him from a death by cancer. When a colleague asked if Paul regretted spending so much money, all for naught, Farmer responded, "I'm not going to stop because we keep losing. . . . You know, people from our background—we're used to being on the victory team, and actually what we're really trying to do [in their medical center] is to make common cause with *the losers*. . . . We want to be on the winning team, but at the risk of turning our backs on the losers, no, it's not worth it. So you fight the long defeat." (p. 289)

I share all this because for me, books were not just part of my education in literacy. They were also part of my education for life. The heroes I met on the pages of books gave me images of possibility for my own life. When I was in high

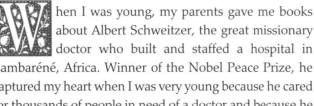

GETTING READY

- Download a photo of Miep Gies from the Internet or print from the *Resources for Teaching Reading* CD-ROM.
- Prepare to add one final bullet to the chart "Making Our Way Through Historical Fiction."

school and college, I thought I might grow up to become a minister. I wanted to spend my life helping people find meaning and majesty in their lives, and I wanted the same for my own life. I wanted to be part of conversations about the important things—to get beneath materialism to a place where human beings really looked each other in the eyes. I remember making a conscious choice against a career in the ministry, thinking, "I don't think my faith is strong enough to build a career on it." And so I became a teacher of reading and writing and a teacher of teachers.

> *The heroes I met on the pages of books gave me images of possibility for my own life.*

Of course, all these years later, I realize that the career I've chosen—that all of us, as teachers, have chosen—is all about helping people find meaning and majesty in their lives. And yes, it's a career that is absolutely all about looking each other in the eyes. Despite my efforts to the contrary, it's a career built on faith—faith that we can take words on a page and breathe life into those words, and faith that those words will breathe life into us as well.

And so this series, and especially this book, would not be complete without a session that acknowledges that we read not only to learn to read but also to learn to live. This session, then, attempts to answer the question, "Why turn to literature? Why beautiful, powerful books? Why historical fiction?"

There are many answers. Surely one answer to the latter question is that as children see the larger historical timeline unfolding and see, also, personal timelines unfolding, they come to realize that these are not parallel tracks. Children can learn to see that the critical choices that their characters have made through the toughest and most challenging of times weren't *inevitable* choices but that willful courage has shaped human history. Everyday courage in the lives of faceless people often goes unreported. Yet such courage, in its silent and unobtrusive way *also* constitutes human history.

In her Newbury Medal Acceptance Speech, author Karen Hesse had this to say: "My inspiration for *Out of the Dust*, Lucille Burroughs, who stared out at me from the pages of *Let Us Now Praise Famous Men*, imploring me to tell her story, even if I had to make it up. . . . *Out of the Dust* is my third historical novel. In the first two, Rifka Nebrot and Hannah Gold brought me back to my Jewish roots. But Billie Jo Kelby brought me even deeper. She brought me back to my human roots." Like Hesse's heroines, all historical fiction protagonists have the potential of bringing readers back to our human roots.

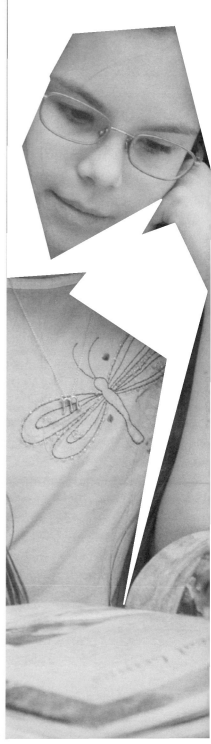

MINILESSON

Making a Mark on History

CONNECTION

COACHING TIPS

Share a true story from a newspaper article that harkens back to a story from your community's shared historical fiction text.

"Readers, this morning, just as I was thinking about what to say to you today as we come to the end of this unit of study, I opened the *The New York Times* to find an editorial that made me gasp. It felt magical that on this day, when I so needed to find a way for us to end this unit of study, this article was here. 'Holy moly!' I thought. 'I absolutely *have* to bring this to our reading workshop.' All morning, I've been watching the clock, quivering with eagerness to read this to you. You'll get what I mean as you listen." Picking up the newspaper, I began reading."

> "I am not a hero," insisted Miep Gies. "I was just an ordinary housewife and secretary." It was Mrs. Gies's habit to deflect accolades for defying Nazi occupiers of Amsterdam to help hide Anne Frank, her family, and three other doomed Jews in a secret annex to the business office of Anne's father, Otto Frank.
>
> But to accept that self-description would be to overlook the remarkable selflessness and courage Mrs. Gies demonstrated, an example so powerful that it continues to inspire nearly 70 years later.

Looking up, I explained a bit of background. "When Anne Frank's family went into hiding in a few little rooms hidden behind a moveable bookcase, hoping to not be deported to a concentration camp, they asked Mrs. Gies to bring them food and supplies, and she agreed—despite the fact that this meant risking her life."

> Working with her husband, Jan Gies, a member of the Dutch resistance and three other employees of Mr. Frank's business, she provided books, emotional support and nourishment. She traveled on her bicycle to spread her food purchases among different grocers in order to avoid suspicion.

This is a true story. The books are finally due to the publisher, and I have just one final minilesson to write. And there, in The New York Times, *is the article I have referenced, feeling like a gift, dropped from the sky. It's a message that I want to say to children and to myself. We have a choice. We can turn our backs on those in need, or we can stand by them. These days, the national news is full of stories of Haiti and of the daily heroism of people who crawl under the rubble of collapsing buildings to bring forth a baby who'd been pinned to the ground. It was not long ago that I read Tracy Kidder's beautiful story of Paul Farmer and of his valiant, over-the-top efforts to address the health crisis in Haiti, and I imagine him there now, laboring among the scenes of such pain. I'm humbled by the choices he's made, and I resolve, in my own way, to do more, to be more. Reading can do that. Howard Gardner, when talking to school leaders, said, "You need to have a way to head to the mountains. You need places that replenish your soul, that feed your spirit." Great literature can give us a way to head to the mountains.*

After the Gestapo raided the hiding place, in August 1944, Mrs. Gies made a bold but unsuccessful attempt to bribe Gestapo officials to spare the lives of the eight arrested Jews. She is owed the world's debt for preserving Anne Frank's diary, which she had kept in the hope that its young author would survive and return to claim it.

Mrs. Gies was the last surviving member of Anne Frank's protectors. Their collective story is an enduring reminder that human beings always have a choice, even when millions were acceding to unspeakable evil. (*New York Times*, "Miep Gies" Wed., Jan. 13, 2010)

I held up the photo of Miep Gies and let children gaze at her kindly face.

Alluding to your community's shared texts, suggest that historical fiction often features characters that are inspired by real people—in particular by the person featured in the newspaper article.

"Readers, something about randomly finding this article in the newspaper today felt too big for words. So you're going to hear me *allude* to books that we've shared in our reading community to explain why I thought it was urgent to share this with you." With my other hand, I picked up my copy of *Number the Stars*—with its image of a young girl with hauntingly wistful eyes on the cover—and held it next to the newspaper snapshot of the white-haired Miep Gies, allowing students to see the two visuals side by side. Leaning in, I said, almost conspiringly, 'Miep Gies—*is* Annemarie Johansen.'

Now that I had students' attention, I set *Number the Stars* down and picked up *The Butterfly* by Patricia Polacco. "Miep Gies is also Monique from *The Butterfly*," I added, holding up this book next so that now children could see the illustration of Monique positioned next to the article. Repeating this process with *Star of Fear, Star of Hope*, I picked that book up next to add, "She is Helen from *Star of Fear, Star of Hope*."

Keeping my voice low so as not to break the spell that these allusions had cast over students, I elaborated further. "Sure, her name is Miep, not Annemarie or Monique. And she wasn't able to save her Jewish friends. But she lived through those times, those circumstances that we've read about. The shiny black boots of Nazi soldiers defined her life as they also defined Annemarie and Monique's lives.

"I'm going to make another allusion to *Number the Stars*. Note what I'm about to say. This diary that Miep preserved in her desk drawer, written by Anne Frank, a young Jewish girl—was no different from the Star of David imprinted upon Annemarie's palm—no different from the tiny Star of David necklace that Monique hid in her dress pocket. If the Nazis had caught her with it, she'd have been arrested—or worse—for aiding Jewish people in their escape. Miep Gies was faced with a critical choice in life: either to help her Jewish friends and risk her life or turn away and stay safe—the same choice that the Johansens faced and that Monique and her mother faced."

Remind children that historical fiction often features two timelines. Add that although a larger historical timeline impacts smaller personal timelines, the small personal choices that people make can also impact history.

"So, readers, there's another reason, too, why it was important to bring this article to share with you all today. This past month we've seen that reading historical fiction involves holding onto two timelines. One is the larger timeline of the nonfiction historical *events* that actually happened. And the other is the *personal* timeline of our fictional characters. You recall how we learned that the larger historical timeline affects a character's personal timeline? For example, the Great Depression affected the smaller timeline of Billie Jo's life by filling it with poverty and hardship. Or the legacy of slavery affected the smaller timeline of Cassie Logan's life by filling it with racial inequality and prejudice.

"At this point near the end of the month, though, I think you're ready to understand something more. Though history affects these small lives, there are ways in which a character's timeline, too, can affect a historical timeline. In other words, there are ways in which small lives can, in turn, define larger history. Miep's was such a life.

"The larger historical events that our books describe are hard or challenging, and some are downright ugly. War, hatred and prejudice, drought, the Great Depression and poverty. None of the themes on the big historical timelines of our books are easy or fun. But the small lives of the people who live through this history are the stories worth telling and repeating. In particular, these small lives are filled with moments where characters have had to stand at critical crossroads and make choices. And in their own right, these small human choices make up the enduring legacy of human history."

You may find yourself wanting to say, "And this is the same choice that you need to make, in moments when you are called upon to make a critical choice." Throughout these units, one of the challenges is to not teach everything at one time, ending up needing to repeat ourselves over and over. The message that children, too, need to make critical choices will be the message for tomorrow, so I am restraining myself from saying it also today. But, yes, you should feel the drumroll.

I think the reason I love this genre so much is that historical fiction is inevitably the story of human beings who affect history. When it is so easy to live without a sense of agency, to feel like a tiny ant, walking through life in ways that leave hardly a trace, this genre teaches children that they can make a difference.

Name your teaching point. Specifically, tell children that paying attention to the choices that characters make gives us a fuller picture of history—and of human nature.

"Readers, today I want to teach you that when characters face critical moments of choice, when a character must decide how he or she wants to respond, we need to remember that it's not just the people around that person who are affected by the choices the character makes. We can be as well. We can learn from characters in books, just as we learn from people in our lives, and we can especially learn from the moments of choice that characters face."

TEACHING

Tell children that parts of a story where characters face critical moments of choice might well be written in bold.

"If we go through our books studying the critical choices that a character makes, we learn not just what kind of character this is. We *also* get a better picture of how people living through that time might have dealt with big historical challenges. We learn about human nature—about *how* humans might choose to survive tough times.

"Readers, remember our conversation earlier about pausing at parts of the text that seem to be written in bold? An example of such parts are specific moments in the story when characters face critical moments of choice—where the character's path opens out into a crossroad, and we see that he or she might choose to go either this way or that. These moments do more than define this one character. In a way, they define human *history*.

"Of course, readers, when I use the word *choice*, I don't mean, 'Hmm, should I wear yellow socks today or blue? Should I have mayo in my salad or not?' Those are small, petty choices that don't really affect anyone but the choice maker—and that, too, in only a small forgettable way. No, I'm talking about what are called 'critical choices.' A critical choice is a fundamental, important, essential, really big choice. It is the kind of choice that affects not just that one character. It affects people around that character." I pointed to a chart I had made, titled "Characters Make Choices."

This minilesson was originally far earlier in the unit, following the minilesson about texts sometimes containing sections that seem as if they're written in bold font. The purpose at that time was to help children find those passages in their own books and mine them for significance. Now, of course, that message continues to shine through, but there is an added message: We human beings make critical choices that shape the history of the world. We can gain inspiration and strength by seeing the choices others have made.

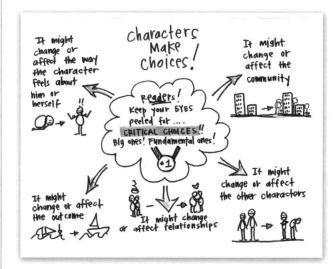

Notice that what you are doing is showing children that characters consider the consequences and risks of their choices.

"Let's recall the moment when the German soldiers come in the night to search for the Rosens, and they awaken Annemarie's family. The Johansens have already made one critical choice—to shelter Ellen and keep her safe. That choice is really put to the test on this night, when those soldiers wake the girls.

"Picture for a moment what the Johansens' situation was. Here they are, asleep in their beds, when there is harsh banging on the door. Angry soldiers with shiny boots and shiny guns walk in and demand to know where the Rosens are.

"Readers, Mr. Johansen really stands at a crossroads at this point. He can choose to do one of two things. If he takes one path (I gestured to my left) and tells them where they are and hands Ellen over, his own family will be safe. He could think, 'The Rosens were fine people and great neighbors, but what's the point of endangering my own little girls? If these soldiers discover that I'm hiding a Jewish girl in my house, I'm as good as *gone*. They'll arrest me! They'll arrest my entire family. I've lost one daughter. Can I bear to put the other two in danger? Just for the sake of the neighbors' girl? This is no time to be emotional. I must protect my family.' He could hand Ellen over, and put his own family out of danger, and he might even have received a reward from the Nazis for doing so. This path (I gestured to my left again) is certainly safer.

"If he takes another path (I pointed right this time), he might decide to protect Ellen. He'd be putting his whole family in danger. He's certainly setting them up for humiliation: The soldier is openly disrespectful of his wife, tears up Lise's photograph, sneers at them. His ploy of pretending that Ellen is actually his own daughter might backfire, and they'd all be arrested. This path (I gestured to the right again) is really one of risk.

"Readers, we know the choice he made. Here's what's worth noting though. Mr. Johansen's choice doesn't *just* tell us about Mr. Johansen. It doesn't just tell us that he was brave or that he was noble or selfless. It also gives us a picture of how, during something as horrific as the Holocaust, small ordinary, everyday people, too, might *yet* have left their mark on history. In one of the ugliest chapters of human history, where the number of people who were killed is too awful to think of, there were some people who *yet* managed to impact history with such choices.

"The Johansens didn't make the Holocaust any less horrific. They weren't in the *position* to do that. Just like Billie Jo is really not in a *position* to bring the rain or end the dust storms. Just like the characters in *If You Travelled in the Underground Railroad* aren't in a position to end slavery. What the characters show us in these books,

Notice that I return for a second time to a scene we've already discussed in great detail in an earlier session. All books have moments, like this one, that are central to the story's larger meaning, that invite interpretation, teach lessons, and beg readers to stop and pause and ponder. As we move toward the end of this unit, it's important that children come to recognize and return to those moments, those passages, in their own reading.

I think this is an important point. The critical decisions that a character makes don't make the war end, the dust storm go away, or the rain come. But they do make life alongside those conditions more bearable.

though, is what people living through war or hardship might do when faced with critical choices in their own lives. And articles like *this* (I held up Miep Gies again) tell us that though the characters in our books are mostly fiction, real human history is full of people who've lived the lives that we find in our books."

ACTIVE INVOLVEMENT

Set clubs up to brainstorm a list of challenges that people living in their assigned historical era might have had to undergo.

"Readers, turn to your clubs and consider the historical timeline that you've read about. Talk about the historical context that provided the backdrop for your story and about the decisions that the context provided to your characters. For instance, immigrants or people who were denied civil rights or the families that lived through war or pioneers or farmers in the Dust Bowl all had big historical challenges that shaped their everyday existence.

"Start talking. Think about the challenges and the difficulties that characters have faced through this historical time. You just have a minute."

Calling the attention of the clubs back to yourself, ask them to now think up one character from their shared books and note a critical moment of choice that this character has faced.

"Club members, eyes up here, please. I'm hearing great conversations: You're talking like historians—with a real sense of the times that your books are set in. Now that you've considered the large historical timelines and set out a list of the general challenges that people faced, I'd like you to think across the books your club has read and choose a character who's been placed at a critical moment of choice. Then talk about how this character's choice tells us something about the way in which an ordinary, everyday person might have dealt with the challenges on your list."

As I named each historical group, I gestured toward the corresponding book club.

LINK

Convene clubs' attentions and allow each club a minute or two to present one character that has faced a critical choice and chosen heroically.

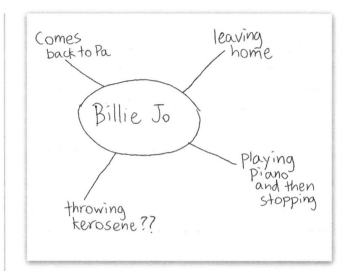

I asked the Dust Bowl Club to tell the class about one of their characters who faced a critical decision. Sarah spoke on behalf of the club, and said, "We talked about Billie Jo, and we thought she made a lot of critical choices in the book. Like she left her home and her pa, and then she decided to come back. We thought those were critical choices."

Kwami chimed in, "I thought it was a big deal that Billie Jo tried to play the piano after she burned her hand, but then she made the choice to stop 'cause it hurt too much. It was like she almost gave up on herself, or kind of like her dream."

Sarah continued, "We weren't sure if throwing the kerosene was a critical choice or not. I mean, it was kind of the biggest thing that happened, but we couldn't figure out if it was really a choice, so we were stuck on that one.

"Hmm," I said., "It is interesting to think about whether or not that's a critical choice. On the one hand, the whole story does turn because of that one action. On the other hand, it wasn't intentional; it was an accident. When your club meets later, you might want to think more about what makes for a critical choice.

"Though small-life heroism goes largely unreported in history textbooks or encyclopedias, historical fiction is often written on behalf of real people like her." I held up the newspaper to denote Miep Gies. "Our books are full of life's most compelling stories—stories that tell us what it means to be human, what it means to make some of the most critical choices that humans have had to make."

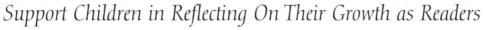

CONFERRING AND SMALL-GROUP WORK

Support Children in Reflecting On Their Growth as Readers

Just as readers have a sense for work that needs to be done at the beginning of a book, in the middle of a book, and at the end of a book, so, too, teachers have a sense for work that needs to be done at the beginning of a unit of study, in the middle of the unit, and at the end of the unit. During the final days of a unit of study, one of your jobs will be to help readers look back over the terrain that they have traveled—not just over the content of a particular book, but over the content of their learning lives. The goal is to be sure that the fruits of experience are harvested. Readers will have done a lot of new work, and in these final days, your goal is to make sure that they come to see themselves as the sorts of readers who do this work continually.

Today, as you draw your chair alongside one reader and another, you may want to talk to readers about ways they've changed. You may say things like, "I've been thinking about the way you've changed as a reader over the last six weeks. Have you noticed the changes as well? Because it seems to be that you used to read at a huge clip, devouring books, reading for what happens next. And the really revolutionary change is that you have learned that huge lesson: to pause. You don't just read on and on and on anymore, do you? Instead, you've become the sort of reader who can put a book down for a moment to think all these huge deep thoughts— like, 'How's my life going to be different because I've read this.' That's gigantic. I bet that years from now, when you make a timeline of your life as a reader, this unit will be on that timeline. 'This is when I learned that reading is not just taking in the words of the text. It is also talking back.'"

MID-WORKSHOP TEACHING POINT

Readers Look for Themes Authors Carry Between Books

"Readers, I want to share some really smart work the Allies did earlier today. They were thinking about some of the books they've read this unit and trying to push themselves to think more about the critical choices characters in those books make. As they were chatting, they realized that one of the books they read as a club—*Autumn Street*—has some interesting parallels with *Number the Stars*, which as you all know is written by the same author, Lois Lowry. Both books are set during World War II, and both tell the story of a friendship between two kids—one who is in a more privileged position and one who is not. As this club was talking, they realized that both Annemarie and Elizabeth (that's the main character of *Autumn Street*) face moments of critical choice that lead to very different outcomes." Interestingly, these two moments occur in the woods, and on another day, this group might look more closely at that setting and think about what it could mean.

"The Allies discovered this. On the one hand, Annemarie risks her life for Ellen and the other Jews who are on the boat, waiting to depart from Denmark. On the other hand, when Elizabeth, who is simply out for an adventure with her friend, Charles, carries the basket through the woods, she decides against her better judgment to leave him behind. She senses danger but can't quite name it, and when Charles refuses to leave with her, she eventually gives up, leaving him to his fate. In the end, Charles is killed by the town's madman. Ellen, meanwhile, and the others on that boat in *Number the Stars* survive.

continued on next page

Of course, you'll support different steps forward for different children. It may be that for some children, you support the fact that they've become the kinds of readers who actually enter conversations expecting to grow new ideas. They come to a conversation with one set of ideas and leave with another. And more than that, they approach a day's reading with one set of ideas and leave with another. Could anything be more important than this—that a child in your care becomes open to continual learning?

For yet another child, the breakthrough may be that this youngster has now become the kind of reader who can handle complexity in books. Perhaps she used to think of characters as all good or all bad, and now she sees them as shades of gray, as nuanced. She may have read

---

MID-WORKSHOP TEACHING POINT

continued from previous page

"Here's the interesting thing the Allies did. They didn't herald Annemarie as a hero—or as "the reason" that Ellen and the others on the boat make it to a safe place. Nor did they condemn Elizabeth (who, after all, is feverish when she and Charles enter the woods, and closer in age to Kirsti than to Annemarie) or say that it is her fault Charles died. Instead, they simply examined these two scenes in these two books, looking at them through the lens of the power of choice. They thought about what might have happened if these characters had made other choices, and they thought, too, about what influenced these characters to make the choices they made. They also thought about how a seemingly small decision can have enormous consequences. They asked themselves, 'What if Elizabeth had stood up for Charles on the hill when the White boys said he couldn't sled? Would he have not stormed off to the woods then? Would he still be alive? Why didn't she feel empowered to speak up?

"A few days ago we talked about theme, and we noticed that many of our books share themes. What's interesting about these two books is that the same author, Lois Lowry, wrote them. It's often the case that writers return to a topic (or an idea or a theme) again and again, exploring different sides of it. The Allies decided that Lois Lowry may have been doing that with these two books. Remember, they're both set during World War II and both are about a friendship between two children who have very different statuses. In *Number the Stars*, Ellen is Jewish and Annemarie is not, and in *Autumn Street*, Charles is Black, and he lacks a lot of the privileges that Elizabeth, who is White and wealthy, has.

continued on next page

---

expecting a single straightforward plotline, ignoring the little subplots, the subordinate characters, but now she's able to hold a larger landscape in mind, thinking about more characters, conscious of strands of the story that are temporarily out of sight but that will surely return as part of the fabric.

As you help youngsters look back on the work they used to do and are now doing, you'll be helping them to tell the story of themselves in ways that provide each learner with a learning trajectory that can influence the child's tomorrows in important ways. If a child comes from this unit saying, "I used to be the sort of reader who made an idea about a text and then gripped onto that idea like a bulldog, not changing it no matter what, but now I make an idea as I read and I know that idea will be revised many times. I enter conversations with others, expecting the idea to be changed, and I read onward in a text, expecting my ideas to be changed," then this work has done its job.

As you work with individuals and small groups today, you may want to think about how to make as big a deal as possible about the insights that you and a child develop together about that child's reading life. You and I tend to publish and celebrate children's written products at the end of a writing unit of study, but often reading units of study come to an end without an equal drumroll. Perhaps you'll want to help each child think about how he or she can use the ending of this unit rather like a New Year's celebration, looking back on the old and looking forward to the new. Can that child think about what she has learned and use that to make New Year's Resolutions for herself, and to even go a step further and think about how her reading notebook might be different or her reading tools might be different as she goes forward? Maybe she plans, from this day on, to make a timeline of her changing ideas about the books she reads. Maybe she'd like to visit the third-grade class as they embark on their first book club unit ever and help those third graders know some of what she's learned about growing ideas in a conversation. Perhaps, this time, you'll want to ask children to look back over their work and to write about ways they've changed as readers, and then to talk about those ways with another person and with their club. Perhaps you'll want to create a bulletin board that is organized around the theme of "I used to be . . . , but now I am. . . ." You will, undoubtedly, invent your own ways to support your children in reflecting on their growth as readers in ways that can encourage future growth.

MID-WORKSHOP TEACHING POINT

continued from previous page

"Listen to what the Allies decided. They felt that whereas in *Number the Stars*, one message might be that there is power in numbers—that friends, and strangers, too, can help others, in *Autumn Street*, Lowry seems to suggest that each of us can only look out for ourselves. They're not sure why, exactly, but it seems to them that whereas one book is very positive about how people can help others with even the smallest choices, the other seems to suggest the opposite. Listen to this quote the Allies found from *Autumn Street*. This is what Elizabeth, the narrator, writes about her decision to leave Charles in the woods: 'I left him there. I left him there alone, because he wouldn't come, and because my head swam with fever and the terrifying knowledge that one can, after all, save only oneself.' Is that so different than the idea we've all grown about *Number the Stars*, about the ability of individuals—and of a nation—to save lives?"

I paused to let that sink in.

"Readers, it's been years since I read *Autumn Street*, and I don't remember the book well enough to add to this conversation, but I do want to congratulate the Allies for doing so many smart things just now—for doing a sort of thematic author study, for considering not just the choices characters make, but other choices they might have made, the influences that lead to those choices, and the outcomes of the choices, for thinking about critical choices critically. All of you can do that. You can step back and ask yourselves, 'What influenced my character to make this choice?' '*How else* might the character have acted?' 'What would have happened if the character decided otherwise?' and 'What might the author be saying by having the character make this choice?'"

Readers Make Connections Between Key Moments Across Books

Mix up the book clubs and invite readers to talk about important choices characters in each book have made.

"Readers, let's try something different. Let's mix up your book clubs." The children looked perplexed. "I'm going to call out a few names, and I want those of you who are called to gather together in the right-hand corner of our room." I called out a new grouping, consisting of one person from each of the clubs, and once those children had settled, I proceeded to convene other groups in each of the other corners of the room, orchestrating things so that each child was in a group consisting of people from other clubs. "All of you are now sitting with members of other book clubs, who read about a very different time period! What I'm hoping you'll discover in a minute is how even when that is the case, there may be instances when a character from your era and a character from another era faced a similar sort of critical decision.

"To prepare for conversation, you are each going to need to think about a big choice one of the characters you've read about in your club has had to make. This might be a choice the character makes during a dramatic moment, like in the race in *Stone Fox*, or during the night when the soldiers intrude on the Johansens. Or the choice might be made during a quieter, less dramatic moment.

"Once you come up with a choice, one of you in each group will need to draw on your best concise (that means brief!) retelling skills to quickly tell your group just the most important information they need to know about what happened in your book to understand the choice your character made. Others in your group will need to listen carefully, noticing possible overlaps between the choices the character described has made and those that your characters have made."

Teachers, you are probably wondering whether overlaps in choices and lessons will, in fact, exist! I can almost hear you asking, 'What if my children can find no universal lessons lurking in their selections?' Put your fears to rest! The truth is that while the time periods and historical events of children's historical fiction cover vast terrain, the challenges people have faced during significant moments in history (and that characters in historical fiction thus face), the choices they've had to make, and the lessons we can learn often overlap. That's the beauty of history, and it's one of the most valuable opportunities available to readers of historical fiction. History—and human error and heroism—repeats itself.

Invite them to draw ideas and life lessons from connections or relationships they may find between the choices they describe.

"Then you'll be able to delve deeper into a conversation about how these choices overlap and, more importantly, about the universal lessons you can derive from all of these moments in different books."

I circulated among the different groups of children as they talked, coaching in when needed to make sure they stayed on track. Then I called out, "Readers, now that you've had a chance to share choices characters made, see if you can find links between the traits your characters displayed by making one choice or another and also the lessons we can learn from those choices."

Again, I walked around the room, this time listening for those "aha" moments when children discovered that characters living on different continents during different time periods might nonetheless have found themselves in similar situations, facing decisions with momentous consequences, making critical choices.

"Readers, we're almost at the end of our unit, so let's not forget to add one last thing to our chart—the work readers do as we examine the significance of the choices characters make and the lessons they teach us."

Making Our Way Through Historical Fiction

- Collect setting details. What kind of place is this? What does it feel like?
- Is trouble brewing? How is it changing? What feels important?
- Collect vital data about characters. Traits? Pressures on them? Problems they face? What drives them?
- What new understanding and historical information do you have?
- What is the sequence of events in the story, including jumps in time?
- Notice what's changing in the book. How are the characters' problems escalating? Has the setting or the mood shifted?
- Think about how characters are reacting differently to big events and what we can learn from this.
- Pause at passages that seem written in bold and ask, "What is significant here?" and "How does it fit with what the whole story is really about?"
- Think about big ideas and the little details that hold those ideas.
- As you read on, carry your theory with you, but be open to new information that might change your theory. Expect to be surprised!
- Look back over the terrain of the text, and ask, "What's this story really about? We take into consideration the beginning, middle, and end of the story."
- See one book as an invitation to do further reading, letting the new information you're learning spark new thinking.
- Think between this book and others you have read earlier, asking, "How are these similar? How are they different?"
- Notice universal themes and ideas across books. Ask, "Does the big idea in this book fit with another book I know well? With the world at large?"
- Consider the critical choices characters have made throughout the book and the consequences of those actions, both personally and historically. Ask, "What are the lessons one can take from this book?"

Celebration

IN THIS SESSION,
you will celebrate with your students the reading and learning of this unit.

nd so another unit of study comes to a close. I hope this is not the final unit of study in your year—I hope there is still time for you to design and teach more units before your year comes to an end, and I hope *Constructing Curriculum* helps you do this. But this unit brings a good portion of our shared teaching to a close. So the session needs to celebrate not only the journey that you and your students have taken together but also the one that you and I have taken together.

In the prelude to *Building a Reading Life*, I suggested you think of the ending of a unit as a beginning, and that as you close one chapter, you help your students take ownership of all they have learned. I wrote, "Your hope on this final day will be to invite children to pack their identity kits and their strategy kits so they go forward with a sense of personal agency, convinced that with resolve, enthusiasm, good books, and good company, they can author lives in which reading matters." You won't be surprised, then, to hear me say that I hope that as we come to the close of this final session, you are packing your identity kit and your strategy kit with new insights and tools, so that you go forward from

our shared work with resolve, enthusiasm, good books, and good company to author your continued teaching.

I have a final bit of advice for you. It is this: Step back and look at the power of all that you and your students have accomplished. Look at the children who have books beside their beds at home. Pay attention to the child who tells you he is teaching his little brother to read, to the one who is reading a book with her mother and getting into quiet talks they never used to have. Watch the way children's reading is giving wings to their writing. Notice that books are being passed from child to child. Hear children attempt to use literary language when they talk about books.

Yes, there are problems. The books that are the hot items in your class may not be the classics some parents want kids to read. Some of your youngsters still resist reading. You don't yet have the classroom library you need. When you invent your own minilessons, you aren't always sure what to do during the active involvement. Your kids still talk on top of each other during their book clubs. Sure, there are problems. It's great that you see those problems and welcome them. After all, in a story the rising action comes when a

GETTING READY

- You'll need a story from your school that shows that sometimes bad things happen in our everyday lives, and we want to make things better but we're not sure how.

- You'll need to reread aloud the ending of *Stone Fox* or another portion of text in which a character makes a choice to do something good.

character (that's you) tackles obstacles. In life, as in stories, we need to "climb every mountain, ford every stream, follow every rainbow, until we find our dream." So, yes, it is wonderful for you to step back and see the problems that still need addressing.

But it is also important for you to look through the problems to see the significance and power in what your children are doing. Remember, teaching is an art, and artfulness comes from a sense of priority, from a vision of what ultimately matters. It's easy to get bogged down in this little

> *Step back and look at the power of all that you and your students have accomplished.*

problem or that one and to lose sight of what matters. You will only be able to take the best of what you have learned and done and build on it if you are able to see the beauty and power and meaning in your students' work—and in your work as well.

I recently spent time in Jordan, working to help Queen Rania's Teachers' Academy help a network of 30 schools pilot a curriculum in teaching writing. My colleagues had been there before me, and the work wasn't unfolding flawlessly. There were problems, confusions, worries. I decided it was time for me to go, myself, to see if I could address the problems that threatened to overwhelm progress.

I saw problems, sure. The setting, culture, and context require that what we once thought were our best ideas about teaching need to be revised. But what I really saw was the gigantic significance of what was happening. You see,

there is no tradition of expressive writing in Jordan's schools. How huge it is, then, that there are teachers in high-poverty schools across Amman who, like the teacher I watched, stand before their students and say, "Watch me as I do this in my writing, and then you try it in your writing." The teacher I observed worked to show rather than to tell her feelings, and then, a few minutes later, forty students did likewise. In the classroom I visited, one girl worked to show, not to tell, about the aching sense of loss she felt when her younger brother was given a bike, and she—who is covered—realized she'd never have the chance that her brother will have to ride over the hills, wind in her hair, the world opening before her. Another girl recalled times when Father rebuked Mother, raising his fist to her. "My mother gets small and says nothing. I say nothing, too, but in my writer's notebook, I'm practicing saying something, and some day I will," she wrote. As I watched this work, I could not help but think of the potential power of this. I saw the problems, sure, and we're addressing them. But what I saw most of all was the significance of what is occurring in those schools. I saw how gigantic and important it is that the queen of this country and an organization she leads is imagining that schools can give young people voices they didn't know they had.

I worried that I wasn't helping. They'd flown me halfway around the world and mostly what I was saying is, "Do you see what is going on? This is huge." Mostly I said, "You need to send the TV cameras. You need to bring scores of other teachers in to see this. It is just so incredible. How will you build upon what you have begun?" But in thinking about this now, I have come to think that whenever any of us are involved in important school reforms, when any of us set out to do work that is complex and important and difficult, it is important that we and our friends are able to pause sometimes and to ask the questions that readers ask, "What's really, really going on here?" What's this about—deep down? What can this teach me about how I can go forward?"

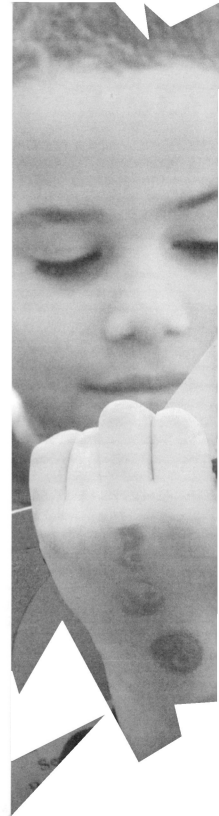

So that is my advice as we come to the close of this unit. Try to see through the problems to that which is big and important, to see that which really matters. Allow yourself to be touched and inspired by the enormity of your students' work—and your work, too. And help your students, as well, see through the problems to that which matters most.

This final session is one more effort to rally students to care about reading. The motif of this year has been that we ask students to author lives in which reading matters. We've urged students to spy on themselves as readers, to collect data on their reading lives, to construct reading identities, to aspire toward goals for themselves as readers, and to draw on their growing repertoire of strategies so they can accomplish big work as readers.

This final session turns their eyes outward toward the world. The session conveys that we read not because we want to author literary lives for ourselves, but because reading enriches our lives. Reading wakes us up. It reminds us of what matters. It helps us to hold onto what is big and beautiful in life. The earthquake in Haiti brought that battered nation to the front of my consciousness, and so I have been rereading Pulitzer Prize-winning author Tracy Kidder's *Mountains Beyond Mountains*. As I've mentioned before, it is the moving story of Paul Farmer, chairman of Harvard Medical School's Department of Global Health and Social Medicine and the Founding Director of Partners in Health, an organization that partners with poor communities—including those in rural Haiti and in the slums of Peru and Rwanda—to combat infectious disease and poverty in comprehensive, large-scale ways.

The book has stopped me in my tracks. Take, for example, as I recounted in the previous session, the account of an emaciated peasant boy, John, who was brought from his rural village to Farmer's hospital in Haiti. His brothers and his father had all died of various ailments, and now John and his mother were the only ones left in the family, and John was suffering from a swelling in his neck. Determined

to not lose him as she had lost the others', John's mother had trekked for days to the clinic. A biopsy revealed that John had a kind of cancer for which the chances of survival were 60% if the cancer had not yet metastasized into the boys' bones and if the boy received the treatment he would need. That treatment would cost $100,000. That was an unimaginable sum for this peasant boy, but Farmer flew to the Massachusetts General Hospital, met with people, and the hospital agreed to donate their services. Still, the boy would need to be flown on a medevac flight. Farmer made the decision to pay for this. "Getting him on a plane is the only chance to save his life, so I am for it," he decided.

As it turned out, the cancer was already in John's vertebrae. He died. Later, reflecting on this, some of Farmer's staff thought about the number of people who could have been cured for the money invested in the boy, and they asked Farmer if he regretted the decision to invest so heavily in him. "No," Farmer said. And then he said words that I will carry with me always. "You know, people from our background—like you, like most Partners in Health people, like me—we're used to being on the victory team, and actually what we are trying to do in Partners in Health is to make common cause with the losers. We want to be on the winning team, but at the risk of turning our backs on the losers, no, it's not worth it. So you fight the long defeat." And he also said, "I have fought the long defeat and brought other people on to fight the long defeat and I'm not going to stop because we keep on losing. Now I actually think we might win. . . .

When I put that book down, I didn't think about my reading strategies or rate or volume. I didn't think about the strategies I'd used to interpret or to envision. I didn't even think about Paul Farmer. I thought about my own work. I thought about how hard it can be sometimes to soldier on in the face of a nation that often seems to have turned its back on children and on teachers. I thought of the times when I am tempted to give up on work that is hard. And I thought, "If Paul Farmer can go to the ends of the earth for his cause, if he can fork out $18,000 for one emaciated peasant boy in a nation filled with starving children, then what am I whining about? And I thought about the title of the book, *Mountains Beyond Mountains*. The title comes from the Haitian proverb, "Beyond mountains there are mountains." As you solve one problem, another will present itself, so onward. Let's go.

Our children may not read *Mountains Beyond Mountains*, but the books they read can also inspire them in similar ways. I was only thirteen or so when I read *Exodus* by flashlight, in my third-floor bedroom under the eaves of our farmhouse. How I recall reading and feeling as if I was on that ship, with Kitty, the American nurse, and Ari, the Israeli soldier, and that group of orphans, refugees from the death camps the Nazis built to exterminate the Jews. It felt as if by reading, I could be with Kitty and help ensure that those orphans would make it to the Promised Land, the only place in the whole world where they could be safe. I still remember that when I put that book down, when I came down from the third-floor bedroom, I felt different. I was less concerned with all the trivia of my life and more concerned with how I could try to live a life of courage and commitment, as Kitty did. That book made me want to make a life for myself that added up, that was big and important.

Teachers, you and I, like Kitty, have found a way to live our lives so that we are part of work that is big and important. Our children need the same chance, the same invitation. Reading can give them that. Our job is not only to help kids author reading lives. It is to help them make their way forward, with hope and resolve, with a sense of agency and a vision of what matters.

Celebration

Remind readers of ways they've marked the end of a unit and celebrated their learning and accomplishments, and let them know that now it is time to honor their learning once again.

"Readers, at the ends of our units of study, we've taken time to make or do things that honor the reading we've done. You'll remember we spread out across the school at the end of our last unit of study to teach people about butterflies, sharks, Greg Mortenson's schools in Afghanistan and Pakistan, and medieval weapons. And when we celebrated the unit prior to that, we made bookmarks so that we'd have a way to carry all we learned with us as we read on.

"I've been mulling over what we could do to honor the unit that is now coming to a close. First, I had an idea that we could all dress up as our favorite characters in the historical fiction books we've read and teach each other about the big things those characters taught us, but that felt a little silly somehow, and not big enough to commemorate our work this year. I kept tossing around other ideas in my head, but somehow, nothing felt quite right. Then it hit me that my problem was that I was trying to come up with one way for all of us to honor what we have learned from this unit and those books, and the truth is, there is not ever going to be one way. The truth is that just as readers need to pause sometimes to think, 'What's important here? How does it fit into the whole of the book?' so, too, people need to pause sometimes and think, 'What's important here? What's this really, really about—for me, for my life?' And that is personal work.

Invite readers to create their own celebrations, continue to build their own reading lives, and more than that, become the kind of people they want to be, as inspired, educated, and influenced by texts.

"Fallon, when you stop to celebrate this unit of study, you'll be doing something that is not the same as the thinking that others in this room will be doing. I know that as you've sat in that corner with your back to the wall, poring over books about strong

You might have some of these artifacts around you as you remind students of prior celebrations. Include any pieces that show students went to extraordinary effort, in order to inspire your students now. As they recall the teaching tools they made, the way students and parents would cluster in the hallways to look at their work, and how they treasured their bookmarks, they'll be eager to outdo themselves in this celebration.

Act as if students have been incorporating ideas from historical fiction into their thinking about the world around them. Some have been doing this visibly. But undoubtedly all your readers have had moments when they have thought to themselves, "I wonder how I could make a difference?" Give a nod to the outspoken students who clearly lead and also to the quiet thinkers who, upon being named, will rise to the call.

women throughout time—women who have made a mark in the world—you are thinking stuff that relates to your family, your old school, your future—stuff the rest of us can't even imagine. And that is true for each one of you. So I have decided that each of you, as authors of your own reading lives, will create your own celebration for this unit. This might be a poster, a picture, a poem, a play. You'll just have today's reading workshop time, so you'll need to think and work fast and furiously, but in this time, I think you will find a way to take all you have been thinking and learning and make something of it.

"I want to make one suggestion though. Until now, we have talked a lot about the fact that your job is to author a reading life for yourself. And I want, at the end of this unit, to point out that really, your job is bigger than that. You job is to make yourself into the person you want to be. And I think that now, as you look back over all the books you have read in this unit and in this year, you'll see something that I've been realizing in my own life. And this is it. Books can inspire us to reach toward becoming the kind of person we want to become."

Tell the story of an incident that might provoke people to want to change or take action.

"This is on my mind partly because this morning I heard about an incident at recess when a group of kids—not from this class—were teasing a boy, calling him names and scaring him. It sounded like the kids were being cruel. I talked to some of you about that incident, and you said to me, 'You know, that sort of thing happens all the time.' When I asked why you and others don't do something, one of you explained, 'People don't stop it because everyone's scared. If you try to stop it, then the bully might turn and pick on you. So it just keeps going.'"

Reread a portion of a familiar text that highlights an incident of a character making a brave choice to do good. Tell children that readers carry with them the characters who have behaved in ways we cherish or wish to emulate to make us better people.

"I've been thinking about how, somehow, it seems to me that the books we've been reading—not just in this unit but all year long, all our lives long—they have something to say to us about times like this, when stuff around us seems wrong and we're not sure how to be. Like, maybe, just maybe, *Number the Stars* has something to say about what a person can do who's afraid, 'cause who wouldn't be afraid to stand up to bullies, to do a whole bunch of other stuff in life that is hard? But I'm thinking that these

In this trilogy, the author shows three characters who are influenced by their reading to act nobly. In the first scene, a bystander, clutching his copy of a novel, interrupts an act of bullying. In the second, another book club member pulls a victim from the deadly path of a speeding car. Finally, in the ultimate scene, a *Number the Stars* reader interrupts an act of unkindness. A story about how stories affect kids daily lives and inspire acts of quiet, unwitnessed heroism.

books help us remember that we are not just the authors of our reading lives. We are the authors of our lives. We make choices. The kids who overheard that bullying on the playground made choices. Stone Fox made choices.

"Do you remember after that final race scene in *Stone Fox*, we dried our tears enough to really think about Stone Fox. We thought about how he might have so easily just kept going when Searchlight collapsed, crossed that finish line and collected the winning prize money. But he didn't, did he? Instead, he stopped."

> Stone Fox stood up slowly.
>
> No one spoke. No one moved. All eyes were on the Indian, the one called Stone Fox, the one who had never lost a race, and who now had another victory in his grasp.
>
> But Stone Fox did nothing.
>
> He just stood there. Like a mountain.
>
> His eyes shifted to his own dogs, then to the finish line, then back to little Willy, holding Searchlight.
>
> With the heel of his moccasin Stone Fox drew a long line in the snow. Then he walked back over to his sled and pulled out his rifle.

"Remember how, after he drew that line in the snow, Stone Fox raised his rifle and his voice to keep the other racers from crossing the line. Then he let little Willy go instead. I don't know if you remember this, Jasmine, but you were very moved by Stone Fox's decision because he let little Willy, a *stranger*, win."

I paused to let the weight of that action sink in all over again. "Readers, the choice Stone Fox made in that moment was in a way just a small gesture, but it had great weight, didn't it? It meant Willy and his grandfather could hold onto their farm, and to each other, and it meant that all of us could learn some big lessons—like that sometimes in life, winning isn't what's most important. Stone Fox did something that was hard for himself, but for Stone Fox, being a man of integrity and of goodness and helping young determined Willy was more important than that winning.

"This is on my mind as we bring this unit to a close and think about how we can honor all we have learned, because from the very start of our year, I think we have been learning not just about reading but about living. And I think these books are not just teaching us about interpretation and envisionment and prediction. I think they are teaching us that human beings are the authors not just of our reading lives but of our lives. And our choices have consequences.

"Big things happened because of Stone Fox's decision. And big things happened because of Uncle Henrik and others like him who, during World War II, helped hide Jews they had never met. People can be afraid and can still, in the face of fear, do what they believe is right. And when people do this, it matters. I'm thinking of Miep Gies, making that brave decision to help Anne Frank and her family."

Give children an example of someone who has carried texts, characters from texts, with them throughout an extraordinary life. Invite them to do the same.

"The other part of this, though, is that books can help us to take the high road. A long time ago, there was a boy hero who became the greatest and youngest general the world has ever known. His name was Alexander the Great, and he conquered all of Greece and Egypt and Persia and a third of the known world in 330 BC. Alexander was always first into battle—the most courageous, the one who led the way. And he was the first one to halt the battle, to call for mercy and justice. Alexander carried only two texts with him through the mountains and deserts, through the hundreds of battles that he fought. One was a book on war strategy. And the other was a story—the *Iliad*. Alexander said that the characters in that story taught him everything he needed to know about courage. When he went into battle, he tried to do it with the fierceness of Achilles. When he ruled his men, he tried to do it with the justice of Hector. Those were some of the heroes of the *Iliad*.

"Readers, I think we can do that, too. We let books be our *Iliad*, inspiring us, through their characters, to try to show courage, even when it's hard. And this can change how we live. That means books can help us not only read differently but live differently. When we feel afraid to do the hard thing, the right thing, we can think of ourselves as standing alongside Annemarie or Cassie or John Henry, and we won't feel so alone."

In this poster, young readers offer advice to their classmates, based on their interpretation of a beloved novel. Book club members have pulled out and celebrated favorite lines from *Number the Stars*—lines that teach them how to live.

Give children time to talk with other children to figure out ways to let their books' big ideas and characters live with them, influencing their behavior.

"So readers, today is for you. I'm going to ask you to talk together with whomever you want about what you are taking with you from this unit, from these books—about lessons that pertain not just to your reading but to your life. And then get started making something that will help you share whatever it is you are taking with you with the rest of us. Get started."

Offer children some examples, hopefully from other classmates, of the work they could do to let their texts and characters influence and inspire them.

After students talked a bit, I shared a few of their ideas with other students. "Some of you are planning to write a letter about some of the injustices that have happened in the school recently. That's great—get started. I'll be eager to see how your reading inspires the content of whatever you have to make or say about that. Some of you want to make posters, showing with pictures and words how *Number the Stars* or other books affect your daily choices. A few of you are going to write poetry or work on your stories. Get started!"

Offer children time and opportunity to share the work they are doing.

"Readers, I love the work you've been making. We're going to need to stop. Will you and your club members count off—1, 2, 3, 4? Readers number 1, meet here at the back table. Share what you have made." Then I pointed to where the readers who were number 2 could meet, and so on. As students met in corners and in the hallway, I cycled among them. I saw that Josh had written a poem about *Freedom Summer*—a poem that grew not only from his reading but also from the recent earthquake in Haiti. [Fig. XX-1]

Gabe had made a drawing in which bullies were depicted as monsters. In one drawing, one of the small plasma-beings who is being bullied rallies others to help by saying "Get our book club!" Another, while being squeezed, waves *Number the Stars* at the bully and says, "Read this now!" [Fig. XX-2]

You could channel students, if you want, toward an image that you have in mind, suggesting people make posters that help them take the high road or help them live differently because of what they have read. We chose to let students do whatever suited them and were astonished at the depth and variety of what they made. Some chose to write poetry. Some wrote letters. Some made posters and charts. Some worked on drafts of stories they had been writing in the writing workshop or at home.

Clearly, having colored pencils, paper, copies of the books, and so forth easily available will facilitate the students' efficiency. The one thing we found we had to remind students of was time. They wanted to embark on super-ambitious projects, such as making a whole cartoon series rather than one drawing, or planning and creating a poster rather than simply getting started. So as you go around the room, you'll find you may need to jump into students' planning sessions and encourage them to "Get started, get it on paper!" The students in the classes we worked with took between forty-five minutes to an hour to make artifacts.

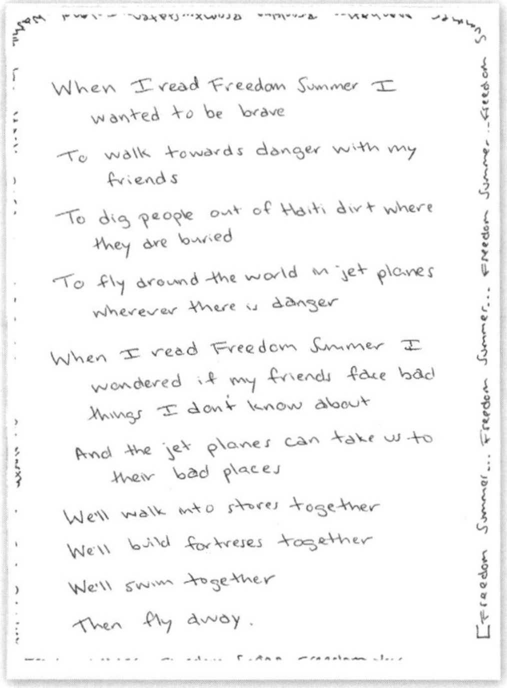

When I read Freedom Summer I wanted to be brave

To walk towards danger with my friends

To dig people out of Haiti dirt where they are buried

To fly around the world in jet planes wherever there is danger

When I read Freedom Summer I wondered if my friends face bad things I don't know about

And the jet planes can take us to their bad places

We'll walk into stores together

We'll build fortresses together

We'll swim together

Then fly away.

Figure XX-1
Young Josh bridges the events of the civil rights era and the current calamity in Haiti in this poem in which, inspired by *Freedom Summer*, he longs to heal hurts around the world.

Figure XX-2
Even monsters are influenced by their book club novels. One victim of the giant/monster/bully calls out for the other book club members, sure that these fearless allies will step willingly into danger. Another fellow victim, while clutched in the massive grip of the bully, advises the giant to "read this," handing him a battered copy of *Number the Stars*.

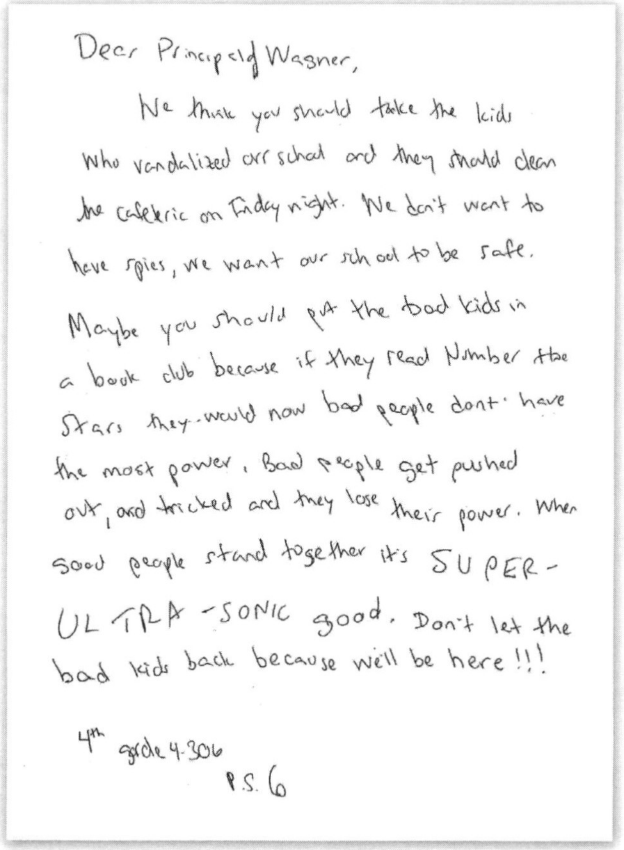

The class had already been in a bit of an uproar because some students from a nearby middle school had broken into and vandalized the elementary school. Two members of the World War II group wrote a letter to the principal of the middle school, suggesting, "Maybe you should put the bad kids in a book club because if they read *Number the Stars*, they would know bad people don't have the most power." [Fig. XX-3]

After listening in, I convened the readers and said, "Readers, it's clear to me that, like Alexander the Great, you will be carrying these books with you as you live. And like Miep Gies, you will try to be brave and to help those who need help. Before we end this conversation, come back to this story of bullying in our schoolyard. Talk with the people in your group about ideas you have for ways you might address that bullying, and talk about whether there are books, or a particular character, that could help."

The children whispered. Gradually, thumbs went up as they had ideas.

Dear Principald Wagner,

We think you should take the kids who vandalized our school and they should clean the cafeteria on Friday night. We don't want to have spies, we want our school to be safe.

Maybe you should put the bad kids in a book club because if they read Number the Stars they would now bad people don't have the most power. Bad people get pushed out, and tricked and they lose their power. When good people stand together it's SUPER-ULTRA-SONIC good. Don't let the bad kids back because we'll be here!!!

4th grade 4-306
P.S. 6

Figure XX-3
These letter writers hope to change the behavior of kids who act badly, by showing them that badness, ultimately, is not rewarded.

Sam began. "Maybe, like Joe in *Freedom Summer*, I could just go stand with the kid who is being bullied? It would be scary, but the bullies in the yard don't usually hit anyone; they're just mean. Maybe if they saw that we would stand with each other, like Joe does when he goes into that store with John Henry, they would stop.

"That's really brave, Sam," I said. "Anyone else?"

Aly added in, "Actually, if we were more like the Danish people in *Number the Stars*, we would *all* go over when we saw the bullies. Then no one would be alone."

Lily jumped in with, "And I liked the pictures some of us made that show how we want to be braver or better. We could put up pictures that show kids standing up to bullies, and maybe that would shame the bullies!"

I nodded at the students. "Readers, these are all brave ideas. Many great activists have talked about how, before you can achieve change, you have to be able to imagine it. Dr. Martin Luther King, Jr. talked about having a dream. Ghandi talked about how we need to be the change we want in the world. I think that's what you're doing. You're dreaming the moments that you want to come true, and even if they don't happen right away, it's only by imagining them that they'll ever come true. I'm going to gather all your beautiful work, and let's put it on display, so others in our school can see what it really looks like when people are different because of what they read. From now on, let's really carry these stories with us, as weapons and as comfort and as sources of courage. And for the rest of the year, I'll be eager to hear how your books are affecting you and to see you teaching each other the lessons that you learn from characters." [*Figs. XX-4 and XX-5*]

I had never heard a braver story than Number the Stars in my life and that's what inspired me to write this story.

Figure XX-4
The Post-it that accompanied a historical fiction story one young writer wrote as an independent writing project. How much their reading affects them!

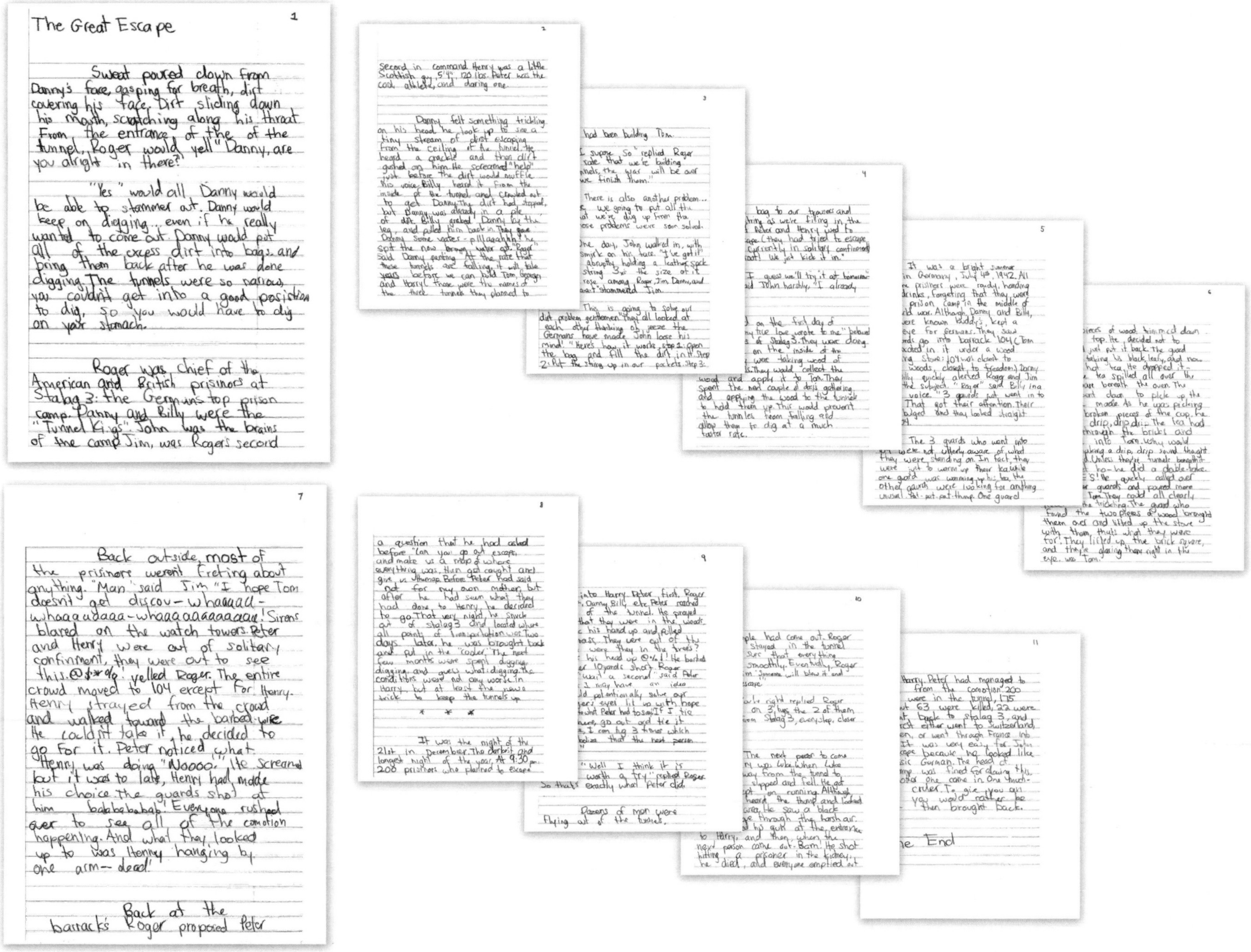

The Great Escape 1

Sweat poured down from Danny's face, gasping for breath, dirt covering his face. Dirt sliding down his mouth, scratching along his throat. From the entrance of the of the tunnel, Roger would yell "Danny, are you alright in there?"

"Yes" would all Danny would be able to stammer out. Danny would keep on digging... even if he really wanted to come out. Danny would put all of the excess dirt into bags and bring them back after he was done digging. The tunnels were so narrow, you couldn't get into a good position to dig, so you would have to dig on your stomach.

Roger was chief of the American and British prisiners at Stalag 3: the Germans top prison camp. Danny and Billy were the "Tunnel Kings". John was the brains of the camp. Jim, was Rogers second

2

second in command. Henry was a little Scottish guy, 5'4", 120 lbs. Peter was the cool, athletic, and daring one.

Danny felt something trickling on his head he look up to see a tiny stream of dirt escaping from the ceiling of the tunnel. He heard a crackle and then dirt gushed on him. He screamed "help" just before the dirt would muffle his voice. Billy heard it from the inside of the tunnel and crawled out to get Danny. The dirt had stopped, but Danny was already in a pile of dirt. Billy grabbed Danny by the leg, and pulled him back in. They gave Danny some water - pllaaahhh! he spit the now brown water out. "Roger" said Danny panting "At the rate that these tunnels are falling, it will take years before we can build Tom, George, and Harry." those were the names of the three tunnels they planned to

7

Back outside, most of the prisiners weren't freting about anything. "Man" said Jim "I hope Tom doesn't get discov- whaaaaa- whaaaaaaa- whaaaaaaaaaa! Sirens blared on the watch towers. Peter and Henry were out of solitary confinment, they were out to see this. @$*%! yelled Roger. The entire crowd moved to 104 except for Henry. Henry strayed from the crowd and walked toward the barbed wire. He couldn't take it, he decided to go for it. Peter noticed what Henry was doing. "Noooo." He screamed but it was to late, Henry had made his choice. The guards shot at him bababababab! Everyone rushed over to see all of the comotion happening. And what they looked up to was Henry hanging by one arm— dead!

Back at the barrack's Roger proposed Peter

8

a question that he had asked before "Can you go out, escape, and make us a map of where everything was, then get caught and give us the map. Before Peter had said not for my own mother, but after he had seen what they had done to Henry, he decided to go. That very night, he snuck out of Stalag 3 and located where all points of transportation were. Two days later, he was brought back and put in the 'cooler.' The next few months were spent digging, digging, and guess what digging the conditions were not any worse in Harry, but at least the new brick to keep the tunnels up

* * *

It was the night of the 21st in December. The darkest and longest night of the year. At 9:30 pm. 200 prisoners who planned to escape

Figure XX-5
These two boys spent hours outside of class writing historical fiction stories, inspired by their novels. Their parents remarked that they had never seen their kids so engaged and so productive. Sometimes some scene, or some act, in the stories they read will inspire your young readers to give historical fiction a try. Get them some paper and tell them you can't wait to read their stories!

Using Assessment to Drive Change Thoughout Our Communities

As we end the final volume of the final unit of study, I want to remind you that you need to assess and watch over not only your students' learning but also your own. Remember that there are mountains of research showing that the one thing students need more than anything in the world is access to a great teacher. That's you. If you pause to think about your own growth, your own learning, and you come to the conclusion that you have been so consumed with concern for your students' growth that you have ignored your growth, don't fool yourself into thinking this is wise. We, as a profession, have a tendency to do that. We work ourselves to the bone; we give and give and then give some more until we are utterly depleted. Then we either leave the field because it just drains too much out of us, or we teach out of that state of depletion, putting one foot in front of the next and trying to get through the day, the week, the year.

Don't let it go that way for you! Roland Barth, the author of a score of books on school change, was wise when he cautioned the principals with whom the TCRWP works especially closely, saying, "In a school, everyone's learning curve needs to be sky-high." And Seymour Sarason echoes Barth's statement, providing me with my favorite quote in the whole field of education: "The notion that teachers can create conditions that are alive and stimulating for children when those same conditions do not exist for teachers has no warrant in the history of mankind." Barth and Seymour are saying something deeply important. For a school to be a vitally alive, humming place, it needs to be a community of practice where it's not only the kids but also the grown-ups that grow. Your school needs to be a place where you and your colleagues outgrow yourselves, over and over again, in palpable and dramatic ways.

Sometimes teachers hear me say this, and they shake their heads, discouraged. "My school just isn't that kind of place," they say. "In my school, everyone teaches with the door closed, and everyone leaves at the end of the school day with the kids. It's each man for himself."

Change Can Begin with One Person: Be that Agent of Change for Your School

My response is this: It doesn't have to be that way. You—just you, just one lone person—can change that. If I know nothing else, I know that one single teacher can provide the turning point around which a whole school changes. I've seen it with my own eyes—not once, but time and time again.

Then again, you may be thinking, "My school is already that sort of community of practice." My response, then, is this: Cherish that community. Nurture it. The learning community in a school is like any other relationship. It needs to be nurtured. And this means that the community itself, like each of you within it, needs its learning curve to be sky-high. My leadership coach began her work with me by asking, "When you dream of where your organization could be, five, ten years from now, what do you see?" That's a question you could ask yourself. Then my coach asked me a question that you could also follow up with: "What positive steps forward could you take to make those dreams come true?"

How do you become an agent of change in your own school? You begin by assessing. Assess yourself and your context, thinking, "What course of study can I construct for myself that will allow me to develop the vision and the strength and the skills—interpersonal as well as professional—necessary so that I can rise to the challenge of being an agent of change in this school?"

"It Takes a Village": Draw on Your Community to Make Big Changes

In the same breath, assess your colleagues, asking, "Who in this school might be yearning to make this into an even richer, stronger learning community? How can those people and I forge some shared images of possibility?" This question is important because when I said that time and again I have seen a single individual become the agent of change for an entire school, that claim is and isn't true. A single individual will never be a strong force for reform unless that individual links with others and unless that individual, in the end, sees the process of change as a community effort. "It wasn't me," that individual will say (and believe). "It was a collection of us." Rufus Jones, the great American Quaker, has said, "I pin my hopes on the small circles and quiet processes in which genuine and reforming change takes place." You need a small circle.

It can be the teachers at your grade level. A decade ago, Amanda Hartman was teaching second grade at a dual-language school not far from Teachers College. She had studied at Teachers College and came to her school with an image of possibility that she was dying to share, but no one seemed particularly interested. "We don't have enough books," they said. "*You* can teach workshop 'cause *you* have the books, but we don't." Amanda listened to her colleagues and then told them she so needed their support, that she really felt she didn't have the strength to teach this way all alone, in isolation. "If I can find a way for you to have books, would you give it a go?" she asked. Then Amanda applied for one of those small grants that are available for resourceful teachers and received $5,000 for children's literature—not for her classroom, but for her colleagues' classrooms. She also met with her principal, Ruth Sweeney, and made a proposal. "If I can raise the money for books for all the second-grade classrooms, would you do what you can to free me up to help in the other classrooms and would you give us some extra time for grade-level planning?"

Two years later, the second grade at PS 165 was the happiest, busiest grade in the school, with teachers in and out of each others' rooms all the time, with a huge binder containing units of study they'd coauthored, and with kids reading and writing up a storm. The principal orchestrated visits from teachers at other grade levels to the second grade, and said to those on other grade levels: "If there is another grade level in the school that wants to forge a similar learning community, come to me with a proposal for what you want to do and for how I can help you do it." Within another few years, the entire school was receiving visitors from across the nation, and Ruth was telling this story to them. "It began with Amanda—she was a new teacher, actually, but still, she made the difference." Hearing Ruth say this, Amanda would inevitably interrupt, chiding her principal. "It wasn't me," she'd say. "It was the whole second grade."

Of course, in your school, the nucleus of change might not be the teachers across your grade level. It might be a scattering of teachers from classrooms that dot the school. That's great. And it may not be you who has the knowledge base to be able to go into other people's classrooms. You needn't change the school from a position of you as the knowledgeable one. To be an agent of change, you needn't start by thinking, "I know how to do this and want to share my knowledge." What schools really need are people who are willing to be contagious public learners. You can change a school just as easily by saying, "I don't know this," as by saying, "I do know this."

Change Can Stem from Acknowledging What You Don't Yet Know and Making a Plan

Absolutely, you can help your school become a vital and alive community of practice by being the person who wears your questions, your curiosity, your humility, and openness on your sleeve. "I've just realized I've got so much to learn," you can say. "I can't do it alone. I'm dying to have a couple people who are willing to study with me." Gather the people and make an appointment with the principal. "We've come to realize that our school could be doing so much more in the teaching of reading (or of anything else). We are starting to see a horizon out there that we're pretty sure we could go for, and we know it would help the school get so much better if we could go for that horizon. We're game to throw ourselves into the project, but it will take a lot of learning on our part, and we're wondering if there is any way we could come up with a plan where you help us do that learning, and in exchange we give back in ways that work for you or for the school."

Then, together with the principal and with your colleagues, make a plan. You and your colleagues will actually have made three or four alternate plans before you even embarked on this conversation. What could help you that wouldn't be too taxing on the system? Are you wondering if you could have a common prep time and schedule it alongside lunch? Are you hoping to have a roving sub who would go between your classrooms one day every six weeks, freeing each of you to observe in each other's rooms? Would you like for your kids to occasionally have movie time in the auditorium so that the teachers in your

study group get some school-supported time to study (as well as your own time that you all devote to this)? Draw on those plans now by making some proposals to the principal, but be ready to revise the plans as well.

You might want to propose a plan that will span just six weeks or three months time. No one will feel overly bound into such a plan—and it is always renewable.

One way or another, try to author a learning life for yourselves that will be intense enough and supportive enough that your learning curve actually will be sky-high, because this will be both an opportunity and a responsibility. If you want to teach your principal that supporting teachers' learning is a wise investment, your study together can't fizzle out and amount to nothing. If you want to teach your colleagues that people get energy from investing themselves in the hard work of outgrowing our own best practices, then it is important that your study together actually leads to better teaching. Better teaching will engine its own rewards.

Assess Your Efforts at Change: Ask Difficult Questions of Yourselves and Others

To author a productive learning life for yourselves, you'll need not only to work hard. You'll also need to work smart. That means you'll need to continually assess. "What's working that we can build upon? What's not working that we can fix?" Don't do this assessment alone. Involve your colleagues. This means being willing to have the hard conversations that tackle obstacles no one wants to admit even exist.

Roland Barth's second piece of advice to the TCRWP principals was that the strength of a learning community was indirectly proportional to the number of elephants in the room. "Every school has them—you know, they are the giant issues that everyone sees, that are right there in the middle of things, but no one admits are there. These are the issues that no one talks about in public—only in the bathrooms, in the parking lot, at home with their family and friends." He then said, "You need to talk about these issues, instead of continuing to avert your eyes from them, to step around them."

Your small circle and quiet processes will have their own elephants in the room. You'd be wise to use your powers of assessment to figure out what those issues might be. The undercurrent of resentment you are starting to feel—is that because of the one teacher who monopolizes every study group and is resented for doing so? Are the tensions coming from jealousies? Might that be because the one teacher who always seems to do everything well has fewer kids or easier kids, and the others find themselves resenting this? Might the issue be that some people feel valued and others don't? Might people be feeling an unspoken fear that this work may be too hard for "our" kids? Whatever these unaddressed issues are, they fester in the dark. They need to be brought to the table, to the light, and talked about.

If you do this, there are some guidelines that tend to work. My husband is a psychotherapist, and it has always been his position that in life, we can't change the other person. It won't work, and it's not our job anyway. The person we can change is ourself. This means that whenever John and I have a fight, after we separate to nurse our wounds and to brood about it, he'll inevitably come back and say, "I've been thinking about my role in this, and I realize I. . . , and I'm going to work on. . . , and I think I can help make things better by. . . ."

I always tended to say, "I'm glad you see the light! I knew it was you all along." Until John said, "Luce, when I say, 'I've been thinking about my role in this and I realize I can do better,' the way the conversation is supposed to go is that you are supposed to say, 'I've also been thinking about my role, and I, too, can do better.'

In any case, whether or not the person responds in kind, it usually works best if you take responsibility for changing yourself and don't take on the job of changing the other. So if you think your colleagues get jealous of the one teacher who has an easier class and is always more successful, you can take this on yourself. "Can we take just a bit of time to talk out some tensions I'm feeling? I know it's not fair for me to feel this way, but I just want to put on the table the fact that I sometimes feel myself getting jealous over all your successes, Patti, because I can't seem to get my kids to do as well. And then I find myself getting all grouchy toward you, thinking, 'It's not fair because she has the easier class.' I know it isn't your fault that this school splits kids up that way, and I'm trying to get over my huffy feelings, but I just figured it might help to put it out there because sometimes when I am short with you, I think that's where it's coming from."

Once you've begun studying with your colleagues, the challenge will be to make sure that this time pays off. Again, you'll want to be continually assessing to determine what does and doesn't work. You'll also want to ask others, from other schools, about the learning community at their school. "What works for you?" you will want to ask. "What doesn't work for you?"

Be on the Same Page: Create and Follow an Agenda, Align Your Teaching to the Group, Share What You Learn, and Imagine and Reimagine Your Vision of Change

Chances are that you'll learn that for study groups to go well, it helps to have and to keep to an agenda. This keeps your study from getting detoured with tangential topics and allows the group to create a plan together that then functions to discipline members of the group to keep that collaboratively constructed plan in mind (or to only alter it after a discussion). Little things like starting and ending on time, even if everyone is not present, convey the message that everyone's time is valued and that collaborative plans matter and are honored. Above all, the study group will go well if people feel themselves learning. For this to happen, it helps if the study group taps funds of knowledge. You'll want to figure out who knows something others want to know or who can be sent out to learn something that others want to know. That learning could be professional reading or a conference or institute or a bit of teaching that one person takes on and then shares with the group. The group will also work well if people's teaching is aligned to the group. So if you and your colleagues are constructing and teaching a unit of study on critical reading, then the study group will be most powerful if members agree to teach in ways that are aligned to the study group. Then the group won't add work onto people's shoulders so much as it will dis-

tribute that work. The discussions in the study group will be directly relevant to people's teaching. These conditions make it likely that the group will thrive.

If it is at all possible to do so, it can be magical to take a day off from school to visit the classroom of someone whose teaching represents that which your study group aspires toward. I won't forget the time I flew to Indiana to visit my friend and colleague, Jerry Harste. "Let's visit a classroom together," I said, and Jerry and I proceeded to drive something like four hours to get to a classroom. I thought at the time, "A plane flight and a four-hour drive to visit one classroom?" But that visit was thirty years ago, and I still remember it vividly. The lectures I've attended have floated out of my memory, and the seminars I participated in are long gone from my mind, but that one late-afternoon visit to a classroom will be with me always. Come to New York City and visit the classrooms here. Or visit the classrooms in the town next door to your own. By all means, visit each other's classrooms.

But assess. Watch over the group. Ask each other, "Is this helping?" and "How could this be more helpful?" And be ready to revise your plans based on those assessments. If you think hard about when you and your colleagues' learning feels especially alive and important, you can examine those moments, asking that question that readers ask so often: "What is this really, really about?" Ask, "What lessons can be learned here that apply not only to today but to every day?" And then you need to do what people the world over do. Build on what is good. Make more of it. Delete or fix what is not good. In this way, you make your learning community match your image of possibility. And you come to a place where you can look at your own learning life and think, "I truly am the author of my learning, of my teaching."

Ada, Alma Flor. 1995. *My Name Is Maria Isabel*. New York: Atheneum.

Agee, James and Walker Evans. 2001. *Let Us Now Praise Famous Men*. Boston: Mariner Books.

Allington, R. L. 2006. *What Really Matters for Struggling Readers: Designing Research-Based Programs*. Boston: Pearson Education.

American Girl series. Middleton, WI: American Girl Publishing, Inc.

Andersen, Hans Christian. 2009. *The Emperor's New Clothes*. Mankato, MN: Stone Arch Books.

Baylor, Byrd. 1995. *I'm in Charge of Celebrations*. New York: Aladdin Paperbacks.

Beah, Ishmael. 2008. *A Long Way Gone*. New York: Farrar, Straus, and Giroux.

Blume, Judy. 1971. *Freckle Juice*. New York: Yearling.

Bomer, Katherine. 2005. *Writing a Life: Teaching Memoir to Sharpen Insight, Shape Meaning—and Triumph Over Tests*. Portsmouth, NH: Heinemann.

Bunting, Eve. 2006. *One Green Apple*. Boston: Clarion Books.

———. 2001. *Dandelions*. Boston: Clarion Books.

———. 1991. *Fly Away Home*. Boston: Clarion Books.

Calkins, Lucy, and Cory Gillette. 2006. "Breathing Life into Essays." *Units of Study for Teaching Writing, Grades 3–5*. Portsmouth, NH: Heinemann.

Chambers, Whittaker. 2002. *Witness*. Washington, DC: Regnery Publishing.

Curtis, Christopher Paul. 2004. *Bud, Not Buddy*. New York: Laurel Leaf.

———. 2004. *The Watsons Go to Birmingham*. New York: Laurel Leaf.

Danziger, Paula. The *Amber Brown* series. New York: Scholastic.

Davies, Bronwyn. 1989. *Frogs and Snails and Feminist Tale: Preschool Children and Gender*. Sydney: Allen and Unwin.

DeJong, Meindert. 1988. *The House of Sixty Fathers*. London: John Murray.

Deutsch, Stacia, Rhody Cohen, and David Wenzel. 2005. *Blast to the Past: Lincoln's Legacy*. New York: Aladdin.

DiCamillo, Kate. 2001. *The Tiger Rising*. Somerville, MA: Candlewick.

Doney, Todd. 2007. *Letters from a Slave Girl: The Story of Harriet Jacobs*. Madison, WI: Perfection Learning.

Erikson, Erik and Robert Coles. 2000. *The Erik Erikson Reader*. New York: W.W. Norton & Company, Inc.

Fariña, Carmen. 2008. *A School Leader's Guide to Excellence: Collaborating Our Way to Better Schools*. Portsmouth, NH: Heinemann.

Frazier, Ian. 1998. *Cold Mountain*. New York: Vintage.

Fritz, Jean. 2001. *The Cabin Faced West*. Madison, WI: Perfection Learning.

Fullan, Michael, Peter Hill, and Carmen Crévola. 2006. *Breakthrough*. Thousand Oaks, CA: Corwin.

Gardiner, John Reynolds. 1980. *Stone Fox*. New York: Scholastic.

Giff, Patricia Reilly. 2008. *Water Street*. Madison, WI: Perfection Learning.

———. 2005. *Maggie's Door*. Madison, WI: Perfection Learning.

Giovanni, Nikki. 2008. *Hip Hop Speaks to Children: A Celebration of Poetry with a Beat*. New York: Sourcebooks Jabberwocky.

———. 2007. *Blink: The Power of Thinking Without Thinking*. New York: Back Bay Books.

Goldstein, Richard. "Miep Gies, Protector of Anne Frank, Dies at 100," *The New York Times*, January 10, 2010.

Greenfield, Eloise. 2008. "Things." From *Honey, I Love and Other Love Poems*. New York: HarperCollins.

Gregory, Kristiana. 1997. *Dear America: The Winter of Red Snow*. New York: Scholastic.

Heard, Georgia. 1998. *Awakening the Heart: Exploring Poetry in Elementary and Middle School*. Portsmouth, NH: Heinemann.

———. 1995. *Writing Toward Home: Tales and Lessons to Find Your Way*. Portsmouth, NH: Heinemann.

Hesse, Karen. 2008. *Brooklyn Bridge*. New York: Scholastic.

———. 1999. *Just Juice*. New York: Scholastic.

———. 1999. *Out of the Dust*. New York: Scholastic.

———. 1992. *Letters from Rifka*. New York: Square Fish.

Hest, Amy, and P. J. Lynch. 2003. *When Jesse Came Across the Sea*. Somerville, MA: Candlewick.

Hoestlandt, Deborah. 1996. *Star of Fear, Star of Hope*. New York: Scholastic.

Homer. 2003. *The Iliad*. New York: Penguin Classics.

Hopkinson, Deborah. 2003. *Sweet Clara and the Freedom Quilt*. New York: Knopf.

Innocenti, Roberto. 1996. *Rose Blanche*. Mankato, MN: Creative Paperbacks.

Johnston, Tony. 2008. *The Harmonica*. Watertown, MA: Charlesbridge Publishing.

Keene, Ellin Oliver, and Susan Zimmermann. 1997. *Mosaic of Thought: Teaching Comprehension in a Reader's Workshop*. Portsmouth, NH: Heinemann.

Kidder, Tracy. 2003. *Mountains Beyond Mountains*. New York: Random House.

Kline, Suzy. The *Horrible Harry* series. New York: Penguin.

Koestler-Grack, Rachel. 2004. *Sacagawea: Native American Biographies*. Chicago: Heinemann Library.

Lamont, Annie. 1995. *Bird by Bird*. New York: Anchor.

Levine, Ellen. 1993. *If You Travelled on the Underground Railroad*. New York: Scholastic.

Lewis, C. S. 1998. *The Lion, the Witch and the Wardrobe*. New York: Scholastic.

Lowry, Lois. 1998. *Number the Stars*. New York: Yearling.

———. 1986. *Autumn Street*. New York: Yearling.

MacLachlan, Patricia. 2002. *Caleb's Story*. New York: HarperCollins.

———. 1997. *Skylark*. New York: HarperCollins.

———. 1985. *Sarah, Plain and Tall*. New York: HarperCollins.

MacNeil, Robert. 1990. *Wordstruck*. New York: Penguin.

McPhillips, Shirley. 2000. *A Note Slipped Under the Door*. Portland, ME: Stenhouse.

Mochizuki, Ken, and Dom Lee. 1995. *Baseball Saved Us*. New York: Lee & Low Books.

Morrison, Toni. 2004. *Sula*. New York: Vintage.

———. 2004. *Beloved*. New York: Vintage.

Mortenson, Greg. 2009. *Listen to the Wind*. New York: Dial.

Oppenheim, Shulamith Levey. 1995. *The Lily Cupboard*. New York: HarperTrophy.

Osborne, Mary Pope. 2002. *Virginia's Civil War Diary*. New York: Random House.

———. 2001. *Revolutionary War on Wednesday*. New York: Scholastic.

Paterson, Katherine. 1995. *Bridge to Terabithia*. New York: HarperTrophy.

Pavel, Thomas. 1986. *Fictional Worlds*. Cambridge: Harvard University Press.

Polacco, Patricia. 1972. *The Butterfly*. New York: Putnam.

Potok, Chaim. 2007. *The Chosen*. New York: Ballantine.

Rawlings, Majorie Kinnan. 2002. *The Yearling*. New York: Scribner.

Rawls, Wilson. 1996. *Where the Red Fern Grows*. Boston: Houghton Mifflin.

Reiss, Johanna. 1973. *The Upstairs Room*. New York: Bantam.

Remarque, Erich Maria. 1958. *All Quiet on the Western Front*. Robbinsdale, MN: Fawcett.

Rinaldi, Ann. 2005. *Girl in Blue*. New York: Scholastic.

Riordan, Rick. 2005. *The Lightning Thief*. New York: Hyperion.

Rock, David. 2007. *Quiet Leadership: Six Steps to Transforming Performance at Work*. New York: Harper Paperbacks.

Ryan, Pam Muñoz. 1999. *Riding Freedom*. New York: Scholastic.

Rylant, Cynthia. 2008. *Hansel and Gretel*. New York: Hyperion.

Sandin, Joan. 1986. *The Long Way to a New Land*. New York: HarperCollins.

Sloane, William. 1983. *The Craft of Writing*. New York: W.W. Norton and Company.

Spufford, Francis. 2003. *The Child that Books Built: A Life in Reading*. New York: Picador.

Steinbeck, John. 2002. *Of Mice and Men*. New York: Penguin.

Stroud, Bettye. 2007. *The Patchwork Path: A Quilt Map to Freedom*. Somerville, MA: Candlewick.

Taylor, Mildred D. 2002. *Let the Circle Be Unbroken*. New York: Puffin.

———. 2002. *Roll of Thunder, Hear My Cry*. New York: Puffin.

———.1998. *The Gold Cadillac*. New York: Puffin.

Tolstoy, Leo. 2008. *War and Peace*. New York: Vintage.

———. 2004. *Anna Karenina*. New York: Penguin Classics.

Turner, Ann, and Ronald Himler. 1995. *Nettie's Trip South*. New York: Aladdin Picture Books.

Uris, Leon. 1983. *Mila 18*. New York: Bantam.

———. 1960. *Exodus*. New York: Bantam.

Wilder, Laura Ingalls. *The Little House* series. New York: Perennial.

Wiles, Deborah. 2004. *Freedom Summer*. New York: Aladdin.

Woodson, Jacqueline. 2001. *The Other Side*. New York: Putnam.

Wyeth, Sharon Dennis. 2002. *My America: Freedom's Wings*. Logan: Perfection Learning.

Zane, J. Peder. 2004. *Remarkable Reads: 34 Writers and Their Adventures in Reading*. New York: W.W. Norton and Company.

Zusak, Marcus. 2007. *The Book Thief*. Logan: Perfection Learning.